THE LITERATURE CONNECTION

Using Children's Books in the Classroom

D1301108

LIZ ROTHLEIN, ED.D.
University of Miami

ANITA MEYER MEINBACH, ED.D.
Department of Special Academic and Arts Programs
Dade County Public Schools

Scott, Foresman and Company
Glenview, Illinois   London

Good Year Books

are available for preschool through grade 8 and for every basic curriculum subject plus many enrichment areas. For more Good Year Books, contact your local bookseller or educational dealer. For a complete catalog with information about other Good Year Books, please write:

Good Year Books
1900 East Lake Avenue
Glenview, Illinois 60025

Copyright © 1991 Scott, Foresman and Company.
All Rights Reserved.
Printed in the United States of America.

8 9 10 11 12 EBL 98 97 96 95 94

ISBN 0-673-38450-0

Library of Congress Cataloging -in-Publication
Rothlein, Liz.
    The literature connection: using children's books in the classroom / Liz Rothlein, Anita Meyer Meinbach.
        p.   cm.—(Good year book)
    Includes bibliographical references (p.)
    ISBN 0-673-38450-0
    1. Children's literature—United States—Study and teaching (Elementary)
2. Children—United States—Books and reading.
I. Meinbach, Anita Meyer. II. Title. III. Series.   90-34953
LB1575.5.U5R68 1991   CIP
372.6'4—dc20

Credits:
iii: "There Is No Frigate Like a Book" by Emily Dickinson. Reprinted by permission of the publishers and the Trustees of Amherst College from *The Poems of Emily Dickinson.* Thomas H. Johnson, ed., Cambridge, Mass.: The Belknap Press of Harvard University Press, Copyright 1951, © 1955, 1979, 1983 by the President and Fellows of Harvard College.
115: "Stopping by Woods on a Snowy Evening," by Robert Frost, from *The Poetry of Robert Frost,* edited by Edward Connery Lathem. Copyright 1923, © 1969 by Holt, Rinehart and Winston, copyright 1951 by Robert Frost. Reprinted by permission of Henry Holt and Company, Inc.
358: "The Pioneer" from *I Sing the Pioneer* by Arthur Guiterman, E. P. Dutton, 1926. Reprinted by permission of Louise H. Sclove.
359: "Immigrants" by Nancy Byrd Turner. Reprinted by permission of Beverley T. Thomas.

There is no frigate like a book
To take us lands away.
Nor any coursers like a page
Of prancing poetry.
This traverse may the poorest take
Without oppress of toll;
How frugal is the chariot
That bears a human soul!

EMILY DICKINSON

For all the children whose pristine innocence is the adult's wisdom and the world's future hope.—L. R.

For Jay, with my appreciation and love, always.—A. M. M.

ACKNOWLEDGMENTS
Our thanks to Christopher Jennison, our editor and "the wind beneath our wings."

For insightful comments and suggestions, a special thank you to Barbara Jouviney, David Yeager, Nancy Whitelaw, Carol George, Carol Katzman, Sam Sebesta, and especially, Anthony D. Fredericks and Bonnie Campbell-Hill.

I N T R O D U C T I O N

The world of books is the most remarkable creation of man.
Nothing else that he builds ever lasts. Monuments fall; nations
perish; civilizations grow old and die out; and, after an era of
darkness, new races build others. But in the world of books are
volumes that have seen this happen again and again, and yet
live on, still young, still as fresh as the day they were written,
still telling the hearts of men of the hearts of men centuries
dead.

Clarence Day
Introduction to
The Story of the Yale University Press

The Literature Connection is intended for all adults who are interested
in bringing children and books together. It is specifically designed for
both preservice and in-service teachers, preschool through grade
eight. *The Literature Connection* has been developed as a text for use in
college-level children's literature classes and as a practical sourcebook
for teachers. The book is also useful for parents and librarians who wish
to expose children to good literature.

For too long, quality works of literature have been read outside the
classroom door. They have been read after the "real work" was completed. Despite the advances in education, teachers have not been
successful in bringing children and books together. Between 1958 and
1980, 95 to 99 percent of American teachers used basal readers to teach
reading (Koeller, 1981), and while children learned reading skills, they
did not develop positive habits and attitudes. Research on illiteracy has
given added impetus for changes in education. One of the changes that
has gained popularity recently is the use of quality literature in the
classroom.

Numerous studies have compared literature-based reading programs with basal reading programs. Eldredge and Butterfield (1986)
studied 1,149 students, comparing a basal approach with five other

experimental methods, including two literature-based programs. They found that "the use of children's literature to teach children to read had a positive effect upon students' achievement and attitudes toward reading—much greater than the traditional methods used."

Similar results have been obtained in studies focusing on students at risk of failure (Larrick, 1987), students in economically depressed rural communities (White, Vaughan, and Rorie, 1986), and remedial readers (Chomsky, 1978). There is no doubt that literature-based reading programs work, that literature can be used to teach children to read, and that literature has a place in the curriculum.

At long last, the tremendous value of literature is being recognized, and many districts and states have made literature use a top priority in revitalizing reading and language arts programs. In California, for example, State Superintendent of Public Education Bill Honig launched the California Reading Initiative Program. The state produced a list of over one thousand books, plus curriculum guides that contain activities, to use in teaching reading through literature.

Literature, however, goes beyond reading and language arts, cutting across all content areas and life experiences. Literature gives children the opportunity to travel to the corners of the earth, to explore the known and the unknown. Literature gives children insight into human nature and motivation. They discover that others have often experienced joys, sorrows, and fears similar to their own, and they gain perspectives on problem solving. Literature is an adventure, and those who work with children have the privilege and responsibility of guiding them on an unforgettable journey that will last forever.

The primary goal of *The Literature Connection* is to serve as a guide for elementary teachers, parents, and librarians in bringing quality literature to children and in instilling in them a lifelong love of reading, a regard for the written word, and an appreciation of the thoughts and ideas presented in literature. We hope that the reading of quality literature will enable the reader to break beyond everyday boundaries, to wonder, imagine, and explore life's endless possibilities.

In keeping with this goal, the book presents approaches and strategies for using children's literature and activities that develop skill in all content areas and that stimulate growth in the areas of thinking and feeling. *The Literature Connection* is divided into four parts, which work together to enrich children's lives through reading quality literature. The following paragraphs describe these four sections.

PART I. DEVELOPING INTEREST IN LITERATURE
The first four chapters describe those approaches that have been most effective in literature-based programs in stimulating children's interest in reading: Chapter 1, "The Read-Aloud Program"; Chapter 2, "Shared

Reading Experience"; Chapter 3, "Sustained Silent Reading"; and Chapter 4, "Storytelling." Guidelines are offered to help implement each of the approaches and activities, and the benefits of each are described.

Chapter 5, "Extending and Sharing Literature," outlines thirty exciting activities that challenge students to extend their understanding of selected literature and encourage them to share good books with others.

PART II. GENRES AND ELEMENTS

Children deserve quality literature and need to be guided in selecting the best literature has to offer. Chapter 6, "Exploring Genres," describes each of the genres (picture books, realistic fiction, historical fiction, fantasy/science fiction, traditional literature [folktales, fables, myths and legends], poetry, informational books, and biographies) to aid adults and children in identifying criteria that will help them select quality literature.

In Chapter 7, "Analyzing Elements," activities involve students in analyzing the elements of literature—characterization, plot, setting, theme, and point of view—and in evaluating literature based on the criteria established in Chapter 6.

Chapter 8, "Involving Students in Selecting Genres," includes activities that encourage and motivate students to select literature that represents a variety of genres.

PART III. LITERATURE AND THE READING PROGRAM

If you are willing to accept the challenge of initiating your own literature-based reading curriculum, Part III details two types of reading programs and addresses many common concerns regarding the implementation of these programs. Chapter 9, "Strategies for Reading," describes several successful strategies for improving comprehension, such as metacognition, directed reading, story mapping, reciprocal teaching, and questioning. The chapter also contains a complete story unit and a description of the integral parts necessary to create similar story units.

Chapter 10, "Literature and the Basal Reading Programs," outlines ways in which you can extend the basal in the reading program to provide students with quality works of literature. A two-hour reading/ language arts block that combines the use of basal and whole books of literature and provides time for skill instruction and application, based on individual and group needs and interests, is suggested. The chapter also includes a comprehensive list of available literature-based materials that will help you extend the basal.

Chapter 11, "A Model for Literature-Based Reading Program," outlines ways in which you can develop a two-hour reading/language arts block that includes the strategies and approaches that are most successful in enhancing the benefits of literature. Two sample lesson plans—one for primary and one for intermediate grades—illustrate how literature can be used as the heart of the reading curriculum. One of the largest concerns of educators using a literature-based reading program deals with evaluation. Chapter 11 also describes methods for formal and informal evaluation and evaluative tools that can easily be adapted to any setting to assess students' growth in reading and skill development. The chapter also offers practical suggestions for organizing a classroom to best facilitate a literature-based curriculum.

Chapter 12, "Using the Library," offers activities for familiarizing students with the use and benefits of the library. The chapter also describes how to organize and operate a classroom library.

The tremendous importance of parents' involvement in their children's education has long been recognized. Chapter 13, "Reaching Beyond the Classroom: Parent Involvement in Reading," includes many suggestions for involving parents and family members in reading with children both at home and at school. Activities, such as a detailed monthly calendar of parent and child activities, extend the benefits of reading and discussing good literature to the home.

PART IV. CONNECTIONS

Part IV describes those connections that extend the benefits of literature throughout the curriculum and to all aspects of life. In Chapter 14, "Affective Response to Literature," specific topics relating to the affective domain, along with appropriate activities and works of literature, are provided as examples of the seemingly unlimited range of themes dealt with in children's literature and the ways in which they can be discussed in the classroom to help children deal successfully with their own lives.

Literature is the perfect vehicle for encouraging children to face issues and problems on an individual basis and from a more global perspective. Many of the models and strategies that foster creative and critical thinking are described in Chapter 15, "Literature for Critical and Creative Thinking," and specific applications illustrate the ways in which these models and strategies can be used with works of literature.

Reading and writing are closely related; each is a catalyst for the other. Chapter 16, "The Reading-Writing Connection," explores this relationship and describes both the writing process and the language experience approach. Guidelines are presented for successful implementation of these techniques, as students realize that they, too, are authors!

The final connection between literature and the curriculum is illustrated in Chapter 17, "Literature and the Curriculum—A Thematic

Approach." Comprehensive, interdisciplinary units, written for primary and intermediate levels, combine theory and practice, as children read for real purposes and make connections between what they are reading and what they are studying. Hopefully, the understandings gained will stay with them long after the last page is read.

APPENDIXES
The appendixes provide a listing of children's book awards, resources for teaching literature, and publishers' addresses.

REFERENCES
Chomsky, Carol. "When You Still Can't Read in Third Grade: After Decoding, What?" In *What Research Has to Say about Reading Instruction*, edited by S. Jay Samuels. Newark, Del.: International Reading Association, 1978.

Eldredge, J. Lloyd, and Dennie Butterfield. "Alternatives to Traditional Reading Instruction." *The Reading Teacher 40* (October 1986): 32–37.

Koeller, Shirley. "25 Years Advocating Children's Literature in the Reading Program." *The Reading Teacher 34* (February 1981): 552–556.

Larrick, Nancy. "Illiteracy Starts Too Soon." *Phi Delta Kappan 69* (November 1987): 184–189.

White, Jane H., Joseph L. Vaughan, and I. Laverne Rorie. "Picture of a Classroom Where Reading Is for Real." *The Reading Teacher 40* (October 1986): 84–86.

C O N T E N T S

x

CONNECTIONS

Affective Response to Literature

Literature for Critical and Creative Thinking

The Reading-Writing Connection:
Writing Process Approach
Language Experience Approach

Literature and the Curriculum —
A Thematic Approach

LITERATURE AND THE READING PROGRAM

Strategies for Reading

Literature and the Basal Reading Program: Extending the Basal Literature-Based Materials

A Model for Literature-Based Reading Programs

Using the Library

Reaching Beyond the Classroom:
Parent Involvement

THE LITERATURE CONNECTION

DEVELOPING INTEREST IN READING

The Read-Aloud Program

Shared Reading

Sustained Silent Reading

Storytelling

Extending and Sharing Literature

GENRES AND ELEMENTS

Exploring Genres:
Picture Books, Realistic Fiction,
Historical Fiction,
Fantasy/Science Fiction,
Traditional Literature, Poetry,
Informational Books, Biographies

Analyzing Elements:
Characterization, Plot,
Setting, Theme, Point of View,
Evaluating Genres and Their
Elements

Involving Students in Selecting
Genres

PART ONE

DEVELOPING INTEREST IN LITERATURE

Most children begin their school life with high expectations. Children, especially those who have been exposed to books at home, anxiously await that special moment when a book is placed in their hands. They open it and read! And all too often, their hopes and expectations are dashed when they are given their first preprimer in reading class. What happened to the magic? What happened to the joy of reading?

Bringing children and books together is one of the most important, rewarding, and perhaps frustrating, outcomes of teaching. Teachers often lament their inability to motivate students to read for the sheer pleasure of reading. And often, teachers are trying to motivate children who wanted desperately to read in the early grades.

There is no magic formula to develop interest in reading. There is no special charm or incantation to recite and no amount of begging will change children's perceptions of reading. Instead, the solution is quite simple and has been in our libraries and classrooms for centuries—books. Real works of literature that are brimming with the knowledge of ages past and ages yet to come, just waiting to excite the imagination and nourish the soul.

Children need to be surrounded by good books. They need to be introduced to and involved with quality works of literature. Many approaches have been successful in bridging the gap between children and books. The first section of *The Literature Connection* focuses on four of these approaches: the read-aloud program, shared reading experience, sustained silent reading, and storytelling. Each approach is described in detail, guidelines for establishing the classroom climate and techniques for developing the approach are offered, and books that meet the criteria for each approach are suggested. In addition, activities that extend the use and impact of each approach are described.

Chapter 5, "Extending and Sharing Literature," the final chapter in Part I, includes thirty meaningful, thought-provoking ideas that are designed to motivate, inspire, and make book sharing a natural outgrowth of reading. The activities, ranging from monologues to mock trials, and from newspapers to time capsules, develop skills in a variety of content areas and extend students' understanding of literature.

As you use the approaches and activities described on the following pages, you will begin to see children's love for books grow and blossom as they discover or rediscover the magic and joy of literature. And perhaps one day, all children will respond to the question, "Which would you rather do, read a book or watch a television program?" as one little first-grader who answered, "I'd rather read because with TV you can't hear what they're thinking."

1

The Read-Aloud Program

More than one-third of the entire population of the United States is illiterate. Jonathon Kozol (1983) reported in "Illiterate America" that 25 million American adults cannot read the poison warnings on a can of pesticide or a note from their child's teacher. An additional 35 million Americans read at a level below the survival needs of society.

These findings cause great concern among educators and leaders in this country. In an attempt to remedy the situation, researchers are investigating those elements that constitute a literate environment. A logical place to begin this investigation is by studying how children learn to read. A great deal of evidence indicates that a person's success in reading depends largely on the experiences with literature and reading that took place during the early years at home and the first few years in school. Also a lot of evidence indicates that some children can read when they come to school.

RESEARCH ON THE IMPORTANCE OF READING ALOUD

A review of the literature to find out why some children can read when they enter school and why some cannot showed one consistently repeated factor. Children who were read to at home were better readers (Durkin, 1966; Sakamato, 1977; Wells, 1986). Reading aloud to children is a valuable activity that improves listening, verbal, and written skills and fosters a lifetime love of books and reading. Children tend to imitate and model adults. If children see adults reading or if they are read to by adults, they are more likely to want to read themselves (Elkind, 1974; Gordon, 1976).

Reading aloud, however, should not be confined to the home. A read-aloud program should be an integral part of the daily classroom curriculum for all students. In fact, reading aloud is just as important for older children as it is for younger ones. Research studies carried out with school-age children show that children who had been read to by their teachers were significantly ahead of the children who had not been given such opportunities in reading, vocabulary development, and comprehension (Cohen, 1968; Cullinan, Jagger, and Strickland, 1974). In addition, Sulzby (1985) strongly suggests that children typically transfer oral language skills to the act of reading and that, as a result of being read to, they progress through developmental stages.

Research has demonstrated that reading to children not only helps them learn to read but also results in additional benefits, such as establishing a mutual bond among listeners. The warmth of the oral reading period, as well as the generally effective climate created during the reading time, helps support the child's emotional well-being and thus helps build self-confidence.

Through the read-aloud process, children learn a lot about books and gain basic understandings about the reading process itself (Durkin, 1970). For example, children learn that print is read from left to right, that books have a top and a bottom and a beginning and an end, and that adults read what is printed in the books.

Language is developed through read-aloud sessions (Durkin, 1970; Flood, 1977; Smith, 1977; Olson, 1977). During the actual reading of the story and follow-up discussions, children hear many words. Many of these words will become part of their listening and speaking vocabularies and later their reading and writing vocabularies.

There is also a connection between being read to and writing performance (Graves, 1983; Clay, 1975). Reading to children sparks their imagination, giving them ideas to write about. Often what is read today will be written about tomorrow.

Firsthand experiences are important, but many children have limited opportunities to acquire all the essential experiences. Still, it is through these experiences that children develop the concepts, knowledge, and thinking skills that are vital to the process of reading. When firsthand experiences are not feasible, one of the next best approaches is to offer them vicariously through reading aloud.

When teachers select a variety of genres to read aloud to children, they help them develop a love and appreciation of books. It is not unusual for a child to want to read a book that has been read aloud, and often they choose to read the book over and over again. As read-aloud books are made available to the children, they can improve their reading skills by rereading familiar books.

Reading to children provides them with an enjoyable and pleasurable activity. It is not surprising that long after the worksheets and textbooks are forgotten, a favorite story that was read by a parent or teacher is still remembered. Reading aloud often whets the children's appetite for more reading and exposes them to literature they would otherwise not be able to experience.

PREPARING A READ-ALOUD PROGRAM

Preparation is needed to establish a successful read-aloud program. You must set the proper classroom climate, select appropriate read-aloud materials, and be aware of those techniques that will help develop the program's objectives.

Setting the Climate

A certain message is sent to children when they realize that their teacher believes reading is important and takes time daily to read to them. Students will begin to look forward to the read-aloud time and savor the moment when their teacher sits down, opens the book, and brings the words and story to life.

Too often, children are credited with being able to choose the best books for themselves. Unfortunately, children frequently select the same genre and do not always choose those books that exemplify good children's literature. A read-aloud program can introduce children to a wide range of outstanding readings. After hearing a book read aloud, children often scramble to locate a copy for themselves to read in their free time. How rewarding to know that reading aloud heightens children's awareness, understanding, and sensitivity to good literature!

It is especially important to set aside specific time for reading aloud, rather than trying to fit it into the schedule haphazardly. The age-old rationalization "There just isn't enough time" is simply an excuse. Making the time for read-aloud sessions should be high on the list of priorities for all teachers. Certainly fifteen minutes a day can be dedicated to enriching students' lives and unlocking the door to the unique and unlimited possibilities that literature holds.

By nature, teachers are rather flexible and creative, and these two traits will ensure that time is found for reading aloud. Many teachers have found that in the morning, right after the bell has rung, is an especially good time for reading aloud. Children quickly settle down for this special time, and it sets the tone for the entire day. Immediately after lunch or just before dismissal have also provided excellent opportunities for reading aloud. Taking just two to three minutes from the class times allotted to other subjects and combining them into a fifteen-minute period can provide the needed time for reading aloud. As a word of caution, avoid beginning the read-aloud session when you only have a minute or two. Little can be accomplished in so short a time and children may lose interest.

Attention span is important to consider when determining the length of read-aloud sessions. Teachers of young children might wish to schedule two or three shorter read-aloud times since their students' attention span is shorter. Generally, stories for children under age seven should be short enough to be completed during a single session. Older children enjoy longer stories that may be completed over a longer period. Teachers may schedule one longer period for the read-aloud session rather than several shorter ones. If children are not used to being read to, the read-aloud sessions should be kept rather short. As they develop skill in listening and interest in the readings, session times can be lengthened.

In addition to setting aside specific times for reading aloud, be sure to consider spontaneous reading. Various lessons might lend themselves to a specific story or poem. For example, Henry Wadsworth Longfellow's poem "The Midnight Ride of Paul Revere" might be appropriate during a lesson on the Revolutionary War. Or perhaps, *And Then What Happened Paul Revere?* by Jean Fritz could be read. A lesson on World War II would be enhanced by reading *Anne Frank: The Diary of a Young Girl.*

Selecting Read-Aloud Books
With the thousands and thousands of books available, knowing how to select the best books for reading aloud is critical. You

must be aware of good children's literature and keep up with the newest additions. Perhaps the most important criterion for a read-aloud selection is how you feel about the book, since this feeling is immediately transmitted to the students. It is crucial that teachers select books that affect them, books that cause them to react in some way, books that challenge their imagination or inspire their dreams, books that make them laugh, cry, or beg for more. Enthusiasm is contagious. A teacher who is excited about reading will have equally motivated students.

The following criteria should be considered when determining your read-aloud book selections:

1. Select well-written books. By first grade, students have expectations of what a story should be and can differentiate between literature that has merit and literature that does not. Children especially enjoy stories that have a strong, fast-paced plot and interesting, well-delineated, and memorable characters with whom they can identify. Children need literature that they can become totally immersed in. *Charlotte's Web* by E. B. White is a classic tale of friendship and giving. Children share Wilbur's feelings of doubt, fear, and need, and they grow to love the assortment of characters that become a real and important part of their lives. Natalie Babbitt's *Tuck Everlasting* is a haunting tale that causes readers and listeners to reflect on their mortality. *Tuck Everlasting* stays with them long after the last word is read. Its words are stirring and challenging, taking its readers beyond the daily routines of life:

> The people would have noticed the giant ash tree at
> the center of the wood, and then, in time, they'd have
> noticed the little spring bubbling up among its roots in
> spite of the pebbles piled there to conceal it. And that
> would have been a disaster so immense that this
> weary old earth, owned or not to its fiery core, would
> have trembled on its axis like a beetle on a pin.

2. Select books that reflect your students' interests. Use interest inventories. Talk to your students—find out what makes them tick, what they love, what they hate, and what they fear. Books become even more appealing when they relate to specific interests or when students can identify with the characters, learning how others deal with situations and problems similar to

their own experiences. Children having difficulty with friendships and with feelings of belonging might identify with Hans Christian Andersen's *Ugly Duckling* or with Wanda, in Eleanor Estes's *The Hundred Dresses*, who longs for acceptance from her peers.

3. Select books that will stimulate your students' imaginations. One of the most rewarding outcomes of reading is that it gives vent to the imagination. It lets the reader dare to dream, to journey to far-off places, to break away from worldly boundaries and take part in wonderful adventures. Laura Ingalls Wilder's *Little House* series allows children to experience life in a different time and share in the excitement, adventure, danger, and happiness of pioneer life. *Johnny Tremain*, by Esther Forbes, transports them to life during the American Revolution and allows children to take part in many of our country's most exciting events.

4. Select books from a variety of genres. Choosing a wide variety of read-aloud books will, in turn, broaden your students' interests as well as their own selection of books. Fiction books (realistic fiction, historical fiction, fantasy, folklore) provide them with characters and emotions they can identify with and establish settings and themes that captivate their imaginations and explore the human condition. Fiction also helps children understand themselves and others.

Poetry should play an important part in the read-aloud program as well. Poems express human feelings and motivation, and students can readily identify with the characters and themes in both contemporary and traditional poetry. In addition, poems provide a natural outlet through which students can express their own feelings, even though students enjoy writing free verse. In general, elementary-age children prefer poetry with a clear rhyme and rhythm, since they have not yet developed the sophistication and skill to become interested in, and to understand poems that are rather abstract or that rely heavily on imagery. Younger children delight in the same nursery rhymes we recited as children, and gradually, as they mature, they can identify with the poetry of Poe, Stevenson, Whitman, Longfellow, and Frost, to name a few. For example, the alliteration and repetition found in "Diddle diddle dumpling, my son John," can later be enjoyed in poems such as Alfred, Lord Tennyson's "Blow, Bugle, Blow,"

The splendour falls on castle walls
   And snowy summits old in story:
The long light shakes across the lakes,
   And the wild cateract leaps in glory.
Blow, bugle, blow, set the wild echoes flying,
Blow, bugle; answer, echoes, dying, dying, dying . . .

Nonfiction books (informational books and biographies) provide students with a wide range of information. Nonfiction arms students with the facts and background they will need to connect new concepts and knowledge. *Harriet Tubman: Conductor on the Underground Railroad*, by Ann Petry, for example, adds another dimension to students' understanding of the Civil War and its consequences.

5. Select books from both traditional and modern literature. Modern literature reflects contemporary settings, language, and characters, but the themes may be contemporary or universal. Traditional literature provides links with the past and carries the reader to another place and time. Traditional literature contains timeless, universal themes that are as relevant today as they were at the time the story was set.

6. Select several books by the same author in order to help your students gain an appreciation for the particular style and work of that author. For example, read several of Ezra Keats's books to your students. Involve them in a discussion that encourages a comparison of the books: How are *The Snowy Day*, *Peter's Chair*, and *Louie* similar? Compare the characters in each. How would you describe books by Ezra Keats? What quality do all his books seem to have? Compare the illustrations in each.

7. Select books that cover a specific theme or concept being developed in class. Students will gain increased understanding of the concept and an additional dimension will be added as you connect good literature and the curriculum. "Arithmetic" by Carl Sandburg or "The Homework Machine" by Shel Silverstein can really enliven a mathematics lesson.

8. Select books that are models for good writing and that are rich in language. Listening to the language of literature affects students' oral and written communication skills. They learn to write not only by becoming involved in the actual process of writing but also by reading the works of others (Smith, 1982). For

example, using Robert Frost's poem "Stopping by Woods on a Snowy Evening," have your students employ the pattern, rhythm, and rhyme in writing another poem. "Whose woods these are I think I know . . ." may become "Whose dreams are these, . . ."

9. Select books that are appropriate to your students' intellectual and emotional levels. No matter how outstanding and worthwhile a book may be, if its subject matter or vocabulary is too sophisticated, students will lose interest. A distinction must be made between the students' listening level and their reading level. For example, first-graders have a reading vocabulary of approximately 350 words, while their listening vocabulary is over 10,000 words.

10. Allow students to help select books for reading aloud. You may want to display a folder that contains Suggestions for Reading Aloud forms, which students can use to suggest books or poems that they would like to have included in the read-aloud program. When a student's book or poem is selected, allow him or her to introduce the selection to the class. Journals such as *The New Advocate* (Boston: Christopher-George Publishers) and *The Reading Teacher* (Newark, Del.: International Reading Association) include columns that review new books.

SUGGESTIONS FOR READING ALOUD

Student's name _____

Suggested Read Aloud Title _____

Author_____

Why I like this book:_____

_____

_____

GUIDELINES FOR READING ALOUD

Certain techniques can help make the read-aloud sessions more successful. The following guidelines describe specific points that you should consider when establishing a read-aloud program:

1. Begin reading to students on their first day in class. Sharing a good book provides a wonderful opportunity for you and your students to share a warm pleasurable moment, determines the climate for the rest of the year, and establishes a close bond.

2. Before reading a story or poem aloud, be familiar with the material. In this way, you will know just what parts should be emphasized, what words or concepts might be introduced prior to the reading to help avoid confusion, what mood should be set, and what tone and pace the reading should take. Do not feel as if you have to read every single word of the text. Often long, overly descriptive passages should be shortened for certain groups. In order for the reading to flow more smoothly, practice reading a story or parts of a story aloud before reading it to children.

3. Hold prereading discussions to establish interest in the book. Children love learning anecdotes about the author or illustrator, and this information brings them even closer to the story or poem. Students may be interested to learn that Robert Louis Stevenson amused his stepson with tales about pirates and buried treasure. These tales grew into *Treasure Island*. Or, knowing that Stevenson fought illness constantly, writing many of his best books and poems from a sickbed, may make children feel more deeply about the poetry of this great writer. Students might be fascinated to know that Robert McCloskey kept ducks in his bathtub to study while writing *Make Way for Ducklings*.

The following questions can be used in a prereading discussion with any form of literature: Look at the title (or cover). What do you think the book might be about? Who is the author? Have you heard of the author before? What other books did this author write? Who is the illustrator? What other books did this illustrator illustrate? How would you describe this illustrator's style?

4. Have children sit comfortably in a semicircle around you and try to eliminate all distractions. Establish eye contact with students throughout the reading.

5. Sit on a low chair close to the students and hold the book so that they can see the illustrations. Illustrations are of particular importance in books for young children. Allow time for students to examine the illustrations and develop their powers of observation. Illustrations for older children might be shown at the end of certain chapters, allowing students to form mental images before they see the accompanying illustrations. Mention the type of illustrations used (i.e., pen and ink, collage, photographs, and so on).

6. Become immersed in the story or poem, express the emotions evoked, and bring the literature to life with gestures, sound effects, and voice inflections. You need not be an actor, but a flare for the dramatic can be a plus. Attempt to be as authentic as possible when reading dialogue. As the reader becomes involved, so do the listeners.

7. Encourage children to participate in the reading when appropriate. For example, they might take part in reciting a repeated word, line, or chorus. Allow them to ask questions and respond to them.

8. Periodically ask questions to enhance comprehension and interest. The main objective for reading aloud is to provide an opportunity for students to sit back, relax, and enjoy the magic that is good literature. So do not constantly ask questions and turn the session into a test of sorts. Perhaps reread certain passages and ask students to give their interpretation of what is happening. At various times, students might be asked to predict outcomes. This heightens interest as they listen to determine whether their predictions were accurate. However, rather than interrupt the continuity of the story, discussion should usually be saved until the end of the session.

9. If it is not possible to complete an entire book or chapter in one reading, try to stop at a cliff-hanger. Leave the children on the edge of their seats, anxious to know what happens next. But don't give the ending away! Spend a few minutes brainstorming about what might come next. Write student responses, accompanied by the student's initials, on the board or on a chart. In subsequent sessions, see how accurate the responses were.

10. At the completion of a story or poem, allow time for the students to silently contemplate what they have heard, explore their own feelings, and internalize the work. Students may wish

to write in their journals at this time as well. Chapter 16 includes suggestions for connecting literature and writing.

11. Once the story or poem is completed, allow time for the students to freely express their feelings, opinions, and conclusions. They usually have a need to respond in some way to what has been read. Student responses may be artistic (illustrating a favorite scene, drawing a picture to represent their feelings about a certain part of the story) or dramatic (puppetry, role playing, miming a scene) rather than verbal.

12. Create open-ended questions that require students to focus on certain elements of the book. Ask only a few well-developed questions. For example, you might ask students to do one of the following:

Analyze character motivation.

Analyze the way in which the setting affected the story.

Discuss favorite events in the story.

Give opinions of the book—what they liked. What they didn't like.

Describe what they might have done differently if they were ___ (name of a specific character).

Identify similarities (or differences) between one of the characters and a character in another book with which students are familiar.

Determine the author's purpose.

Describe how the story made them feel.

13. If a book selected for a session does not hold a majority of the students' attention, do not continue reading it. Instead, suggest that those students who are interested in the book read it independently and then select another book for the read-aloud session.

14. Include copies of books that have been read aloud (and other books by the same author) in the classroom library. This provides children with the opportunity to read and reread their favorites, as well as others in a series (i.e., *The Little House* series).

15. To evaluate student participation and interest in the read-aloud stories, consult the Shared Reading Observation Sheet (p. 29). Most of the questions are appropriate for evaluating the success of read-aloud sessions.

EXTENDED ACTIVITIES FOR READING ALOUD

The following activities can extend the use and impact of a read-aloud program:

1. Allow children to help prepare their own class lists of recommended books for the read-aloud program. The books should meet specific criteria that you and the students have discussed. These criteria can be based on the list given in the section "Selecting Read-Aloud Books."

2. Set up a program for older students to create a read-aloud program for younger students at the school. Before implementing the program, introduce students to the fifteen guidelines for reading aloud discussed in the previous section and give them the opportunity to practice reading aloud the selections they want to read to the younger students.

3. Beyond the traditional approach to reading aloud, you might incorporate other strategies into the classroom discussion:

- Tape relevant and strong sections on cassettes for groups or individuals to enjoy.
- Pair students so that a more powerful reader and a weaker one take turns reading a section to each other.
- Allow students to time themselves as they read a specific portion of a book. Have them time themselves at different sessions and record their progress.

4. Hold a class discussion in which each student discusses his or her favorite scene. Divide the class into groups according to their favorite part. Create a class mural on which each group draws a picture showing the part of the story selected. The scenes should be drawn sequentially according to the plot so that the completed mural is a pictorial representation of the book.

5. To determine the effectiveness or enjoyment level of the book, have the students complete the following Read-Aloud Evaluation Form after a read-aloud session. The form is short to ensure that it is not seen as "just another book report."

READ-ALOUD EVALUATION FORM

Student's name: _____

Date: _____

Title: _____

Author: _____

The part I enjoyed most was when _____

_____

_____

_____

_____

The part I liked least was when _____

_____

_____

_____

_____

On a scale of 1 to 5 (5 meaning you loved it and 1 meaning

you didn't enjoy it at all), I would rate the

selection a _____ .

SUGGESTED BOOKS FOR
THE READ-ALOUD PROGRAM

Picture Books

Allard, Harry. *Miss Nelson Is Missing!* Illustrated by James Marshall. Houghton Mifflin, 1977. (Grades 2–5)

Andersen, Hans Christian. *The Ugly Duckling.* Retold and illustrated by Lorinda Bryan Cauley. Harcourt Brace Jovanovich, 1979. (Grades K–6)

Bemmelmans, Ludwig. *Madeline.* Viking Press, 1962. (Grades K–3)

Carle, Eric. *The Very Hungry Caterpillar.* World, 1968. (Grades K–2)

Cooney, Barbara. *Miss Rumphius.* Viking Press, 1982. (Grades K–3)

DePaola, Tomie. *Nana Upstairs, Nana Downstairs.* Penguin, 1978. (Grades 2–4)

De Regniers, Beatrice S. *May I Bring A Friend?* Illustrated by Beni Montresor. Atheneum, 1964. (Grades K–3)

Flack, Marjorie. *Ask Mr. Bear.* Macmillan, 1968. (Grades K–1)

Freeman, Don. *Corduroy.* Viking Press, 1968. (Grades K–2)

———. *Dandelion.* Viking Press, 1964. (Grades K–2)

Gag, Wanda. *Millions of Cats.* Coward-McCann, 1928. (Grades K–2)

Kantrowitz, Mildred. *Maxie.* Illustrated by Emily A. McCully. Parents, 1970. (Grades 2–4)

Keats, Ezra J. *Snowy Day.* Viking Press, 1962. (Grades K–1)

Kraus, Robert. *Leo the Late Bloomer.* Illustrated by Jose and Ariane Aruego. Thomas Y. Crowell, 1971. (Grades 2–4)

McCloskey, Robert. *Make Way for Ducklings.* Viking Press, 1941. (Grades K–6)

Martin, Bill, Jr. *Brown Bear, Brown Bear.* Hold, Rinehart & Winston, 1983. (Grades K–2)

Moore, Elaine. *Grandma's House.* Illustrated by Elsie Primavera. Lothrop, 1985. (Grades K–3)

Musgrove, Margaret. *Ashanti to Zulu: African Traditions.* Illustrated by Leo and Diane Dillon. Dial, 1976. (Grades 3–6)

Ness, Evaline. *Sam, Bangs and Moonshine.* Holt, Rinehart & Winston, 1966. (Grades 2–4)

Seuss, Dr. [Theodore S. Geisel, pseud.]. *The Cat in the Hat.* Random House, 1957. (Grades K–3)

Steig, William. *Doctor De Soto.* Farrar, Straus & Giroux, 1980. (Grades 1–3)

Stevenson, James. *That Dreadful Day.* Greenwillow, 1985. (Grades 1–3)

Viorst, Judith. *Alexander and the Terrible, Horrible, No Good, Very Bad Day.* Illustrated by Ray Cruz. Atheneum, 1972. (Grades 1–6)

Waber, Bernard. *Ira Sleeps Over*. Houghton Mifflin, 1972. (Grades 1–3)

Williams, Margery. *The Velveteen Rabbit*. Illustrated by William Nicholson. Doubleday, 1958. (Grades 2–4)

Zion, Gene. *Harry, the Dirty Dog*. Illustrated by Margaret Bloy Graham. Harper & Row, 1956. (Grades K–3)

Zolotow, Charlotte. *My Grandson Lew*. Illustrated by William Pene du Bois. Harper & Row, 1972. (Grades K–3)

————. *Mr. Rabbit and the Lovely Present*. Illustrated by Maurice Sendak. Harper & Row, 1962. (Grades K–3)

Realistic Fiction

Burch, Robert. *Queeny Peavy*. Illustrated by Jerry Lazare. Viking Press, 1966. (Grades 5–6)

Byars, Betsy C. *The Summer of the Swans*. Illustrated by Ted Coconis. Viking Press, 1970. (Grades 5–6)

Cleary, Beverly. *Dear Mr. Henshaw*. Illustrated by Paul O. Zelensky. Morrow, 1983. (Grades 5–6)

Cohen, Barbara. *Thank You, Jackie Robinson*. Illustrated by Richard Caffari. Lothrop, 1974. (Grades 4–6)

Estes, Eleanor. *The Hundred Dresses*. Illustrated by Louis Slobodkin. Harcourt Brace Jovanovich, 1942. (Grades 3–6)

Paterson, Katherine. *Bridge to Terabithia*. Illustrated by Donna Diamond. Thomas Y. Crowell, 1977. (Grades 5–6)

Rawls, Wilson. *Where the Red Fern Grows*. Doubleday, 1961. (Grades 4–6)

Saint-Exupery, Antione. *The Little Prince*. Translated by Katherine Woods. Harcourt Brace Jovanovich, 1943. (Grades 2–4)

Sperry, Armstrong. *Call It Courage*. Macmillan, 1968. (Grades 4–6)

Yep, Laurence. *Child of the Owl*. Harper & Row, 1971. (Grades K–3)

Historical Fiction

Benchley, Nathaniel. *Sam the Minuteman*. Harper & Row, 1972. (Grades 4–5)

Brink, Carol R. *Caddie Woodlawn*. Illustrated by Kate Seredy. Macmillan, 1936. (Grades 3–6)

Dalgliesh, Alice. *The Courage of Sarah Noble*. Illustrated by Leonard Weisgard. Scribner's, 1954. (Grades 2–4)

Forbes, Esther. *Johnny Tremain*. Illustrated by Lynn Ward. Houghton Mifflin, 1946. (Grades 4–8)

Fox, Paula. *Slave Dancer*. Illustrated by Eros Keith. Bradbury, 1973. (Grades 2–4)

Holling, Holling C. *Paddle-to-the-Sea*. Houghton Mifflin, 1941. (Grades 5–6)

Lobel, Arnold. *On the Day Peter Stuyvesant Sailed to Town*. Harper & Row, 1981. (Grades 1–4)

Maclachlan, Patricia. *Sara, Plain and Tall.* Harper & Row, 1985. (Grades 4–6)

O'Dell, Scott. *Island of the Blue Dolphins.* Houghton Mifflin, 1960. (Grades 5–6)

Petry, Ann. *Harriet Tubman: Conductor on the Underground Railroad.* Thomas Y. Crowell, 1955. (Grades 6–10)

Wilder, Laura Ingalls. *Little House in the Big Woods.* Illustrated by Garth Williams. Harper & Row, 1953. (Grades 2–4)

Fantasy/Science Fiction

Andersen, Hans Christian. *The Emperor's New Clothes.* Illustrated by Virginia Lee Burton. Houghton Mifflin, 1949. (Grades 3–6)

Banks, Lynne Reid. *The Indian in the Cupboard.* Illustrated by Brock Cole. Doubleday, 1981. (Grades 2–4)

Babbitt, Natalie. *Tuck Everlasting.* Farrar, Straus & Giroux, 1975. (Grades 5–6)

Carroll, Lewis. *Alice's Adventures in Wonderland.* Macmillan, 1963. (Grades K–6)

Grahame, Kenneth. *The Wind in the Willows.* Illustrated by Beverly Gooding. Scribner's, 1982. (Grades 4–6)

Kipling, Rudyard. *Just So Stories.* Illustrated by Etienne Delessert. Doubleday, 1972. (Grades K–6)

Lawson, Robert. *Rabbit Hill.* Viking Press, 1944. (Grades K–3)

L'Engle, Madeline. *A Wrinkle in Time.* Farrar, Straus & Giroux, 1962. (Grades 4–6)

Lewis, C. S. *The Lion, the Witch, and the Wardrobe.* Illustrated by Pauline Baynes. Macmillan, 1961. (Grades 4–6)

Milne, A. A. *Winnie the Pooh.* Illustrated by Earnest Shepard. Dutton, 1926. (Grades K–4)

Norton, Mary. *The Borrowers.* Illustrated by Beth and Joe Krush. Harcourt Brace Jovanovich, 1963. (Grades 4–6)

Tolkien, J. R. R. *The Hobbitt.* Houghton Mifflin, 1938. (Grades 1–3)

White, E. B. *Charlotte's Web.* Illustrated by Garth Williams. Harper & Row, 1952. (Grades 2–6)

Folklore

Aardema, Verna. *Why Mosquitos Buzz in People's Ears: A West African Tale.* Illustrated by Leo and Diane Dillon. Dial, 1975. (Grades K–3)

Aesop. *Aesop's Fables.* Illustrated by Heide Holder. Viking Press, 1981. (Grades 2–6)

Asbjornsen, Peter Christian, and Jorgen E. Moe. *East of the Sun and West of the Moon and Other Tales.* Illustrated by Tom Vromay. Macmillan, 1963. (Grades 3–5)

Brown, Marcia. *Stone Soup.* Scribner's, 1947. (Grades 1–4)

D'Aulaire, Ingri, and Edgar P. D'Aulaire. *Norse Gods and Giants*. Doubleday, 1967. (Graes 3–5)

Gag, Wanda. *Tales from Grimm*. Coward-McCann, 1978. (Grades 4–6)

Galdone, Paul. *Henny Penny*. Seabury, 1968. (Grades 1–4)

————. *The Little Red Hen*. Seabury, 1974. (Grades K–2)

Grimm, Jacob, and Wilhelm Grimm. *Rapunzel*. Illustrated by Trina S. Hyman. Holiday House, 1982. (Grades 2–5)

Perrault, Charles. *Cinderella*. Illustrated by Marcia Brown. Scribner's, 1954. (Grades 1–4)

Ross, Tony. *The Three Pigs*. Pantheon, 1983. (Grades K–2)

Stoutenburg, Adrien. *American Tall Tales*. Illustrated by Richard M. Powers. Viking Press, 1966. (Grades 4–6)

Yagawa, Sumiko. *The Crane Wife*. Translated by Katherine Paterson. Illustrated by Suekichi Akaba. Morrow, 1981. (Grades 3–5)

Poetry

Benet, Rosemary, and Stephen Benet, eds. *A Book of Americans*. Holt, Rinehart & Winston, 1987. (Grades 3–6)

Brewton, Sara, and John Brewton, eds. *American Forever New: A Book of Poems*. Thomas Y. Crowell, 1968. (Grades 2–6)

Cole, William. *A Book of Animal Poems*. Illustrated by Robert Andrew Parker. Viking Press, 1973. (Grades 2–6)

Dickinson, Emily. *I'm Nobody! Who Are You? The Poems of Emily Dickinson*. Stemmer, 1978. (Grades 5–6)

Dunning, Stephen, Edward Lueders, and Hugh Smith. *Reflections on a Gift of Watermelon Pickle and Other Modern Verses*. Scott, Foresman, 1966. (Grades 4–9)

Fisher, Aileen. *Out in the Dark and Daylight*. Illustrated by Gail Owens. Harper & Row, 1980. (Grades 2–6)

Fleischman, Paul. *Joyful Noise*. Illustrated by Eric Beddows (Charlotte Zolotow). Harper & Row, 1988. (Grades K–6)

Froman, Robert. *Seeing Things: A Book of Poems*. Thomas Y. Crowell, 1974. (Grades 4–6)

Frost, Robert. *Stopping by Woods on a Snowy Evening*. Illustrated by Susan Jeffers. Dutton, 1978. (Grades 5–7)

————, compiler. *How Pleasant to Know Mr. Lear!* Holiday House, 1982. (Grades 4–6)

Merriam, Eve. *Independent Voices*. Illustrated by Arvis Stewart. Atheneum, 1968. (Grades 1–3)

Prelutsky, Jack. *New Kid on the Block*. Illustrated by James Stevenson. Greenwillow, 1984. (Grades 3–6)

Silverstein, Shel. *Where the Sidewalk Ends: Poems and Drawings*. Harper & Row, 1974. (Grades 1–6)

————. *A Light in the Attic*. Harper & Row, 1981. (Grades 2–6)

Sutherland, Zena, and Myra Livingston. *The Scott, Foresman Anthology of Children's Literature*. Scott, Foresman, 1987. (Grades 2–6)

Thayer, Ernest L. *Casey at the Bat*. Illustrated by Patricia Polacco. Putnam, 1988. (Grades 2–6)

Nonfiction

Alki. *Dinosaur Bones*. Thomas Y. Crowell, 1988. (Grades 1–3)

————. *Dinosaurs Are Different*. Thomas Y. Crowell, 1985. (Grades 1–3)

Anderson, LaVere. *The Story of Johnny Appleseed*. Garrard, 1974. (Grades 2–4)

Arnosky, Jim. *Secrets of a Wildlife Watcher*. Lothrop, 1983. (Grades 3–6)

DePaola, Tomie. *The Quicksand Book*. Holiday House, 1977. (Grades 2–5)

Isenbart, Hans-Heinrich. *A Duckling Is Born*. Photographs by Othmar Baumli. Putnam, 1981. (Grades 2–4)

Kushkin, Karla. *The Philharmonic Gets Dressed*. Illustrated by Marc Simont. Harper & Row, 1982. (Grades 2–5)

Lauber, Patricia. *Seeds: Pop Stick Glide*. Photographs by Jerome Wexler. Crown, 1981. (Grades K–3)

Paterson, Francine. *Koko's Kitten*. Photographs by Ronald H. Cohn. Scholastic Hardcover, 1985. (Grades 1–3)

Sattler, Helen R. *Dinosaurs of North America*. Illustrated by Anthony Rao. Lothrop, 1984. (Grades 3–6)

Selsam, Millicent E. *Cotton*. Photographs by Jerome Wexler. Morrow, 1982. (Grades 3–5)

————. *See Through the Forest*. Harper & Row, 1956. (Grades 2–4)

Biography

Alki. (Brandenberg). *The Many Lives of Benjamin Franklin*. Prentice-Hall, 1977. (Grades 1–3)

Clayton, Edward. *Martin Luther King: The Peaceful Warrior*. 3rd ed. Illustrated by David Hodges. Prentice-Hall, 1968. (Grades 4–6)

Faber, Doris. *Eleanor Roosevelt: First Lady of the World*. Illustrated by Donna Ruff. Viking Press, 1985. (Grades 3–6)

Feinberg, Barbara S. *Franklin D. Roosevelt: Gallant President*. Lothrop, 1981. (Grades 5–6)

Fritz, Jean. *And What Happened to Paul Revere?* Illustrated by Margot Tomes. Coward-McCann, 1973. (Grades 3–6)

McGovern, Ann. *The Secret Soldier: The Story of Deborah Sampson*. Illustrated by Ann Grifalconi. Four Winds, 1975. (Grades 4–6)

Syme, Ronald. *Magellan: First Around the World*. Burdett, 1983. (Grades 4–6)

REFERENCES

Clay, Marie. *What Did I Write?* London: Heinemann Educational Books, 1975.

Cohen, Dorothy. "The Effect of Literature on Vocabulary and Reading Achievement." *Elementary English 45* (1968): 209–213, 217.

Cullinan, Bernice E., Angela Jagger, and Dorothy Strickland. "Language Expansion for Black Children in the Primary Grades: A Research Report." *Young Children* (1974): pp. 29, 98–112.

Durkin, Dolores. *Teaching Them To Read.* Boston: Allyn & Bacon, 1970.

———. *Children Who Read Early.* New York: Teachers' College Press, 1966.

Elkind, David. "Cognitive Development and Reading." *Claremont Reading Conference Yearbook 38* (1974): 10–20.

Flood, James. "Parental Styles in Reading Episodes with Young Children." *The Reading Teacher 35* (1977): 864–867.

Gordon, Ira. "Parenting, Teaching, and Child Development." *Young Children 31* (1976): 173–183.

Graves, Donald. *Writing: Teachers and Children at Work.* London: Heinemann Educational Books, 1983.

Kozol, Jonathon. "Illiterate America." *Marketing News*, May 1983, p. 18.

Olson, D. "From Utterance to Text: The Bias of Language in Speech and Writing." *Harvard Educational Review 47* (1977): 257–281.

Sakamoto, T. "Beginning Reading in Japan." Paper presented at the annual meeting of the International Reading Association, Miami, May 1977.

Smith, Frank. *Writing and the Writer.* New York: Holt, 1982.

———. "Making Sense of Reading—and Reading Instruction." *Harvard Educational Review 47* (1977): 386–395.

Sulzby, Elizabeth. "Children's Emergent Reading of Favorite Story Books." *Reading Research Quarterly 20*, no. 4 (1985): 458–481.

Wells, Gordon. *The Mean Maker: Children Learning Language and Using Language to Learn.* London: Heinemann Press, 1986.

2

Shared
Reading
Experience

Very closely related to the read-aloud program is a classroom version of the bedtime story called the Shared Reading Experience. Just as a parent shares a book with a child as a bedtime story, a teacher shares a book with a group of children. One of the most popular types of book for this approach is a Big Book, which is an oversized book that contains illustrations and text large enough for an entire group of children to see. In shared reading, the teacher and children share in the reading and rereading of books that include favorite stories, rhymes, songs, chants, and poems.

RESEARCH ON THE SHARED READING EXPERIENCE

Holdaway (1979) is credited with discovering the effectiveness of the Shared Reading Experience. This discovery came about as a result of his investigation into the alarming increase of illiteracy in New Zealand. During the investigation, instead of looking at what caused readers to fail, Holdaway and a team of teachers began looking at what was different about successful readers. They found that the most successful readers came from homes in which books, reading, and bedtime stories were part of their everyday lives. Holdaway's team studied the bedtime story setting to find out what gave these children such an advantage. They found that during the bedtime story, the reader usually snuggled close to the child as the story was being read. When the story was completed, the child typically asked the reader to read it again. As the reader read the same story over and over again, night after night, the child learned what the story said. When the reader skipped a few pages, the child insisted that the reader read the whole story exactly as written. As the reader read the story, the child often turned the pages, becoming familiar with the illustrations and learning that the book had a top and a bottom, that words were read from left to right, and that print represented what was being read. Often, as the reader pointed to the words being read, the child repeated the words he or she recognized. From these investigations, Holdaway's team found that many children actually learned to read during the bedtime story time even though the reader made no conscious effort to teach reading. In fact, the reader was usually not trained in methods of teaching reading. The child learned to read naturally.

Research from several countries supports the belief that children can learn to read naturally through a literature-based language arts program. Doake (1979), Durkin (1966), and Smith (1971) found that preschool children learned to read without formalized reading instruction. They learned to read by being read to. Clay (1977) and Sulzby (1985) found that the strategies used in the Shared Reading Experience, which were so effective in teaching reading to preschoolers, were also valuable for classroom use. Butler (1985) reported that children in Australia and New Zealand have successfully been taught to read using Big Books through the Shared Reading Experience. Thus, the use of Big Books for shared reading is becoming more widely used. This approach is especially effective with young children.

It is no surprise that children learn to read when the Shared Reading Experience is used, since many of the important beginning reading skills are introduced during the process. Children learn that there is a connection between the written and spoken forms of language. Because they repeatedly hear the words and see the print, they begin to associate letters and sounds. Many children figure out the code by themselves. In addition, they learn that reading is a pleasurable and enjoyable activity, which is the ultimate goal of any reading program.

SELECTING SHARED READING BOOKS
Choosing the right book for the Shared Reading Experience is crucial. It is much easier to select a book for a bedtime story than for the classroom Shared Reading Experience. For the bedtime story, you can easily cater to the individual child's preference, whereas in the classroom setting, you have to select a book that appeals to every child.

Selecting books for the Shared Reading Experience is similar to selecting books for reading aloud; however, there are a few aspects of a story that are particularly important for a successful Shared Reading Experience:

1. Select books that are predictable; that is, ones whose outcome can be imagined very easily from the reading. This predictability allows children, after reading a few pages, to tell what they think will happen next or how the story will end. For example, in the book *Danger*, after you have read a few pages such as "Look out for the chairs. They are full of bears. Look out for the cakes. They are full of snakes," the children are ready to predict and call out "witches" when you read, "Look out for ditches. They are full of ___ (witches)." The children are using meaning clues as well as rhyming clues to predict words and happenings.

2. Select books that are repetitious; that is, ones whose patterns repeat over and over again. Repetition allows the children to actively participate by joining in a chant or chorus that repeats itself frequently. For example, in the book *Who's in the Shed?* the sentence pattern "What did she see" is repeated on nearly every page. Therefore, when you come to this repeated phrase, the children join in. This kind of repetition is important when learning to read because research indicates that words need to be repeated many times before they actually become part of a child's reading vocabulary. Repeating the words in a Shared Reading Experience is much more interesting and fun than learning them from a list on the chalkboard.

3. Select books that contain rich, descriptive, and memorable language with lots of rhythm and rhyme. An example of this rich, descriptive language can be found in the story *The Night Train*. In this story, the words sound like a train making its way along the track: "They go along the hallway, Ticketty-tat, Ticketty-tat. They go along the hallway, Tania and Jessie and Cat."

4. Select books that reflect warmth, humor, and fun. Children enjoy the story *A Monster Sandwich* because it is fun to see the huge amounts of things being put on the sandwich. For example, whole heads of lettuce are used instead of a single piece of lettuce. Children have fun imagining what a big sandwich like this would truly look like.

5. Children love nonsensical words and lines such as those

found in the story *Mrs. Wishy-Washy.* They love repeating "In the tub you go . . . wishy-washy, wishy-washy."

6. Select books with attractive and appropriate illustrations that enhance the text. For example, within the book *The Enormous Watermelon*, two full pages reveal an *enormous* watermelon. Children squeal with delight at the sight of this big, tremendous, enormous watermelon. What a wonderful way to exhibit what enormous really means!

7. Select books that have characters and situations with which children can identify. As the story *In a Dark, Dark Woods* is being read, children often identify with darkness and their own scary fantasies and dreams, the darkness of their rooms, the darkness of outside, and so on. Therefore, the children can especially relate to the last line of the book, "And in the dark, dark box, THERE WAS A GHOST."

8. Select books that have an active story line. The book *Three Little Ducks* demonstrates this kind of action. In this book, the ducks "paddle, paddle, paddle" and they "waddle, waddle, waddle" and they "gobble, gobble, gobble." All of these actions are enjoyable to read about or to act out.

GUIDELINES FOR READING
THE SHARED READING SELECTION USING BIG BOOKS

According to Butler (1987), the Shared Reading Experience secret of success is creating the right environment, one in which a trusting, exciting, and secure feeling is established. In addition, the environment must be free of competition, criticism, and constant correction. The children and teacher usually develop a feeling of intimacy that is much like the feeling established during bedtime story hour. Therefore, when conducting a Shared Reading Experience in a classroom setting, it is important to consider the following guidelines:*

1. Seat the children on the floor as close to you as possible so that all can see the illustrations and print. It is best if the Big Book is placed on an easel so that you can conveniently turn the

---

*Since Big Books allow children to see the text and illustrations more clearly, these guidelines focus on Big Books. However, the guidelines can be adapted for use with other books.

pages and point to the words as the book is being read. It may be desirable, at times, to have a child turn the pages.

2. Introduce the story. This can be done by discussing the front cover illustration, the title, any connections with past experiences, and so on. The introduction should be brief. For example, when introducing Ezra Jack Keats's *The Snowy Day*, the following questions may be used as an introduction: What is snow like? How does it feel? Have you ever played in the snow? If not, what do you think it would be like to play in the snow? The aim of the introduction is to whet the appetite of the listeners so they are interested in hearing what the story is about.

3. Read the story. The first time, read the story for pure enjoyment and pleasure; subsequent readings should provide a means for learning to read. Since many teachers find it difficult to point to the words while reading with expression, that can come with future readings. You may want to use a pointer so that the children can see exactly what is being read. As you reread the Big Book, point to the words and invite the children to participate. They can repeat a familiar refrain or chant or make simple hand actions or appropriate sound effects. As you point to the words, they are able to see that print follows certain conventions, and they begin to recognize sound-symbol relationships and words.

4. Following the initial reading, discuss the illustrations, characters, or favorite part of the book. Remember that at this point the discussion should flow naturally. Making connections with the author's intended meaning or testing for comprehension is not appropriate. You will return to this story many times; therefore, this initial discussion should be brief and end before the children lose interest.

5. After the initial or subsequent rereadings of the Big Book, be sure to conduct appropriate follow-up activities. These activities may include independent reading of the story, dramatization, art, music, and writing. Of all the follow-up activities, independent reading is the most important because it allows the children to become part of a reading community. Small versions of the Big Books are available for independent reading. These should be made readily available to the children so they can reread their favorite books as often as possible. The ultimate goal of the independent reading is for the children to learn to read by reading.

SHARED READING OBSERVATION SHEET

Names of Students

Does the student . . .

1. show interest in the story?

2. become actively involved?

3. participate in responses to key words or phrases?

4. participate in predicting happenings?

5. react appropriately to the emotions conveyed?

6. demonstrate curiosity about the story's characters and plot?

7. take part in discussions before or after the story is read?

8. show interest in reading the book independently?

9. show a desire to read and reread the book?

10. transfer ideas from the story to his or her own writing?

6. During and after the Shared Reading Experience, evaluate the progress of each student. Once the child has accomplished a particular skill, check the appropriate column next to the questions provided on the Shared Reading Observation Sheet (see page 29).

EXTENDED ACTIVITIES FOR THE SHARED READING EXPERIENCE

There are many stimulating and useful follow-up activities to extend the Shared Reading Experience using either existing text or creating new Big Books. You may need to provide both independent and group activities, depending on the children's needs.

Using Existing Text

The following activities use existing text to teach reading skills.

1. After you have read the text at least two or three times to the students, use the popular cloze technique to develop word recognition skills. To do this, place blank pieces of paper over key words in the selection. Then reread the text, stopping at each blank and allowing the children to supply the missing word.

Another way to do the cloze technique is to write the words from a page of the text on individual cards. For example, using the book *Bedtime for Francis*, write the following words on the cards:

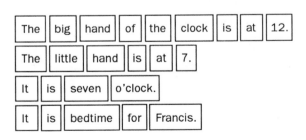

Tape the word cards on the chalkboard, omitting some of the words as follows:

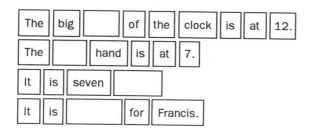

Have the students read the paragraph, supplying the missing words as they read. The missing words can then be taped to the chalkboard and the paragraph can be reread.

2. Use a story such as *Woosh* to make up new stories by replacing characters and actions. For example, the original story reads "I had a little dog. His name was Dandy. His tail was long. And his legs were bandy." You can help the children make innovations in the text that may read something like this: "I had a little cat. His name was Tingle. He had a bell around his neck. It went jingle, jingle." This is fun to do and extends the use of available books. In addition, children are being creative as they develop skills necessary to learn to read.

3. Using the vocabulary words from a Big Book story, make word cards on 5-by-8-inch index cards. Line up these word cards along the chalkboard tray. Display the Big Book pages so that everyone can see them. Direct a child to select a word from the tray and then find the same word in the story. This activity can be used as a readiness activity to reinforce visual discrimination skills or with beginning readers to reinforce the recognition of words. Students can also make their own word cards to create individual word banks.

4. Discuss sentences by pointing out that sentences begin with capital letters and have punctuation marks at the end. Discuss the different punctuation marks, explaining the purpose of each. While you read the text aloud and the children follow along, they have the opportunity to observe that punctuation marks help guide reading. As you draw attention to the functions of the punctuation marks, children will begin to make the connection between reading and writing. This will help guide them

in their reading and help them with their writing. For example, in the Big Book T*he Big Toe*, when you read the line, "Then something by the gate said, 'Who's got my big toe?'" you can point out that the line "Who's got my big toe?" is in quotation marks to indicate that someone is speaking. As a result, when the student is writing, he or she may transfer this knowledge to the works being created.

5. Present a play based on a story. It is an excellent motivation for getting the children to read and reread a story. The children can make costumes, masks, and props. The book *The Farm Concert* is an excellent book to act out. Have the children help make masks for a farmer, dog, duck, frog, pig, and sheep. Next, choose a child to be the farmer and other children or groups of children to represent the animals. You and the remaining children can read the story as each animal character joins in with their parts as the text is being read. For example, when the character of the cow says "Moo-moo," the group reads "went the cow."

6. Invite the children to identify repetitive lines and indicate which words are the same. Discuss how some words sound the same, but look different, such as *heard* and *herd* or *hear* and *here*. Discuss the concept of rhyming words. Select words that rhyme from the story. Encourage the children to think of other words to rhyme with these words.

7. Once the children are familiar with the story, select a page or two and copy them, leaving spaces where children can add their own words, phrases, or lines. Read the story, substituting words, phrases, or lines suggested by the children. Then discuss the differences and similarities between their version of the story and the original version.

8. Using a Big Book such as *Bedtime for Francis*, discuss the idea of selecting symbols to represent each of the characters. For example, Francis may be a circle, Mother Bear may be a triangle, and Father Bear may be a square. Allow the children to create the symbols from flannel and then retell the story on a flannel board using these symbols. This activity will also aid in the development of abstract thinking skills.

9. Introduce children to word attack skills. It is important that children know how to approach an unfamiliar word. They can be introduced to the use of context clues, phonic analysis,

structural analysis, and syllabication. For example, if a child comes to the word *caterpillar*, discuss how that word can be divided into smaller units (syllables). Once the word is divided into syllables, discuss how the reader can then pronounce each small unit and then finally put it together to pronounce the whole word.

Making Big Books

Big Books, as well as copies of smaller versions, are readily available from a variety of publishing companies. However, the lack of availability of specific titles and the cost may cause you to make your own Big Books. Students can help in the production process. This involvement stimulates interest in reading and fosters a feeling of ownership and pride in the product. There are several different ways to make Big Books.

The first step is to select a favorite story. This may be a story that children have rated highly in the read-aloud session. Once the story is selected, copy each page of the text onto blank pieces of paper that are approximately 25 inches by 15 inches. An older student can help with this. The text must be duplicated exactly and the print must be large enough for a group of children to see. Once the text is written, reread the story and discuss possible illustrations. Give each student (or pairs of students) one page of the text to illustrate. You need to circulate while the illustrations are being created and ask relevant questions to ensure that the pictures adequately illustrate the text. When the illustrations are completed, bring the children together as a group and display the pages of illustrated text. As a group, decide on the correct sequence for the pages. Once the sequence is determined and coincides with the order of the original text, the book can be bound. Before binding, however, display the pages along the chalkboard, bulletin board, or clothesline for a time. This gives the children an opportunity to read and reread the story. Once the decision to bind the book is made, the pages can be put together into a Big Book, adding a cover and a title page. A heavy-duty stapler, metal rings, or heavy stitching (dental floss works well) can be used for binding. You may want to reinforce the spine of the book with heavy book-binding tape. A nice addition to a student-created Big Book is to prepare a book information page that lists the names of the illustrators, a photograph of the class, the date of publication, and a make-believe publishing company. It is a good idea to laminate the covers. Then place a loan pocket on the inside of the back cover so children can check out the books.

A second way to make a Big Book is to select a favorite book, following the same procedures as in the previous example, except that you use the illustrations from the original book instead of illustrations done by the children. Enlarge the original illustrations using a duplicating machine or an opaque projector, and then color the illustrations. Finally, adhere the illustrations to the large sheets of paper and sequence them to make the Big Book.

A third way to produce Big Books for a classroom is to encourage children to write and illustrate their own books. This can be done by following the guidelines for the writing process (Chapter 16). Instead of publishing a regular-size book, you can provide large sheets of paper on which to publish the books. Illustrations can include original photographs or pictures from magazines.

SUGGESTED BIG BOOKS FOR SHARED READING

The following Big Books are available from Rigby Education, 4545 Virginia Street, Crystal Lake, Illinois 60014.

Prekindergarten to First Grade

Danger
The Enormous Watermelon
The Gingerbread Man
Gobble, Gobble, Glup, Glup
Interruptions
Jack and the Beanstalk
The Little Red Hen
A Monster Sandwich

The Night Train
Oh No!
The Three Billy Goats Gruff
The Three Little Pigs
The Ugly Duckling
When Goldilocks Went to the
     House of the Three Bears
Who's in the Shed?

First to Second Grade

The Bean Bag Mom Made
Breakfast in Bed/Green Bananas
Debra's Dog
Excuses, Excuses
The Greedy Gray Octopus

The Horrible Black Bug/On A Cold,
     Cold Day
Munching Mark
Tricking Tracy
The Trolley Ride
When Lana Was Absent

The following Big Books are available from Wright Group, 10949 Technology Place, San Diego, California 92127.

Kindergarten to First Grade

The Big Toe
Boo-hoo
Cat and Mouse
Dan, the Flying Man
The Farm Concert
Grandpa, Grandpa
Harry Bears
The Hungry Giant
In a Dark, Dark Woods
The Jigaree
Lazy Mary
The Monsters' Party
Mrs. Wishy-Washy

Obadiah
One Cold Wet Night
Poor Old Polly
Rat-a-Tat-Tat
The Red Rose
Sing a Song
Smarty Pants
Three Little Ducks
To Market, To Market
To Town
Who Will Be My Mother?
Woosh
Yes Ma'am

First to Second Grade

Cat on the Roof
Clever Mr. Brown
Cooking Pot
Fast and Funny
Fiddle-Dee-Dee
Grandma's Stick
Help Me
Just Like Me
Let Me In

More! More! More!
The Pie Thief
Roly-Poly
Sing to the Moon
Sun Smile
Tiddalik
Wet Grass
Will I Never?
Yum and Yuk

The following Big Books are available from Scholastic Inc., P.O. Box 7501, 2931 East McCarty Street, Jefferson City, Missouri 65102.

Kindergarten to Third Grade

All the Pretty Horses
Bedtime for Francis
Boss for a Week
Bunches and Bunches of Bunnies
Caps for Sale
Cats and Mice
Chicken Soup and Rice
Clifford's Family
Farmer Joe's Hot Day
Have You Seen Birds?

A House Is a House for Me
How Much Is a Million?
I Said to Sam
Jump, Frog, Jump
The King's Cat
The Little Red Hen
Madeline
More Spaghetti, I Say?
The New Baby Calf
Noisy Nora

On Market Street
The Owl and the Pussy Cat
Sing a Song of Mother Goose
Snowy Day
The Three Billy Goats Gruff

What Do You Do with a Kangaroo?
Where Have You Been?
Why Can't I Fly?
Wynken, Blynken and Nod

REFERENCES

Butler, Andrea. The Story Box in the Classroom Stage 1. Australia: Rigby Education, 1987.

————. Shared Book Experience: An Introduction. Australia: Rigby Education, 1985.

Clay, Marie. Reading: *The Patterning of Complex Behaviour*. London: Heinemann, 1977.

Doake, David. "Book Experience and Emergent Reading Behaviour." Paper presented at Preconvention Institute No. 24, Research on Written Language Development, International Reading Association Annual Convention, Atlanta, Ga., April 1979.

Durkin, Dolores. *Children Who Read Early*. New York: Teachers' College Press, 1966.

Holdaway, Don. *The Foundations of Literacy*. Toronto: Ashton Scholastic, 1979.

Smith, Frank. *Understanding Reading*. Toronto: Holt, Rinehart & Winston, 1971.

Sulzby, Elizabeth. "Children's Emergent Reading of Favourite Story Books." *Reading Research Quarterly 20*, no. 4 (1985): 458–481.

3

Sustained Silent Reading

Sustained Silent Reading (SSR), first initiated by Lyman C. Hunt, Jr., in the early 1960s, is an accepted component of many reading programs. It can be used in a single classroom, in a school building, or in an entire district. The process is very simple. In a single classroom setting, each student, and the teacher, chooses something to read and then everyone reads silently, without interruption, for a specific amount of time. When an entire school or district initiates the SSR program, everyone in the school or district selects something to read and then reads silently. This includes principals, custodians, secretaries, librarians, and so on. The amount of time allotted to SSR may differ in each situation.

RESEARCH ON SUSTAINED SILENT READING

What is referred to here as SSR has also been called Uninterrupted Sustained Silent Reading and Student Quiet Uninterrupted Reading Time. In recent years, SSR has attracted more attention because of claims that reading is overtaught and underpracticed. Too many teachers give students little time to practice the word recognition and comprehension skills they teach. This is like learning the names of the notes on a piano and then not playing the piano. In many classrooms, a disproportionate amount of time is spent on skill-building activities such as completing workbook pages or filling in the blanks. Reading is a skill and, like all other skills, the more you use it the better you become. Anderson et al. (1985) substantiates the importance of practicing reading, recognizing that the best readers are those who read the most. Researchers agree that the amount of reading done outside school relates consistently with achievement gains (as measured on standardized tests). Mork (1972) went so far as to suggest that the ratio of reading practice to reading instruction should be as high as 80 to 20. However, when Goodlad (1984) studied schools in America, he found that only 6 percent of the classroom time in the elementary schools was actually spent reading.

In addition to providing the opportunity for transferring and applying reading skills to actual reading, SSR may help create an interest in reading and thus develop lifelong readers. Today, more than ever before, producing lifelong readers seems to be a very worthwhile goal of the SSR program. Research indicates a decline in how much reading is done and how many people are reading. Long and Henderson (1973) reported that during a two-week period, a group of fifth-grade students spent an average of only three hours reading compared to thirty hours watching television. Other studies (i.e., Anderson et al., 1985) have revealed similar findings. Thus, it appears essential for schools to provide an independent, silent time for reading. If the SSR period lasts only 15 minutes a day, five days a week, that is more than an hour of reading per week.

Since the inception of SSR, many studies have been conducted to determine the effectiveness of such programs on reading achievement and changes in attitudes. Research studies, such as those done by Reed (1978) and Sadowski (1980), did not find any significant gains in reading achievement, especially at the secondary level. However, Allington (1977) found that younger readers did show improvement in both attitude and achievement skills. Other studies have found that positive attitude changes occurred (Petre, 1977; Cline and Kretke, 1980). The positive attitude changes toward reading included (1) students spent more time reading and discussing books, and (2) more students were motivated to go to the school library and were happier about overall reading-related assignments.

SELECTING SUSTAINED SILENT READING MATERIALS

One of the most important considerations for a SSR program is that a variety of reading materials must be provided. Although students select their own material, your responsibility is to make a wide assortment of materials available. Sustained Silent Reading is a time for reading enjoyment, and the materials provided should promote reading for the sheer pleasure of it. These materials should include representation from the various genres, reflect the vast interests of the students, and meet a wide range of independent reading abilities.

It is especially important to give beginning readers the opportunity to select from familiar books, such as display books that have been previously used in the read-aloud program or books that they have listened to at home. Their knowledge of the story, coupled with their interest and use of context clues and decoding skills, will have them "reading the story" and feeling quite proud of their accomplishment!

For the nonreader, provide a selection of wordless picture books. These books should be carefully chosen based on their ability to adequately relate the story through the pictures. As children "read" wordless books, they develop independence and enjoy an actual sense of reading. Many of the reading readiness skills are fostered as children read their picture books. They learn to turn pages, practice "reading" from left to right, and grow in their love and respect for books.

In order for SSR to be successful, you must have a well-stocked classroom library! When books are easily accessible, children are much more likely to reach out for one. Periodicals, newspapers, and reference books, as well as quantities of books from the various genres, should be included. Chapter 12 discusses, in detail, the design, planning, organization, and implementation of a classroom library.

In addition to using a well-stocked classroom library, give students ample opportunity to use the school library. Make arrangements with the school librarian to give students a guided tour, pointing out the locations of various genres and explaining the procedures for locating and checking out materials, the rules of the library, and so on. Chapter 12 also provides activities to acquaint students with the library. Encourage students to visit local public libraries and to become acquainted with the materials and services offered there.

As previously mentioned, newspapers are a valuable classroom resource. Arrange for a local newspaper to be delivered daily or at least twice a week. This will help keep students abreast of current events. To help intermediate students become aware of different viewpoints, arrange to have papers delivered from at least two different publishers. Introduce students to the features of the newspaper (i.e., editorials, international news, national news, local news, advice columns, and weather reports) before the SSR time and involve them in activities that will foster their understanding of the publication and its organization. Many local newspapers provide educational consultants who will conduct sessions on using the newspaper. In addition to subscribing to local newspapers, subscribe to weekly classroom newspapers such as *Scholastic, News Ranger,* or *Weekly Reader*.

Children's periodicals are also valuable sources of reading materials. These include *Highlights*, *Ranger Rick*, and *Jack and Jill*.

Students, especially in the intermediate grades, enjoy reading reference books. For example, *The Guinness Book of World Records* contains many interesting facts. Students are fascinated by the world's largest roller coaster, the most difficult tonguetwister, or the records set in their favorite sports. The encyclopedia is another reference material that should be available for selection during SSR. Often students like to browse through an encyclopedia, reading articles that piqué their interest and curiosity. Other reference books that should be displayed include *Famous First Facts*, *Familiar Quotations*, almanacs, and biographical dictionaries.

Often, teachers find it difficult to interest students in reading a variety of books. The following suggestions may help motivate students to select reading materials for SSR:

1. Provide a time for students to share books and magazines or newspaper articles. Encourage them to read or tell about a part of their selection that was particularly interesting.

2. Borrow a cart from the school library to use for a "Book Show on Wheels." Display books, magazines, and newspapers that you have collected from the library, and give students a brief introduction or booktalk on each of the selections. The introductions should be stimulating and provide just enough information to whet the students' appetites so that they can't wait to get their hands on the materials and read! You must be quite knowledgeable about the content of the materials for this type of presentation.

3. As a project, allow a group of students to prepare their own "Book Show on Wheels." They may collect books relating to

a specific theme or selections may be made based on individual literary leanings. Provide time for students to share their selections with the rest of the class.

4. Conduct a "Literary Rap Session" in which each student has an opportunity to discuss a special interest. Encourage others in the class to suggest related reading materials that the student might enjoy.

5. Recommend books based on or used as the motivation for popular movies or television programs. Encourage students to write short scripts, scenes, and story narratives.

6. Organize a paperback bookstore in your class or involve the school's parent association in such an endeavor. The bookstore could be operated at selected times, such as before classes begin in the morning, during lunch, or after school. The store could promote both new and used books. Encourage students to bring in books that they have already read and trade them for other used books or apply their credit to newer books. Students may even take turns being the store's manager or salesperson.

ESTABLISHING THE SUSTAINED SILENT READING PERIOD

Although establishing an SSR period is relatively simple and requires little preparation, certain procedures should be followed to help ensure a successful program. In order for SSR to establish and nurture the habit of sustained reading of self-selected materials, acquaint students with the purpose of the SSR period and the rules that must be followed. It is important that students recognize that the only thing they are expected to do is read. This is a time for free, uninterrupted reading.

There are few rules for SSR. Do not permit talking, and do not allow students to roam about the room or reading area. To prevent students from constantly searching for new reading materials during SSR, each student should have three items of reading material at his or her desk. Then if a book proves to be uninteresting or too difficult, another selection is readily available. During class time, either before or after SSR, give students the opportunity to replenish their stock of reading materials. Encourage students to suggest books for the read-aloud program that they are interested in but that proved too difficult for independent reading.

The most basic rule for SSR is that the only activity going on is reading. *No one* is exempt, not even the teacher. As a matter of fact, as the teacher becomes involved in SSR, he or she provides an excellent role model. Sadly, the teacher may be the first adult students have seen who is involved in reading for pleasure, and therefore, it is imperative that the teacher read and not be allowed to get sidetracked by daily classroom tasks. These can wait! In many schools, SSR is implemented as a schoolwide effort. Everyone from the principal to the custodial staff reads at the appointed time!

Discussion of SSR and its rules should take place several days before the program's implementation. You may want to brainstorm the rules with your students. Once the rules have been established, they should be prominently displayed. If a rule is broken, the infraction should simply be pointed out to the student and SSR should continue. At the onset, students will be more likely to interrupt their reading. However, as they become more familiar with the process and as the SSR habit is established, there will be fewer problems.

RULES FOR SUSTAINED SILENT READING

Select a book—one that's just right

Silently enjoy it—let your imagination take flight

Read it tomorrow, read it today

Everybody reads—that's the way!

Sustained Silent Reading should be scheduled for the same time each day. Students look forward to SSR and should be able to expect it as a permanent part of their daily routine. As you first implement SSR in your curriculum, begin with shorter periods and gradually increase the time. The following chart provides guidelines, but your own experiences will be the best guide. Experiment with the time frame that works best for your students. Often, for younger children whose attention span is short, it is advantageous to plan two shorter SSR periods rather than one longer one. As a rule of thumb, it is always better to schedule too short a time rather than too long a time. In that way, children will anxiously be awaiting the next day's SSR.

SSR TIME GUIDE

Grade Level	Minimum Time	Maximum Time
K–1	3–5 minutes	10–15 minutes
2–3	5–10 minutes	15–20 minutes
4–6	10–15 minutes	20–30 minutes

Since the purpose of SSR is to make reading an enjoyable part of the student's world, make the SSR period as comfortable as possible. As adults, we usually do not sit in an upright position when we read for enjoyment; therefore, students shouldn't be required to sit at their desks and read. Allow them to find their own niche or corner of the room. They may wish to decorate it with a banner or poster and bring in pillows, towels, or cushions to sit on. If the weather permits, take them outside to read. Let them find a tree, lean against its trunk, and start to read.

FOLLOW-UP ACTIVITIES

Sustained Silent Reading is not be used as a prerequisite for a book report. Essential to the success of the program is the students' realization that the SSR period has been established to give them an opportunity to read whatever they choose. Reserve some time at the end of the period for students to share something special from their readings if they desire. You may want to share as well, but begin this sharing time only after the program is well established.

To vary the sharing sessions, you might ask students to share specific portions of their readings. Again, student participation should be encouraged, not forced. You might ask the students to read or share one of the following: a part that felt good, a part that made you wish you were somewhere else, the part that you liked best, a part that made you wish you were someone else, or a part that made you feel happy, uneasy, or surprised.

Students should be encouraged to keep a log of the books they read during SSR and during other parts of the day. Younger students will need help in keeping their records; perhaps a class record would be more appropriate. You may want to reproduce the Independent Reading Log (page 46) for more mature students and allow them to keep a copy at their desk to fill in whenever they finish a book.

As an alternative to a log, create a booklet in which students can record their readings. Fold a sheet of 8-by-11-inch paper into book form. On the cover, write "Reading for Pleasure" and then draw lines for the student's name and grade. Inside, on both sides, and on the back cover, put numbered lines on which the student can list each book he or she has read and the name of the author. At the end of the year, students should have a fairly impressive list of the books they have read just for the fun of it!

INDEPENDENT READING LOG

Student's name:_____

Books I Have Read . . .

Date   Title of Book   Author

_____

_____

_____

_____

_____

_____

_____

_____

_____

_____

_____

_____

_____

REFERENCES

Allington, Richard. "If They Don't Read Much, How They Gonna Get Good." *Journal of Reading*, October 1977, pp. 57–61.

Anderson, Richard C., Elfrieda H. Hicbert, Judith A. Scott, and Ian A. G. Wilkinson. *Becoming a Nation of Readers: The Report of the Commission on Reading*. Washington, D.C.: National Institute of Education, 1985.

Cline, Ruth K. J., and George L. Kretke. "An Evaluation of Long-Term SSR in the Junior High School." *Journal of Reading 23* (March 1980): 503–506.

Goodlad, John I. *A Place Called School*. New York: McGraw-Hill, 1984.

Long, Barbara H., and Edmund H. Henderson. "Children's Use of Time: Some Personal and Social Correlates." *The Elementary School Journal 73* (January 1973): 193–199.

Mork, Theodore A. "Sustained Silent Reading in the Classrooms." *The Reading Teacher 25* (February 1972): 438–441.

Petre, Richard M. "On the Job Reading for Teachers." *Journal of Reading 20* (January 1977): 310–311.

Reed, Kathleen. "An Investigation of the Effect of Sustained Silent Reading on Reading Comprehension Skills and Attitude Toward Reading of Urban Secondary School Students." Paper presented at the National Reading Conference, St. Petersburg Beach, Florida, November 1978.

Sadowski, Mark C. "Ten Years of Uninterrupted Sustained Silent Reading." *Reading Improvement 17* (Summer 1980): 153–156.

4
Storytelling

Storytelling is nothing new. It began thousands of years before written language, as early people spun tales to depict the human experience and to attempt to understand the unknown. These tales expressed the human qualities of hope, fear, love, and jealousy and represented interpretations of phenomena that confused, awed, and terrified their creators. As stories were passed orally from generation to generation, details were changed based on the times, the style and creativity of the teller, and the needs of the audience, yet the themes remained constant. These themes have survived over the ages due to their universal appeal, and these stories are the myths, legends, and folktales we enjoy today.

As people traveled from country to country and continent to continent, they brought their culture and heritage in the form of stories. Most myths and legends, whether Greek, Roman, or Norse, contain similar plots, characters, and themes. Likewise, popular folktales retain those elements basic to understanding human motivation, and they reflect the values of good versus evil and right over might. Although each country has its own tales that mirror the values of its people, such as the American Tall Tale that reflects the vast open spaces of the American West and the sense of "bigness," the themes transcend time and place.

One of the main reasons for the popularity and longevity of these tales is the talent and skill of the storyteller who breathes life into them. Storytelling is an art; in fact, it is one of the oldest art forms. The storyteller captures the images, recreates the story, and captivates the audience. The storyteller does what the name implies, he or she *tells* the story rather than reads it. A good storyteller must not only be able to communicate the plot, he or she must also convey the mood, the sense of being there.

THE IMPORTANCE OF STORYTELLING

The classroom is a perfect setting for storytelling—a strategy that is too often overlooked. Storytelling fulfills two main purposes: to entertain and to inform. A teacher can make the past come alive for his or her students and help them understand our culture as well as the cultures of other places and times. As they are transported through time, children gain an appreciation for the values that have shaped our lives. Storytelling can also bring much of the classroom curriculum to life. A lesson in electricity will be much more meaningful, for example, if students first listen to a story about the life of Edison, his successes, his failures, and especially his perseverance.

Through storytelling, students find that they are not alone. They experience the story together and realize that others share their feelings, insights, and understandings, and the impact of the story on their lives. When children share a story, they enjoy it more. They laugh harder, they feel more deeply, and they become part of a bonding process that includes their classmates and the storyteller.

Storytelling is a perfect strategy for improving the communication skills of listening, writing, and speaking. Because of its very nature, children must focus on the story, the action, and the dialogue in order to capture the meaning. Children are better able to draw inferences when they listen rather than read. As this skill is developed through strategies such as storytelling, students will be better equipped to improve their ability to draw inferences when reading silently.

Storytelling encourages children to appreciate and respect our language, to develop their own use of language, both written and oral, and to organize their thoughts and ideas.

Finally, through storytelling, the teacher can foster a love of literature. Introducing students to the various genres encourages them to seek similar books for their independent reading. Storytelling gives vent to their emotional needs, allows their imaginations to soar, and gives them the opportunity to share in the experiences that have shaped our world.

SELECTING THE STORY

One of the most important criteria to remember when selecting material for storytelling, as when choosing read-aloud materials, is the way in which the book or poem affects the storyteller.

Since the storyteller has an intimate relationship with the audience, his or her feelings toward the story will be transferred to them.

Folklore, which includes myths, legends, fairy tales, and fables, is perhaps the most popular genre for storytelling. Children love these stories, and they contain elements that children relate well to, such as a fast-moving plot, realistic and convincing characters, little unnecessary detail, and universal themes. These stories transmit their message in an appealing and easy-to-understand manner, never in a didactic, pedantic tone. And the tales affect young and old alike. Even as adults, we cherish the belief that good will triumph over evil, that each ugly duckling will one day awaken to find that he or she has been transformed into a graceful and glorious creature.

Poetry is another genre that lends itself well to storytelling. Children soon learn to appreciate the beauty of poetry, its rhythm, rhyme, and verse. Through nursery rhymes, young children become familiar with alliteration. They look forward to the repetition that involves them in the actual storytelling. Older children also enjoy the ballads and narrative poems whose verses tell of life, at times tragic and frustrating but always exciting.

Realistic stories and biographies are also easily adapted for storytelling. Children thrill to those stories that satisfy their own needs for love, security, and adventure. These genres allow students to identify with the plot and character, depicting life the way it is—good and bad.

When choosing materials for storytelling, consider the following criteria:

1. Choose books for a variety of purposes. Storytelling can inform and entertain. Match the stories to the needs of the children. Choosing the right materials can help students better understand themselves and others, gain insight into specific problems, become aware of past cultures as well as their own, and learn to appreciate the various genres.

2. Make sure that the story fits your own style, talents, and personality. For example, if a book requires the use of dialects, you may find it difficult to reproduce the needed dialect effectively.

3. Select materials in which there is sufficient action and

dialogue. You may often need to add dialogue when adapting a story; however, stories that are completely determined by dialogue and that rely on "exact wording" or illustrations to play an integral part are usually better selections for reading aloud. For example, because the illustrations in *The Very Hungry Caterpillar* are so realistic, colorful, and alive, they play a significant part in the story, helping children to understand the metamorphosis of a butterfly. This concept would be much more difficult to demonstrate through storytelling; thus, the book is far more appropriate for reading aloud.

4. As you build a repertoire of materials for storytelling, select materials that reflect a variety of genres. It is helpful to keep a separate Story Folder for each story you learn and then keep all pertinent information and needed materials inside that folder (see the following section on "Preparing the Story"). On the outside of the folder, include the following information: name of the story or poem, author, and genre. Check your files to be sure that each genre is represented.

5. Base selections on your knowledge of the audience, their age, interests, and maturity. Be sure that the vocabulary used fits the listening level of your audience rather than their reading level. Students can understand stories far beyond their reading level. The reverse is also true. A story may be written at a lower reading level, but if the theme is of interest to older children, it could easily be adapted for storytelling. Listening levels can be determined by using instruments such as Informal Classroom Reading Inventories. Informal reading inventories are available from many publishers, such as Scott, Foresman.

PREPARING THE STORY

A cardinal principle underlying the process of storytelling is *DON'T MEMORIZE the story*. Each time a story is told, it should take on a personality of its own, reflecting an understanding of the audience, their needs, interests, maturity level, and listening level. It is crucial that the storyteller establish a rapport with the audience. Memorization usually hampers this rapport, preventing the storyteller from being natural and responding to the audience's feedback.

Good storytelling does not come without effort. Just as an actor must rehearse lines, reaching into his or her soul for just the right blend of honesty and emotion, so must the storyteller. In order to be an effective storyteller, you must know the story and become part of it. You must understand the motivations and conflicts of the characters, feel what they must feel, and become sensitive to the images and mood created by the author. There is no magic recipe for becoming a good storyteller. Preparation, practice, and experience are the main ingredients, for only through trial and error will you become successful. The following steps will help you prepare stories for storytelling and should serve as a checklist:

☐ 1. Read the story several times.
☐ 2. Analyze the plot to determine the introduction, the conclusion, and the various scenes.
☐ 3. Analyze the story to determine the action, conflict, and climax. These will merit emphasis during storytelling.
☐ 4. Notice the repetition of words and phrases.
☐ 5. Visualize the characters in order to bring them to life for the audience.
☐ 6. Visualize the setting and determine the mood of the story.
☐ 7. Consider what gestures, facial expressions, and voice tones would be most appropriate in establishing the mood of the story.
☐ 8. Outline the story. Your outline should include the introduction, the main scenes, the climax, and the conclusion. In folklore (folktales, myths, legends, and fables), memorize a few sentences of the introduction and conclusion since they immediately set the stage for the story and envelope students in their magic. Include any specific words or phrases that are repeated throughout the story so that they can be repeated accurately and can be used to involve students in the actual storytelling. The following sample outline may serve as a guide.

Rumpelstiltskin

I. Introduction

"There was once a miller who was very poor, but he had a beautiful daughter. Now it once happened that he had occasion to speak with the King, and in order to give himself an air of importance, he said, 'I have a daughter who can spin gold out of straw.'"

II. Scenes
   A. King puts girl into chamber filled with straw, a
      reel, and a spinning wheel and tells her that
      unless she can spin all the straw into gold she
      will be killed. As girl cries, she is visited by a
      strange little man. "What will you give me if I
      spin it for you?" She gives him her necklace.
   B. Scene is repeated only this time she is put into
      a larger room filled with straw. She is visited
      again by the strange man. "What will you give
      me if I spin it for you?" She gives him her ring.
   C. The third time, she is put into a still larger
      room and again visited by the strange man.
      "What will you give me if I spin it for you?" This
      time she has nothing and offers him her first-
      born child.
   D. The girl becomes queen and a year later a
      child is born. The strange little man comes to
      claim the child. The queen begs him to give up
      his claim, and he says he will if, within three
      days, she can guess his name.
   E. Queen sends messengers all over the land.
      First two times the strange man appears she
      tries all types of names. After each he says,
      "No, no, that's not my name."
   F. Finally, a messenger in the woods hears:
      "Today I bake; tomorrow I brew my beer;
      The next day I will bring the Queen's child
         here.
      Ah! lucky 'tis that not a soul doth know
      That Rumpelstiltskin is my name. Ho! Ho!"

III. Climax
     The queen guesses Rumpelstiltskin's name.

IV. Conclusion
    After the queen guesses his name, Rumpel-
stiltskin becomes enraged: "In his rage, he stamped
his right foot into the ground so deep that he sank
up to his waist. Then in his rage he seized his left leg
with both hands and tore himself asunder in the
middle."

□ 9. Practice telling the story in front of a mirror, using gestures, facial expressions, and proper voice inflections and tone. Practice the story until it becomes second nature, until you have become part of the story yourself. Use vocabulary that will captivate the audience and carry the story.

□ 10. If possible, tape yourself (video or cassette). Be objective in your critique. Did you capture the mood of the story? Did you use rich language? Did you pace the story well? Was your diction clear? Did you use expressions and gestures to convey the mood and plot? Were you successful in transporting the audience to another place and time? Did you lose your own identity and become part of the story? Make any necessary changes based on your analysis.

□ 11. Save your outline in a Story Folder for future reference. In this way, you will build a repertoire and be in constant demand as a storyteller.

GUIDELINES FOR GOOD STORYTELLING

A good storyteller can capture the hearts and minds of his or her listeners. This ability is developed through careful preparation and lots of practice. But, in addition, there are several other guidelines for becoming a good storyteller:

1. Before beginning the storytelling session, establish a purpose for the story. This preintroduction does not have to be long, yet it should cause the audience to sit up and take notice. For example, before recreating *The Ugly Duckling*, you might say, "Did you know that one of Hans Christian Andersen's fairy tales was a lot like his life?" Before reading *Rumpelstiltskin*, you might ask, "Have you ever made a promise that you knew you couldn't keep? What would cause you to make such a promise? I'm going to tell you a story about how a promise got a queen into a lot of trouble."

2. Watch for the audience's reactions. Be receptive to both verbal and nonverbal indicators. Watch the students' faces. Do they seem to be feeling the emotions you are attempting to convey or do they appear to be confused? Are they interested or are they restless? Are they involved or are you losing their attention? Are you speaking too quickly or too slowly? Are they taking part in the repetitions of words or phrases? Be cognizant

of the audience's reactions, and be prepared to change your style and technique based on their feedback.

3. If possible, set aside a special area of the classroom for storytelling. You may even want to decorate the area to resemble a theater.

4. Have the children sit in low chairs or on cushions, carpet, foam, or towels. It is important that children sit close to one another since this helps create a close, warm environment and contributes to the group's feelings of oneness.

5. Prepare any props in advance, and have them easily accessible. You don't want to interrupt the continuity and flow of the storytelling by having to search for needed materials.

6. Many storytellers believe that sound effects detract from the overall effect. Modulate your voice, its pitch and tone, to convey the mood or feeling. For example, rather than emulate the sound of galloping horses, project the mood with the rhythm of the words you are using.

7. Do not quiz the audience after the storytelling session. Instead, allow discussions to flow naturally, based on the children's questions and comments. You may want to ask a few thought-provoking questions, however, to help foster meaningful dialogue among members of the audience. For example, you could ask, "Based on the story *The Ugly Duckling*, what do you think Hans Christian Andersen's life might have been like?" or "Was Rumpelstiltskin evil or good? What makes you believe this?" Encourage children to support their answers with specifics from the story.

8. Take care to modify the storytelling for the individual audience. Take into account the group's maturity level, listening level, interests, and needs. Never talk down to your audience. You can modify almost any story to fit the audience by selecting appropriate language and degree of sophistication needed.

9. Establish eye contact and attempt to involve members of the audience in the story. Encouraging children to take part in the repetition of words and phrases is one way of involving them. Repeat the chant that Rumpelstiltskin sang and have students sing it together. Personalize the story, mentioning names of members of the audience when appropriate, such as, "Alan, can you guess what happens next?" or "Amanda, would you help Ali Baba repeat the magic words?"

10. Prepare an evaluation form to aid in your evaluation of your performance and complete it after every storytelling session. The self-evaluation chart below will provide the feedback you will need to help you prepare for your next storytelling session. Keep this chart in the Story Folder for future reference.

STORYTELLING SELF-EVALUATION FORM

Title of story: _____

Date presented: _____

Age of group: _____

Props used: _____

Modifications made for specific audience prior to

presentation: _____

_____

Part of story that seemed most effective: _____

_____

Part of story that seemed least effective: _____

_____

Reactions of audience: _____

_____

What I should do differently next time: _____

_____

Questions that initiated meaningful discussion: _____

_____

Additional comments: _____

_____

11. Prepare an evaluation form in which the audience can critique the storytelling session. You may want to duplicate the following Audience Evaluation Form. This form will be particularly useful with intermediate grades.

AUDIENCE EVALUATION FORM FOR STORYTELLING

Title: _____

Was rapport established?	1 2 3 4 5*
Was there eye contact?	1 2 3 4 5
Was storytelling dramatic?	1 2 3 4 5
Was voice level appropriate?	1 2 3 4 5
Did the storyteller appear to know the story well?	1 2 3 4 5
Did the storyteller hold your attention?	1 2 3 4 5

Total points _____

Comments: _____

_____

_____

Name of evaluator: _____

Date: _____

*Note: 5 is the highest point score; 1 is the lowest.

CHOOSING APPROPRIATE PROPS OR MEDIA

Often, authorities in the area of storytelling advise against the use of props or other types of media. Instead, they suggest relying on the storyteller's talents to create and enhance the plot and mood. However, those working with small children may want to use a variety of media such as flannel boards, puppets, and music to add a further dimension to the storytelling.

Flannel characters can be made from flannel or pellon, a fabric used to stiffen collars and cuffs. Pellon is often preferred since it is easy to see through and can be used to trace illustrations from any source. Paper cutouts can also be used with a flannel board by gluing small pieces of sandpaper to the back of the cutout. Children can then decorate and color their cutouts. Flannel boards can be purchased, but you can also make them simply by covering a sheet of cardboard with a piece of flannel material. Ready-made flannel-board stories are available for the primary grades. Each kit contains a summary of the story, which provides the teacher with sufficient information for storytelling, and large cutouts of the characters. *Flannelboard Stories for the Primary Grades*, by Paul Anderson, is one example of commercial materials that are available to aid in developing flannel-board characters. It offers a variety of titles.

Flannel-board stories lend variety to storytelling, and they provide material that allows students to reenact the story as reinforcement. As the story is told, the flannel (or pellon) characters are placed on the flannel board and moved about as the story dictates. Stories that have only a few characters and a rather simple plot are more adaptable to flannel boards. Stories in which new characters or events are added (cumulative stories), such as *Ask Mr. Bear*, are especially effective, allowing children to watch as the plot unfolds. Once a flannel-board story is told, allow it to remain in the classroom so that children have the opportunity to retell the story and manipulate the figures. Once you are finished with the flannel-board characters for a story, file them in the Story Folder for future reference.

Puppets, whether paper bag, stick, or sock, are easy to make and again lend variety to storytelling. The puppets can be used to tell the story, to introduce the story, or, at the end, to prompt discussion. Puppets can represent animate and inanimate story characters.

Often, a storyteller will use several props. These props can simply symbolize the character. For example, an egg might introduce *The Ugly Duckling*, or a rock might introduce *Sylvester and the Magic Pebble*.

Finally, music can really enhance the atmosphere before the story is presented. Choosing the right music is important, however, because you will want to establish just the right mood. A lively, toe-tapping number might be perfect for *Mama Don't Allow*, but it would not be appropriate for *Goodnight Moon*, where a more serene selection would enhance the feeling of peace and contentment.

ALTERNATIVES TO STORYTELLING AND EXTENDED ACTIVITIES

Storytelling is only one way of orally communicating a story. Over the years, alternatives have been developed that benefit listeners in similar ways and also involve them to a greater degree. Story Theatre and Reader's Theatre are two such alternatives that strengthen reading and listening skills and help children to develop confidence as they perform in front of others. The dramatization of a story also helps to improve comprehension skills. Perhaps the most important outcome, however, is that these techniques are fun, bringing the joy of literature that much closer to children.

Story Theatre

In this technique, stories or poems are read or told while they are being mimed. Materials that lend themselves best to Story Theatre contain quite a bit of action. Folktales, myths, and legends are particularly good. Once the book or poem is selected, you must determine how much of the material will be performed. A key here is to make sure that the section, whether it is a chapter or specific scene, has some type of closure.

To prepare for Story Theatre, students must first have experience with mime. Warm-up activities should be developed to allow students to become comfortable with mime and to help them develop skill in the technique. The following activities can be used, with some adaptation, with students in the elementary grades. Encourage students to rehearse in front of a mirror and concentrate on every facial and body movement.

1. Pretend you are walking through snow, mud, high grass.
2. Pretend you are eating something you detest.
3. Mime an activity that you do everyday, such as brushing your teeth, making the bed, or fixing a sandwich. Take care to include every move that you follow when you are actually involved in the activity.
4. Mime the action of a player in your favorite sport (i.e., a catcher in baseball, a goalie in soccer).
5. Mime an emotion, such as terror, surprise, worry, impatience. See if the audience can determine what you are feeling.
6. Become a wild animal. Move as that animal might move. See if the audience knows what type of animal you are.
7. Select a partner. Imagine you are looking in the mirror and become the mirror image of your partner, doing what he or she does.
8. Become a robot, moving as a robot might move.

Once the selection for Story Theatre is made and students have the background needed for mime, the selection must be carefully analyzed. Students must be able to visualize the setting, characters, and action. While only a part of the story may be used, students should be familiar with the entire work in order to better understand the characters, their motivation, and how they might think and move. Gestures, posture, and facial expressions must be well planned to recreate the mood of the story.

If the narration is told rather than read, follow the guidelines outlined for storytelling earlier in this chapter. If the narration is read, follow the guidelines described for reading aloud in Chapter 1.

Poems that are well suited for Story Theatre include "My Shadow," by Robert Louis Stevenson, and "Casey at the Bat," by Earnest L. Thayer. Readily adaptable stories for Story Theatre include "Cinderella" (and most folktales, legends, and myths) and *Just So Stories* by Rudyard Kipling.

Reader's Theatre

Some stories contain a large amount of dialogue that determines the plot and action. Reader's Theatre is an excellent technique to use for these stories. In Reader's Theatre, a narrator describes the action while children act out the dialogue of specific characters. Props or other media are not important for this technique. The story is revealed through the characters' portrayal and the narration.

Since Reader's Theatre necessitates the creation of a script based on the story selected, reading and writing skills are enhanced. The narrator's part must be developed to help introduce the characters, to help describe the plot, and to simplify the narrative passages in the book. The dialogue in the story, however, should not be changed, although it may be necessary to shorten it. When preparing the script, it is often helpful if you first script part of the story and allow the children to compare the original and the newly written script. Next, work with the class on scripting a portion of the text. Finally, allow pairs of students to write the script based on a certain part of the story. Time should be allotted for students to help edit each portion of the script. As students write the script, you may need to question them to make sure they understand how their portion fits in with the entire story and to ensure that their piece keeps with the story line and tone.

When students take part in Reader's Theatre, they read from their scripts. However, students must feel comfortable with what they are to read, and they must have ample opportunity to rehearse before performing the story for others. With younger children, it is often advisable for the teacher to take the part of the narrator. Older students will easily assume this role.

Once student parts have been determined, they must become familiar with the entire work, not just the portion being used for Reader's Theatre. In this way, they will become more sensitive to their character. Remind students that to become the character, they must assume the voice inflections and accent that the character might use. Students should be guided in their understanding and interpretation of the characters and their movements, tone of voice, dialects, and so on.

Students can prepare for Reader's Theatre by first developing skill in speaking using different inflections or accents. Provide them with situations in which they can practice this skill. For example, "You are the owner of a plantation in the Deep South. Your crops will be destroyed unless the rains come"; "You are an elderly woman, praying for a visit from your son";

"You are a young child who has just learned that he or she must move to the other side of the country, far from friends and family"; "You are a salesperson, trying to persuade a reticent audience to buy a special chair you have developed"; or "You are living in a large urban area. It is cold and dark outside. You are alone at home, when suddenly you hear noises."

You can create your own scripts or you can order scripts that have already been adapted by contacting Reader's Theatre, Box 17193, San Diego, California 92117. Books that lend themselves well to Reader's Theatre include those in which the plot is developed and the characters are revealed through dialogue. Try to choose books that will not need a great deal of adaptation. The following stories (or portions) lend themselves well to Reader's Theatre: *The Little House* series by Laura Ingalls Wilder, *Charlotte's Web* by E. B. White, and *The Borrowers* by Mary Norton. Most books suitable for storytelling are also adaptable, provided they contain the criteria listed earlier.

After a story has been prepared, arrange for an audience of other students, school staff, or parents to view the finished production. Try to arrange to have the presentation videotaped. Children love to see themselves on television, and videotaping provides an excellent strategy for self-appraisal.

Storytelling can also be extended through the following classroom strategies and activities:

1. Allow children to prepare a story and present it to the class, the school, or other selected audience. Remind students to consider the audience when selecting and preparing the story.
2. Videotape the storytelling session. Allow students to critique the session, emphasizing "constructive criticism."
3. Allow students to present a story for younger children at a local library.
4. Allow students to prepare a storytelling session based on a story they have written. Stories can be written by individuals, small groups, or the entire class.
5. Involve the class in group storytelling, where each class member has a part in recreating the story.
6. Involve students in a storytelling session that is done completely through mime with no narration. This could be followed by a discussion to get the audience's interpretation of the story and to learn what mime techniques worked best.

SUGGESTED BOOKS FOR STORYTELLING

Andersen, Hans Christian. *The Complete Fairy Tales and Stories*. Doubleday/Anchor, 1983.

Brothers Grimm. *Grimm's Fairy Tales*. Grossett & Dunlap, 1945.

Bryant, Al. *Stories to Tell Boys and Girls*. Zonderman, 1952.

Bulfinch, Thomas. *A Book of Myths*. Macmillan, 1970.

D'Aulaire, Ingrid, and Edgar D'Aulaire. *Book of Greek Myths*. Doubleday, 1962.

————. *Norse Gods and Giants*. Doubleday, 1967.

Green, Roger L. *A Book of Myths*. Dutton, 1965.

Jacobi, Frederick, Jr. *Tales of Grimm and Andersen*. Modern Library, 1952.

Lyttle, Kirk. *Pleasant Journeys. Twenty-Two Tales from Around the World*. Writing Works, 1979.

McDermott, Gerald. *Daughter of Earth: A Roman Myth*. Delacorte Press, 1984.

Mathon, Laura E., and Thusnelda Schmidt. *Treasured Tales*. Abingdon Press, 1960.

Untermeyer, Louis. *The World's Great Stories: 55 Legends that Live Forever*. Lippincott, 1964.

White, Anne Terry. *The Golden Treasury of Myths and Legends*, Illustrated by Alice and Martin Provensen. Golden Press, 1959.

REFERENCES

Teacher

Anderson, Paul S. *Language Skills in Elementary Education*. New York: Macmillan, 1964.

————. *Flannelboard Stories for the Primary Grades*. Minneapolis: T. S. Dennison & Co., 1962.

Baker, Augusta, and Ellin Greene. *Storytelling: Art and Technique*, 2nd ed. New York: R. R. Bowker, 1987.

Bauer, Caroline. *Handbook for Storytellers*. Chicago: American Library Association, 1977.

Briggs, Nancy E., and Joseph A. Wagner. *Children's Literature Through Storytelling and Drama*. Dubuque, Iowa: William C. Brown, 1970.

Cathon, Laura, et al., eds. *Stories to Tell to Children: A Selected List*. Pittsburg: University of Pittsburg Press, 1974.

Coody, Bernice, ed. *Children's Literature in the Reading Program*. Newark, Del.: IRA, 1987.

Huck, Charlotte S., and Doris Young Kuhn. *Children's Literature in the Elementary School*. New York: Holt, Rinehart & Winston, 1968.

Johnson, Terry D., and Daphne R. Louis. *Literacy Through Literature*. Portsmouth, N.H.: Heinemann, 1987.

Ross, Ramon R. *Storytelling*, 2nd ed. Columbus: Charles E. Merrill, 1980.

Sutherland, Zena, and May Hill Arbuthnot. *Children and Books*, 7th ed. Glenview, Ill.: Scott, Foresman, 1986.

Sutherland, Zena, and Myra Cohn Livingston. *The Scott, Foresman Anthology of Children's Literature*. Glenview, Ill.: Scott, Foresman, 1984.

Children

Andersen, Hans Christian. *The Ugly Duckling*. Retold and illustrated by Lorinda Bryan Cauley. Harcourt Brace Jovanovich, 1979.

Brown, Margaret Wise. *Goodnight Moon*. Illustrated by Clermont Hurd. Harper & Row, 1947.

Carle, Eric. *The Very Hungry Caterpillar*. World, 1968.

Flack, Marjorie. *Ask Mr. Bear*. Macmillan, 1968.

Hurd, Thacher. *Mama Don't Allow*. Thacher Hurd, 1984.

Kipling, Rudyard. *Just So Stories*. Illustrated by Etienne Delessert. Doubleday, 1972.

Norton, Mary. *The Borrowers*. Illustrated by Beth and Joe Krush. Harcourt Brace Jovanovich, 1953.

Steig, William. *Sylvester and the Magic Pebble*. Windmill, 1969.

Stevenson, Robert Louis. *A Child's Garden of Verses*. Illustrated by Brian Wildsmith. Oxford, 1966. (1885)

Thatcher, Hurd. *Mama Don't Allow*. Thatcher Hurd, 1984.

Wilder, Laura Ingalls. *Little House Series*. Illustrated by Garth Williams. Harper & Row.

White, E. B. *Charlotte's Web*. Illustrated by Garth Williams. Harper & Row, 1952.

5

Extending and Sharing Literature

Reading aloud, shared reading, sustained silent reading, and storytelling are just a few techniques that bring children and the world of literature together by stimulating their imagination and creating a desire to read. As children enjoy and are touched by books, they should have an opportunity to share their treasures with classmates through "peer sharing." Children delight in telling their friends about a wonderful book, just as adults love to turn their friends onto a book they "just couldn't put down."

Traditionally, however, the desire to share books has been stifled because the children must write meaningless, often laborious reports. These reports take the excitement and creativity out of sharing by asking for a plot summary or a description of the main characters. Ironically, the very reports teachers have used to stimulate reading and sharing have caused a negative attitude toward books.

Book reports do have a place in the curriculum. They provide a vehicle through which the reader interacts with the characters and the plot. Children need a way in which they can react to a particular story, whether their reaction takes the form of written, artistic, dramatic, or oral expression. Reports can be formal or informal, but they must give students an opportunity to talk about books rather than merely evaluate them.

ALTERNATIVES TO THE TRADITIONAL BOOK REPORT

The following ideas for extending and sharing literature provide alternatives to the traditional book report and are designed to motivate and inspire students and to make book sharing a natural outgrowth of reading.

Book Week

Celebrate National Book Week by organizing a variety of activities related to the books that the children have read. Give them an opportunity to create a classroom in which they are enveloped in literature. The classroom may reflect a cornucopia of literature or a specific theme or author. For example, decorate the classroom door in the likeness of the class's favorite book character. Just imagine walking up to the door only to be greeted by the Cat in the Hat! Students can create puppets or dress dolls to represent specific characters. Grinches, Thing One and Thing Two, Bartholomew Cubbins, and other Seuss creations can fill the room and serve as props for student plays, mimes, and other dramatic activities. Students can create their own artistic model representations of green eggs and ham or the hats of Bartholomew Cubbins. As a culminating activity, they can dress as their favorite character and parade through the school. Imagine children watching as their favorite characters stroll by and deliver invitations to a Dr. Seuss Fantasy Festival! At the festival, storytelling and student dramatic presentations can be the main events, and refreshments can reflect the theme.

Slide Show

Have students create their own slide show based on a specific book by taking photographs of book illustrations or photographic representations of the plot. For example, consider *Charlotte's Web*. Students can either take pictures from the text or go to the zoo or a farm and photograph a pig, a sheep, or a goose. Characters such as Charlotte the spider can be made from pipe cleaners or clay. Students can then make an audiocassette that tells the story and correlates with the pictures. Slide shows can be put into a Literature Corner to give students the opportunity to enjoy them time and time again.

Time Capsule

Discuss with students the purpose of a time capsule; that is, to preserve information for the future. In this case, the time capsule would allow students in another era to become aware of the books enjoyed by children today. Brainstorm about the items they might put into a time capsule that would be representative of a favorite book. For example, for the story *Corduroy*, they might include a small teddy bear with green overalls and a missing button; or, based on *Little House in the Big Woods*, they might include a letter that could have been written by Laura Ingalls telling a friend about her life; or they could create an illustration representative of a selected scene. As each child decides on a favorite book, he or she is responsible for selecting specific memorabilia and providing the following information:

Title
Author/illustrator
Publisher/date of publication
Summary of the story
Reason for selecting the book

Have students create their own time capsule that relates to the book in some way. For example, if they select *Corduroy*, they might make a time capsule in the shape of a bear, cutting out a pattern from a paper bag and stapling the sides together after inserting all the memorabilia. Get permission from your school's principal to bury the time capsule(s). Prepare a map that gives the location of the time capsule and the date that it is to be opened. Present this map to the school's principal with the stipulation that it be turned over to each succeeding principal until the specified time.

Diary

After reading a particular selection, have students become one of the characters and record the events of the story in diary form from that character's viewpoint. It will be interesting to compare diaries based on the same book but written from the perspectives of different characters. For example, in *The Emperor's New Clothes*, one student must take the emperor's point of view, another the tailor's, and another the child's. Allow time for students to read their diaries aloud and discuss their feelings, as if they were still the character.

Newspaper

Students can create a classroom Literary Newspaper, as each student develops a specific section of the paper, relating to a book they have read. For example, assign students sections of the paper such as comic strips, editorials, classified ads, advice columns, headlines, sports, advertisements, and book reviews. The articles can be based on actual events as relayed in the story or they can be an elaboration as in the *Island News* based on *Island of the Blue Dolphin* by Scott O'Dell. Students may create the headline, "Corduroy Loses Button in Department Store," and write a humorous column related to it as it ties in with the book,

 # ISLAND NEWS

By Kenny

Vol. 1 March 14, 1989

Tragedy on Island of the Blue Dolphins

Today on the island, an unfortunate event occured. Chief Chowig, who rules the island, was killed in a battle. The Russian hunter who makes trades with us for the hides of animals, shot the chief when he refused to take just one chest of treasures for the skins. A battle was fought between us and the Russian with the help of the Aleuts. They emerged victorious. We hope no tragedy like this ever occurs again.

Karana and Ramo — Alone

After a storm, all people of the island prepared to leave. When everyone had boarded, Ramo realized he had forgotten his spear. He went back to the village to retrieve it. Karana went after him. While they were gone, the boat left, leaving them behind. They are now on the island alone.

Wild Dogs!

Karana and Ramo spotted a pack of wild dogs today. They built a house with a fence around it in order to protect themselves from the dogs. We hope it works out for them. Later Karana plans to build a device that will shoot an arrow into any dog that approaches the fort. Good luck to them both.

Dog Found

Today on the island Karana found a big gray dog. The dog had been shot with an arrow. Karana named him Rontu which means "Fox Eyes." Rontu was a little frightened at first, but is now getting used to Karana.

or they may take the story a step further and develop other events that might have occurred but didn't.

Another type of newspaper is a monthly Book Review, in which students write reviews of books they have read. In preparation, have students read reviews from other publications such as local newspapers and children's magazines. Reviews must include bibliographic information such as title, author, illustrator, publisher, date of publication, number of pages, and age appropriateness. Reviews should also include a summary of the plot, as well as the students' reactions based on specific details. Have students, as a class, devise a rating scale and symbols to evaluate the books.

$\ominus$ = Ho-hum, a real sleeper
$\bigcirc$ = OK, but could be replaced
$\oplus$ = Good book
$\circledast$ = A *must read*

Book of Quotes

Have students compile a book of quotations by selecting and illustrating their favorite quotations from a specific book. Illustrations can be photographs that the students have taken or cartoons and pictures that they have cut from periodicals. These pictures, along with the quotation, can create various moods, depending on the way in which the quotation is illustrated. For example, the following quotations from Shakespeare's *Julius Caesar*, although serious when taken in context, take on a different meaning when combined with certain illustrations.

You shall not stir out of your house today!
(Calpurnia, Act II, Scene 2)

In contrast, when coupled with a different type of illustration, the result can be quite poignant.

His life was gentle, and the elements so mixed in him that Nature might stand up and say to all the world, "This was a man!" (Anthony, Act V, Scene 5)

When compiling their quotation booklets, students should include the name of the person who is being quoted and the page number on which the quotation appears. All pages should be put together in booklet form with a clever title and illustration.

Poetry

Encourage students to react to a particular book, specific story element, or character through poetry. Poems can be created based on plot, setting, theme, or characters in the story. Poems should be saved in an individual Poetry of Literature booklet. Students should become familiar with a variety of poetic forms and read several examples before writing their poetry. Poetic forms include haiku, cinquain, diamonte, clerihew, bio-poem, and limerick.

The *haiku* is a poem with only three lines and seventeen syllables; it usually depicts some aspect of nature:

Line 1: Five syllables
Line 2: Seven syllables
Line 3: Five syllables

The *cinquain* is a five-line poem, written in the following format:

Line 1: One word (which may be the title)
Line 2: Two words (describing the title)
Line 3: Three words (an action)
Line 4: Four words (a feeling)
Line 5: One word (referring to the title)

When completed, the *diamonte* takes on a diamond-shaped form. It is written in the following format:

Line 1: One word (a noun or pronoun)
Line 2: Two words (adjectives describing line 1)
Line 3: Three words ("ing" verbs showing action, related to line 1)
Line 4: Four words (nouns: the first two relate to line 1, the last two to line 7)
Line 5: Three words ("ing" verbs showing action, related to line 7)
Line 6: Two words (adjectives describing line 7)

Line 7: One word (a noun or a pronoun, often the opposite of the word in line 1)

Clerihew poetry contains four lines with an *aabb* rhyme scheme. The poem is usually written about a well-known person, either living or dead, or a fictional character. The person's name becomes the first line of the poem.

A *bio-poem* tells about a famous person, real or fictitious, using the following format:

Line 1: First name
Line 2: Title
Line 3: Four words (that describe the person)
Line 4: Lover of (three or more things or ideas)
Line 5: Who believed (one or more ideas)
Line 6: Who wanted (three things)
Line 7: Who used (three things or methods)
Line 8: Who gave (three things)
Line 9: Who said (a quote)
Line 10: Last name

A *limerick*, made popular by Edward Lear, is a humorous poem. Limericks have five lines. Lines 1, 2, and 5 rhyme and have a similar rhythm, while lines 3 and 4 are shorter, have a similar rhythm pattern, and rhyme with each other.

Puzzles

Students love to create and solve puzzles of various sizes and shapes. Have students select a favorite book and create a puzzle. Duplicate the puzzle and provide time for others in the class to solve it. Puzzle forms include word searches, crosswords, secret codes, riddles, "What's wrong with this picture?" (both pictorial and written), rebuses (pictures represent words), and jumbles. A jumble and its solution appear on pages 76 and 77.

JUMBLE

Directions: The thirteen characters listed below are found in a well-known piece of literature. Unscramble their names and write the letters that fall within the circles on the blanks provided. Finally, unscramble those letters to discover the name of the book.

1. W O W D I   D U G O S A L
   _ _ _ _ _   _ _(_)_ _ _ _

2. U A T N   P L O L Y
   _ _ _ _   _ _ _ _(_)

3. M T O   W Y E R S A
   _ _ _   _ _ _ _(_)_

4. J E O   R P H E A R
   _ _ _(_)_ _ _ _ _

5. B K E Y C   T T H H C A R E
   (_)_ _(_)_   _ _ _ _ _ _ _ _

6. A M U S E L   L M C E S E N
   _ _ _ _ _ _   (_)(_)_ _ _ _ _

7. V L E A S
   _ _ _ _(_)

8. G G E R F S A N D R O R
   _(_)_ _ _ _ _ _ _ _ _

9. P H S O E E R S D H N
   _ _ _ _ _ _(_)_ _ _ _

10. F R A T
    _ _(_)_

11. K R M A   W I T A N
    _ _ _ _   _ _ _(_)

12. J U I N N   O E J
    (_)_ _ _   _ _ _

13. S I M S   W T N O A S
    _ _ _ _   _ _ _ _(_)

Write the letters that are circled above on the following blanks:

_ _ _ _ _ _ _ _ _ _   _ _ _ _

What is the name of the book?_ _____

Created by David

JUMBLE: ANSWER KEY

Directions: The thirteen characters listed below are found in a well-known piece of literature. Unscramble their names and write the letters that fall within the circles on the blanks provided. Finally, unscramble those letters to discover the name of the book.

1. W O W D I   D U G O S A L
   <u>W I D O W   D O U G L A S</u>

2. U A T N   P L O L Y
   <u>A U N T   P O L L Y</u>

3. M T O   W Y E R S A
   <u>T O M   S A W Y E R</u>

4. J E O   R P H E A R
   <u>J O E   H A R P E R</u>

5. B K E Y C   T T H H C A R E
   <u>B E C K Y   T H A T C H E R</u>

6. A M U S E L   L M C E S E N
   <u>S A M U E L   C L E M E N S</u>

7. V L E A S
   <u>S L A V E</u>

8. G G E R F S A N D R O R
   <u>G R A N G E R F O R D S</u>

9. P H S O E E R S D H N
   <u>S H E P H E R D S O N</u>

10. F R A T
    <u>R A F T</u>

11. K R M A   W I T A N
    <u>M A R K   T W A I N</u>

12. J U I N N   O E J
    <u>I N J U N   J O E</u>

13. S I M S   W T N O A S
    <u>M I S S   W A T S O N</u>

Write the letters that are circled above on the following blanks:

<u>U Y E H B K C L E R R</u>   <u>F N I N</u>

What is the name of the book? <u>HUCKLEBERRY FINN</u>

Literary Word Bank

Students will undoubtedly come across unfamiliar words and terms in the literature they read. Ask them to jot down these words and the appropriate page numbers as they are reading. Once they have finished reading, they should enter each word into their Literary Word Bank and copy the sentence in which the word appeared. Next, students should try to determine the meaning from context clues. Then they should find the word in the dictionary, copy the definition, and compare it with their own definition. Finally, have them illustrate the word so that its meaning becomes evident. For example:

The words included in each student's Literary Word Bank can become part of the individual's or the class's weekly spelling or vocabulary lesson.

Literary Letters

Have students react to reading from a specific work of literature. Reactions can be in the form of a letter that you read and answer. To encourage students, share your own reactions to serve as a model. Letters should not simply summarize what has been read. Instead, they should reflect the students' impressions of story elements (character, plot, setting, mood, and theme) or contain their predictions, questions, opinions, and insights. Literary letters are personal interpretations. For children to feel free to express their thoughts, your feedback must be supportive and show respect for each student's ideas and conclusions. Your responses should also encourage students to clarify and extend their ideas in order to promote growth in their awareness of themselves and others.

Literary letters are an effective tool for providing additional information on students' comprehension and communication skills, which, in turn, can help guide subsequent lessons. Often the ideas and conclusions expressed in the letters can serve as the focus for small-group and whole-class discussions.

ADDITIONAL ACTIVITIES
FOR EXTENDING AND SHARING LITERATURE

The following activities are alternatives to the traditional book report and to the strategies suggested earlier.

1. Create caricatures of favorite characters.
2. Write to the author. Authors' addresses can be found in books such as *Something About the Author: Facts and Pictures About Authors and Illustrators of Books for Young Children* and *Yesterday's Authors for Children*.
3. Develop a book review using video or radio to broadcast it to the entire school. A different student can present the review each day.
4. Design a bulletin board to depict a particular book or book theme.
5. Create a book jacket with a clever cover and inside blurb to lure readers.
6. Conduct a debate based on either a particular issue related to a book or their opinions of a specific book or author.
7. Create a peep box. Inside a shoe box, design a scene from the story. Punch a hole in the lid so the scene can be viewed once the lid is put back onto the box.
8. Develop a time line or story map to indicate events of the story.
9. Create a lost or found advertisement to recover either a character or item from the story.
10. Make a collage by cutting out pictures, words, or letters from periodicals to reflect a story theme or particular action.
11. Indicate the book's setting on a world map that is posted in the classroom. Often books will have multiple settings; each setting should be labeled.
12. Record a favorite segment of the book on an audiocassette. Label the tape and keep it in a special "listening area" of the room so that others may listen. If possible, along with the tape, display a copy of the book and a brief summary.
13. Retell the story with musical accompaniment. Choose music that best reflects the story line and mood. A variety of music

may be chosen for the same story as the action and characters dictate. The story can also be told through mime.

14. Create a meeting between the book's main character and the main character from another favorite story. Illustrate the meeting or write a brief story that describes the meeting.
15. Create a mural to retell the story.
16. Create a book of interesting facts. This activity works especially well with biographies and informational books.
17. Design a mosaic that symbolizes the book in some way. The mosaic can be created with various pasta shapes, shells, fabrics, peas, beans, and so on.
18. Prepare and deliver a monologue that was either part of the story or that is original yet might have been said by a main character.
19. Create a wanted poster for a character in the book. As an alternative, create a missing persons poster or a reward poster. Information included on the poster can be humorous or serious.
20. Create a costume and dress a doll or stuffed animal to represent a favorite character.
21. Write a television news report detailing a special event in the book. A special news bulletin, "We interrupt this program to bring you this special bulletin . . . ," can also be created.
22. Organize a panel discussion among several students who have read the same book. Develop thought-provoking questions as the basis for discussion.
23. Compare the book with the movie or television version. Which form developed the characters better? Which form made you more sensitive to the story and the characters? Which form did you enjoy more?
24. Write a twenty-five-, fifteen-, or ten-word telegram that one character might have sent to another character. As an alternative, send a telegram to a friend telling him or her about the book and why he or she must read it!
25. Create flannel-board characters, and retell the story using them.
26. Create a humorous skit between a person who is trying to sell the book and an uncooperative customer.
27. After reading a nonfiction book dealing with how to make something, create two charts. On the first chart, list the

materials needed to create this item, and on the second, list the procedure. Display the finished product along with the posters.

28. Create a story map by sketching the main events of the story. Below each picture write a *brief* sentence to describe the specific part of the story being illustrated.

29. Create a comic book, cartoon, or comic strip based on a favorite character or setting. Students should study the way in which these forms are designed before attempting to create their own.

30. Prepare a mock trial in which a character is charged with a "crime" relating to the story. For example, Jack (*Jack and the Beanstalk*) is tried for trespassing, or Wanda (*A Hundred Dresses*) is tried for exaggerating. Select classmates to serve as judge, defense attorney, prosecuting attorney, defendant(s), plaintiff(s), witnesses, and jurors. The students involved must be familiar with their roles and with the story in terms of how it affects their roles.

BOOKS FOR CHILDREN

Andersen, Hans Christian. *The Emperor's New Clothes*. Illustrated by Virginia Lee Burton. Houghton Mifflin, 1949.

Babbitt, Natalie. *Tuck Everlasting*. Farrar, Straus & Giroux, 1975.

Cauley, Lorinda Bryan. *Jack and the Beanstalk*. Putnam, 1983.

Estes, Eleanor. *The Hundred Dresses*. Illustrated by Louis Slobodkin. Harcourt Brace Jovanovich, 1944.

Freeman, Don. *Corduroy*. Viking, 1968.

O'Dell, Scott. *Island of the Blue Dolphin*. Dell, 1960.

Seuss, Dr. (pseud. for Theodore Seuss Geisel). *The Cat in the Hat*. Random House, 1957.

White, E. B. *Charlotte's Web*. Illustrated by Garth Williams. Harper & Row, 1952.

Wilder, Laura Ingalls. *Little House Series*. Illustrated by Garth Williams. Harper & Row.

REFERENCES

Commire, Anne (Ed.). *Something About the Author: Facts and Pictures About Authors and Illustrators of Books for Young Children*. Detroit: Gale Research, 1971–1989.

Commire, Anne (Ed.). *Yesterday's Authors for Children*. Detroit: Gale Research, 1977–1978.

THE LITERATURE CONNECTION

CONNECTIONS

Affective Response to Literature

Literature for Critical and Creative Thinking

The Reading-Writing Connection:
Writing Process Approach
Language Experience Approach

Literature and the Curriculum —
A Thematic Approach

LITERATURE AND THE READING PROGRAM

Strategies for Reading

Literature and the Basal Reading Program: Extending the Basal Literature Based Materials

A Model for Literature-Based Reading Programs

Using the Library

Reaching Beyond the Classroom: Parent Involvement

DEVELOPING INTEREST IN READING

Read Aloud Program

Shared Reading

Sustained Silent Reading

Storytelling

Extending and Sharing Literature

GENRES AND ELEMENTS

Exploring Genres:
Picture Books, Realistic Fiction, Historical Fiction, Fantasy/Science Fiction, Traditional Literature, Poetry, Informational Books, Biographies

Analyzing Elements:
Characterization, Plot, Setting, Theme, Point of View, Evaluating Genres and Their Elements

Involving Students in Selecting Genres

PART TWO

GENRES
AND
ELEMENTS

Walking into a library, we are struck by the rows and rows of titles. Knowing which to select for our students should not be left to chance. An understanding of children and of the criteria to apply when selecting and evaluating literature provides the framework for finding just the right book. The right book could be that one special story that will open the door to the world of literature for a reluctant reader, or stimulate a child's curiosity, or help a child who is going through a troubled time not feel so alone. Between the covers of books, children can visit the past, explore the wonders of our universe, and find special friends. Books invite children to become one with the characters and vicariously experience their joys, sorrows, hopes, and fears. And, as they turn the last page, the "right book" will stay with them, exciting their imaginations and challenging them to search for another book that is "just right."

Part II of *The Literature Connection* is designed to familiarize students with the tremendous variety of literature available and to help them develop the skills and understanding necessary to select the best literature has to offer. Books are categorized according to certain characteristics, and these categories are referred to as *genres*. A book's genre is often easily established, however, many books do fall into one or more genres. Children's literature can be categorized into the following genres (described in detail in Chapter 6): picture books, realistic fiction, historical fiction, fantasy/science fiction, traditional literature, poetry, informational books, and biographies. Although these classifications are surrounded by debate, they introduce us to the scope of books available and remind us of the importance of exposing children to the wealth of literature that exists.

Each genre contains certain elements of literature; namely, characterization, plot, setting, theme, and point of view. However, these elements are developed differently, depending on the nature of the genre. In Chapter 7 these literary elements are described to help develop in children an awareness of their importance and the way in which they interact to weave the magic that is good literature. Chapter 7 also includes a variety of motivating activities that will help further children's understanding of these elements. Other activities present opportunities for students to evaluate specific works of literature based on appropriate criteria.

All too often, students tend to select books that represent only one or two genres. The activities in Chapter 8 involve students in reading a variety of genres. As they become more familiar with each genre, its elements, and benefits, students will be more motivated to read across the genres depending on their interests, needs, and purposes for reading.

No matter what their age, all children can and should be taught to be discriminating readers. The most important objective of Part II, then, is to develop in children an awareness of the variety of available literature and an understanding of the evaluative criteria that will help them select and read exemplary books that will guide them in discovering themselves and their world.

6

Exploring Genres

PICTURE BOOKS

Long before they can decode the written word, young children
are fascinated by picture books. A good picture book is a source
of delight and enrichment. The pictures leap off the pages, weave
magic tales, and spark the imagination. Generally, books for
young children are grouped together and referred to as picture
books. Illustrations play an integral part in these books. Instead
of simply being an extension of the text, illustrations are necessary for understanding the book's content. The elements of a
picture book are heightened by the way in which the illustrations
create mood, depict the characters, and develop the action.
Interestingly, almost every artistic medium and technique has
been successfully used in picture books, from watercolors to
collage and pen-and-ink sketches, photographs, and linoleum
prints.

Usually children's first books, picture books encourage an
appreciation and love for reading as they allow children to
participate in the literate community. As children listen to
picture books being read, or as they "read" them aloud, they are
developing their reading readiness skills and language development. Since so much of their speech and vocabulary has been
developed by the time they are six years old, it is vital that young
children be provided with literature to stimulate and nurture
their language development.

The classification of picture books has been a subject for
debate. Is it a genre of its own or is it subsumed within other
genres? A case can be made for each side: picture books do have
certain qualities in common, yet, because of their subject matter, they cross into other genres. For example, *Where the Wild
Things Are* is a picture book, yet its text would be classified as
fantasy, while *The Snowy Day* is a picture book that could also be

classified as realistic fiction. To best focus on the qualities, benefits, and appeal of this special group of books, we will treat picture books as a distinct literary genre. Picture books include a variety of books such as alphabet books, counting books, books of Mother Goose rhymes, toy books, wordless picture books, concept books, predictable books, easy-to-read books, and picture storybooks.

Types of Picture Books

Alphabet Books. In an alphabet book, each letter of the alphabet is matched with an illustration of an object that begins with that letter. The illustrations must clearly match the key letters and the objects pictured must be easily identifiable. Some alphabet books are organized around a specific theme such as farm animals or modes of transportation. In such cases, the illustrations must be consistent with the theme of the book.

One of the primary benefits is that an alphabet book helps children identify letters and corresponding sounds. Children may also identify the specific words that accompany the objects pictured. Alphabet books help develop visual literacy, stimulate object definition, and enhance vocabulary development.

They are used primarily for younger readers; however, alphabet books such as *Animalia*, by Graeme Base, with its hidden pictures and wonderful vocabulary, delight older children as well as adults.

Counting Books. Counting books present numbers and number concepts in a variety of ways. Often, numbers are matched with illustrations containing familiar objects. The number of objects depicted depends on the number or number concept being stressed. It is important that both numbers and objects are clear and easily identifiable. Extraneous details in the illustrations should be avoided so that the children readily understand what is being counted and can focus on the objects and number concepts.

Counting books develop the concept of one-to-one correspondence and aid in the development of sequential counting, usually one through ten. In addition to numerical concepts, many counting books incorporate the concepts of size and shape. Language development is also enhanced when rhyming is used to convey the message; for example, "One, two, buckle my shoe/Three, four, shut the door . . ."

Mother Goose. Mother Goose rhymes are usually a child's first introduction to the literary world. Their appeal lies in their fast-paced action, rhyme, rhythm, mood, and nonsensical verse. Mother Goose rhymes contain a variety of characters and subject matter, and they create various moods. Humor and musical qualities are important aspects of these rhymes. They are magical. Children react spontaneously to the verse by laughing, clapping, or singing along.

The varied language patterns allow children to experiment with the sounds and uses of words as they develop their own language skills. In addition, these well-loved nursery rhymes instill a love of poetry, prepare their young readers for more sophisticated forms of poetry, and acquaint them with poetic devices such as alliteration, repetition of initial sounds, and onomatopoeia (the imitation of natural sounds in word formation). It is wonderful to watch young children at play, unconsciously singing their favorite Mother Goose rhyme. The verses become a common bond among children. No matter what their background, culture, or heritage, all children can share in the magic of Mother Goose.

Toy Books. Toy books employ an unusual way of presenting content. They include pop-up books, cardboard books, cloth books, finger puppet books, and flap books. Toy books are becoming increasingly popular. They entice children to become involved with the text as they explore letters, numbers, concepts, rhyming words, and story plots. Their unique format encourages involvement with the book as children open doors, look under flaps, and unfold pages to discover hidden secrets. As a result of this involvement, children develop cognitive skills, improve their language and social skills, and grow to love books. Their positive attitudes toward reading should eventually extend to other types of literature.

Concept Books. Both concrete and abstract ideas can be represented pictorially and made more easily understandable through concept books. A good concept book clearly presents objects and includes one or more examples to foster understanding of the concept being developed. Sometimes, the concepts being emphasized are taught through the story line or are explained through repetition of examples and ideas or through comparisons. Although certain concepts such as colors, shapes, and sizes lend themselves more readily to demonstration, other concepts such as position (up, under, through, etc.) and emotions are more difficult to explain. And concept books provide an additional dimension of explanation.

Concept books foster cognitive development. Children seek to identify relationships as they become aware of the differences and similarities among objects and transfer these newly integrated concepts into other areas. The books stimulate vocabulary and language skills as children match words with pictures of objects. Children may become active participants as they underline, point, or verbally respond to various items in response to a teacher's or parent's directions. Their affective development is also enhanced through the use of those books based on children's values, feelings, and the everyday events in their lives.

Wordless Picture Books. These books tell a story through illustrations alone. Wordless picture books have become increasingly popular, appealing to a society of youngsters who delight in television, comic books, and other visual forms of communication. If a story line is intended, the pictures must be properly sequenced and the action clearly drawn. Wordless picture books take many forms; they can be humorous, serious, informational, or fictitious.

These books offer many benefits. They are instrumental in developing reading readiness skills such as left-to-right progression, the concepts of top and bottom, the turning of pages, and an appreciation and respect for books. Wordless picture books foster oral and written language development as children produce the text to accompany the pictures. Teachers may then record the generated text and use it in language experience lessons or children may produce their own text. As children create their own versions of the story, the wordless picture books provide a catalyst for creative thought processes.

Comprehension skills are also developed as children "read" the story through the use of the illustrations. Children analyze the author's intent, identify main ideas, and recognize details as the story unfolds.

Predictable Books. Predictable books include repetitive language patterns, phrases, or questions, refrains, strong rhythm and rhyme, sequences of numbers or days of the week, and so forth that help the emergent reader gain meaning from the text.

Predictable books allow children to actively participate by joining in on a repetitive chant or chorus. This is important because research shows that words need to be repeated many times before they become part of a child's reading vocabulary. Through the repetition, children quickly learn the language patterns. Repetitive story patterns also help the child predict the action in the plot. In predictable texts, the outcome can be imagined very easily. After reading a few pages, children can tell what they think will happen next or predict how they think the story will end. Predictable books also provide great models for writing. Children can follow the same rhythm, pattern, or style as the author and substitute their own content and write their own versions.

Easy-to-Read Books. Easy-to-read books are designed to allow children with beginning reading skills to read independently. Similar to picture books, easy-to-read books contain a large number of illustrations that are suggestive of the written text. Unlike other picture books, which are written at various reading levels and are designed for adults to read to children, easy-to-read books are written with a controlled vocabulary, easily understandable words, and limited sentence and text length. Generally, they are a bridge between the basal reader and the trade book.

Whether mystery or sports, fact or fantasy, easy-to-read books give children the opportunity to make their own selections based on their own needs and interests. Using these books, children practice and reinforce their reading skills. They feel a sense of accomplishment and independence as they actually read a book. Easy-to-read books provide the vehicle for such independence.

Picture Storybooks. A picture storybook conveys its message through illustrations and written text; both elements are equally important to the story. These books cover a wide range of topics, and their themes are often based on everyday life experiences that children can readily identify with. Characters in these books, whether human or animal, display human qualities, characteristics, and needs that children can understand and relate to.

A well-written and well-illustrated storybook gives children a sense of what constitutes good literature. Good picture storybooks contain elements intrinsic to other literary forms: well-structured plot, well-defined characters, style that has movement, authentic and accurate settings, and interesting themes. In addition, these books are original and imaginative and provide stimulus for creative thought. As with other good literature, picture storybooks foster an appreciation of language, encourage oral communication, expand cognitive thought processes, foster the expression of feelings, and increase sensitivity to the arts.

Selecting and Evaluating Picture Books

When selecting and evaluating picture books, certain criteria must be considered. The following checklist can be used to help in the selection and evaluation of picture books. However, not all ten criteria will apply to all types of picture books.

☐ 1. Do the pictures extend the text rather than conflict with it?
☐ 2. Are the pictures clear and easily distinguishable? Are extraneous details avoided?
☐ 3. Do the illustrations enhance the setting, plot, mood, and characterizations?
☐ 4. Will children be able to identify with the characters and the action?
☐ 5. Are the style and language appropriate for young children?
☐ 6. Do the illustrations avoid stereotypes?
☐ 7. Is the theme significant?
☐ 8. Is the concept or theme appropriate for young children?
☐ 9. Have a variety of books been chosen to reflect multicultural awareness?
☐ 10. Have books been chosen that reflect a variety of genres?

Suggested Picture Books

Alphabet Books

Anno, Mitsumasa. *Anno's Alphabet*. Thomas Y. Crowell, 1975.
Azarian, Mary. *A Farmer's Alphabet*. Godine, 1981.
Base, Graeme. *Animalia*. Harry N. Abrams, Inc., 1987.
Bayer, Jane. *My Name Is Alice*. Dial Books, 1984.
Bruna, Dick. *B Is for Bear*. Methuen, 1987.
Duke, Kate. *The Guinea Pig ABC*. Dutton, 1983.
Eichenberg, Fritz. *Ape in a Cape*. Harcourt Brace Jovanovich, 1980.
Kitchen, Bert. *Animal Alphabet*. Dial Books, 1988.
Lear, Edward. *An Edward Lear Alphabet*. Illustrated by Carol Newsom. Lothrop, 1983.
Lobel, Arnold. *On Market Street*. Illustrated by Anita Lobel. Greenwillow, 1981.
Oxenbury, Helen. *ABC of Things*. Watts, 1972.
Ryden, Hope. *Wild Animals of America ABC*. Lodestar/Dutton, 1988.
Stock, Catherine. *Alexander's Midnight Snack: A Little Elephant's ABC*. Clarion, 1988.
Van Allsburg, Chris. *The Z Was Zapped*. Houghton Mifflin, 1987.
Wilks, Mike. *The Ultimate Alphabet*. Holt, Rinehart & Winston, 1987.

Counting Books

Anno, Mitsumasa. *Anno's Counting House*. Thomas Y. Crowell, 1983.
————. *Anno's Counting Book*. Thomas Y. Crowell, 1975.
Bang, Molly. *Ten, Nine, Eight*. Greenwillow, 1983.
Carle, Eric. *My Very First Book of Numbers*. Thomas Y. Crowell, 1974.
Hoban, Russell. *Ten What? A Mystery Counting Book*. Scribner's, 1974.
Hoban, Tana. *1, 2, 3*. Greenwillow, 1985.
Hutchens, Pat. *I Hunter*. Greenwillow, 1982.
Oxenbury, Helen. *Numbers & Things*. Watts, 1983.
Potter, Beatrix. *Peter Rabbit's 1 2 3*. Warne, 1988.
Sis, Peter. *Waving: A Counting Book*. Greenwillow, 1988.
Testa, Fulvio. *If You Take a Pencil*. Dial Books, 1983.
Wildsmith, Brian. *Brian Wildsmith's 1, 2, 3's*. Watts, 1988.

Mother Goose Books

Brian, Aldersen. *Cakes & Custard*. Illustrated by Helen Oxenbury. Morrow, 1975.
Brooks, Leslie. *Ring O'Roses*. Warne, 1972.
de Paola, Tomie. *Tomie de Paola's Mother Goose*. Putnam, 1985.
Greenaway, Kate. *Mother Goose*. Warne, n.d.

Hague, Michael. *Mother Goose: A Collection of Classic Nursery Rhymes*. Holt, Rinehart & Winston, 1984.

Lobel, Arnold. *Whiskers & Rhymes*. Greenwillow, 1985.

Marshall, James. *James Marshall's Mother Goose*. Farrar, Straus & Giroux, 1979.

Tudor, Tasha. *Mother Goose*. Walck, 1944.

Wildsmith, Brian. *Brian Wildsmith's Mother Goose*. Watts, 1965.

Wright, Blanche Fisher. *The Real Mother Goose*. Rand McNally, 1965.

Toy Books

Bond, Michael. *Paddington's Pop-Up Book*. Illustrated by Igor Wood. Price, Stern, Sloan, 1977.

Carle, Eric. *The Very Busy Spider*. Philomel, 1984.

Crowther, Robert. *The Most Amazing Hide-and-Seek Alphabet Book*. Viking, 1978.

Goodall, John. *Paddy Finds a Job*. Atheneum, 1977.

Hill, Eric. *Where's Spot?* Putnam, 1980.

Kunhardt, Dorothy. *Pat the Bunny*. Golden, 1962.

Munari, Bruno. *Who's There? Open the Door*. Philomel, 1960.

Oxenbury, Helen. *Friends*. Simon & Schuster, 1981.

Roffey, Maureen. *Home Sweet Home*. Coward-McCann, 1983.

Spier, Peter. *The Pet Store*. Doubleday, 1973.

Concept Books

Coleridge, Sara. *January Brings the Snow*. Illustrated by Jenni Oliver. Dial Books, 1986.

Crews, Donald. *Freight Train*. Greenwillow, 1978.

Fisher, Leonard. *Look Around: A Book About Shapes*. Viking, 1987.

Hoban, Tana. *Look! Look! Look!* Greenwillow, 1988.

———. *26 Letters & 99 Cents*. Greenwillow, 1987.

Kraus, Ruth. *A Hole Is to Dig By*. Illustrated by Maurice Sendak. Harper & Row, 1982.

McMillan, Bruce. *Growing Colors*. Lothrop, 1988.

Martin, Bill Jr., and John Archambault. *Here Are My Hands*. Holt, Rinehart & Winston, 1987.

Rockwell, Harlow. *My Kitchen*. Greenwillow, 1980.

Spier, Peter. *Crash! Bang! Boom!* Doubleday, 1972.

Tudor, Tasha. *First Delights*. Platt & Munk, 1988.

Wordless Picture Books

Anno, Mitsumasa. *Anno's Journey*. Philomel, 1980.

Carle, Eric. *Do You Want a Friend?* Harper & Row, 1971.

de Paola, Tomie. *The Knight and the Dragon*. Putnam, 1980.

———. *Pancakes for Breakfast*. Harcourt Brace Jovanovich, 1978.

Handford, Martin. *Where's Waldo*. Little, Brown, 1988.
———. *Find Waldo Now*. Little, Brown, 1987.
Hutchins, Pat. *Changes, Changes*. Macmillan, 1971.
Keats, Ezra. *Kitten for a Day*. Watts, 1974.
McCully, Emily Arnold. *First Snow*. Harper & Row, 1985.
Mayer, Mercer. *One Frog Too Many*. Dial Books, 1975.
Omerod, Jan. *Picnic*. Harper & Row, 1984.
———. *Moonlight*. Lothrop, 1982.
Spier, Peter. *Peter Spier's Rain*. Doubleday, 1982.
———. *Noah's Ark*. Doubleday, 1977.

Predictable Books

Brown, Ruth. *A Dark Dark Tale*. Dial Books, 1981.
Carle, Eric. *The Very Busy Spider*. Philomel, 1984.
Emberly, Barbara. *Drummer Hoff*. Prentice-Hall, 1967.
Galdone, Paul. *The Teeny Tiny Woman*. Clarion, 1984.
Ginsburg, Mirra. *Across the Stream*. Illustrated by Nancy Tafuri. Greenwillow, 1982.
———. *The Chick and the Duckling*. Illustrated by Jose and Ariane Aruego. Macmillan, 1972.
Hill, Eric. *Spot Goes to the Beach*. Putnam, 1985.
Hutchins, Pat. *Rosie's Walk*. Macmillan, 1971.
———. *Titch*. Macmillan, 1971.
Kraus, Robert. *Where Are You Going, Little Mouse?* Illustrated by Jose Aruego and Ariane Dewey. Greenwillow, 1986.
Martin, Bill Jr. *Brown Bear, Brown Bear, What Do You See?* Illustrated by Eric Carle. Holt, Rinehart & Winston, 1983.
Nerlove, Miriam. *I Meant to Clean My Room Today*. McElderry, 1988.
Numeroff, Laura J. *If You Gave a Mouse a Cookie*. Harper & Row, 1985.
Roy, Ron. *Three Ducks Went Wandering*. Illustrated by Paul Galdone. Clarion, 1979.
Sendak, Maurice. *Chicken Soup with Rice*. Scholastic, 1962.
Sundgaard, Arnold. *The Lamb and the Butterfly*. Illustrated by Eric Carle. Orchard Books, 1988.
Slate, Joseph. *Who Is Coming to Our House?* Illustrated by Ashley Wolff. Putnam, 1988.
Tolstoy, Alexei. *The Great Enormous Turnip*. Illustrated by Helen Oxenbury. Watts, 1968.
Voirst, Judith. *Alexander and the Terrible, Horrible, No Good, Very Bad Day*. Illustrated by Ray Cruz. Atheneum, 1972.
Wildsmith, Brian. *Toot Toot*. Oxford, 1984.
———. *The Cat Sat on the Mat*. Oxford, 1983.

Easy-to-Read Books

Adler, David A. *My Dog and the Birthday Mystery*. Illustrated by Dick Gackenbach. Holiday House, 1984.

de Brunhoff, Laurent. *Babar's Little Circus Star*. Random House, 1988.

Hoff, Syd. *Sammy the Seal*. Harper & Row, 1959.

Lobel, Arnold. *Grasshopper on the Road*. Harper & Row, 1978.

Minarick, Else Homelund. *Little Bear*. Illustrated by Maurice Sendak. Harper & Row, 1957.

Seuss, Dr. (Theodor, Geisel). *The Cat in the Hat*. Beginner Books, 1957.

———. *And to Think That I Saw It on Mulberry Street*. Vanguard, 1937.

Picture Storybooks

Aardema, Verna. *Why Mosquitoes Buzz in People's Ears*. Illustrated by Leo and Diane Dillon. Dial Books, 1975.

Ahlberg, Janet, and Allen Ahlberg. *The Jolly Postman*. Little, Brown, 1986.

———. *Each Peach Pear Plum*. Puffin, 1978.

Allard, Harry, and James Marshall. *Miss Nelson Is Missing!* Houghton Mifflin, 1977.

Brett, Jan. *Annie and the Wild Animals*. Lothrop, 1987.

Calhoun, Mary. *Cross Country Cat*. Mulberry Books, 1986.

Cooney, Barbara. *Miss Rumphius*. Puffin, 1982.

de Paola, Tomie. *Strega Nona*. Prentice-Hall, 1975.

de Regniers, Beatrice Schenk. *May I Bring a Friend?* Illustrated by Beni Montresor. Atheneum, 1965.

Fleishman, Syd. *The Scarebird*. Greenwillow, 1988.

Galdone, Paul. *The Little Red Hen*. Seabury, 1973.

Keats, Ezra. *The Snowy Day*. Viking, 1962.

Lionni, Leo. *Swimmy*. Pantheon, 1963.

Munsch, Robert. *Love You Forever*. Firefly Books, 1986.

Ness, Evaline. *Sam, Bangs, & Moonshine*. Holt, Rinehart & Winston, 1966.

Sendak, Maurice. *Where the Wild Things Are*. Harper & Row, 1963.

Steig, William. *Sylvester and the Magic Pebble*. Windmill/Simon, 1969.

Steptoe, John. *Mufaro's Beautiful Daughter*. Lothrop, 1987.

Van Allsburg, Chris. *Polar Express*. Houghton Mifflin, 1985.

———. *The Mysteries of Harris Burdick*. Hougton Mifflin, 1984.

———. *Jamanji*. Houghton Mifflin, 1981.

Ward, Lynd. *The Biggest Bear*. Houghton Mifflin, 1952.

Williams, Vera B., and Jennifer Williams. *Stringbean's Trip to the Shining Sea*. Greenwillow, 1988.

Yolen, Jane. *Owl Moon*. Philomel, 1987.

REALISTIC FICTION

Childhood is a special time of wonder, joy, and growth. Yet growing up is often a difficult and sometimes painful process. Children face many of the same hopes, fears, and doubts as adults, and they need reassurance and help in dealing with their feelings. In realistic fiction, children can identify with certain characters and situations and thereby gain understanding and insight into their own lives.

Also referred to as contemporary or modern realistic fiction, this genre includes books that are imaginatively and realistically written and that deal with all aspects of life. Humorous stories, animal stories, sports stories, and mysteries are all realistic fiction. Each of these forms leads to a better understanding of the human condition here at home and in other countries.

Books of realistic fiction have certain qualities in common. While they are fictitious, they are set in a plausible place and time, and they contain believable characters who are involved in situations that could conceivably happen. This allows the reader to identify with or relate vicariously to the settings and characters.

Many realistic fiction stories focus on everyday problems such as family issues, interpersonal problems, handicaps, sexism, sexuality, aging, death, nontraditional living styles, and growing up. Realistic fiction offers children an opportunity to better understand and resolve their problems. Selected books can help them realize that they are not alone and gain some understanding about ways to face and cope with reality. Realistic fiction can also help children discover and experience unfamiliar problems. For example, a child who has never experienced death may identify and mourn with the characters as he or she reads Tomie de Paola's *Nana Upstairs, Nana Downstairs* or Judith Viorst's *The Tenth Good Thing About Barney*. Children can also learn about different lifestyles. For example, if children living in the rural Midwest read Eleanor Schick's *City in the Winter*, which portrays a little boy without a father, a mother who goes to work, a grandmother who wears old sneakers and socks, and an impoverished-appearing apartment, they will realize that not everyone lives as they do. Realistic fiction also builds a sense of empathy in the reader. In William Armstrong's *Sounder*, the reader is forced to deal with the way a boy is treated, thus empathizing with him. Finally, realistic fiction can help children identify their roles in society. This is not done by telling children what to do or by preaching to them, but rather by incorporating their problems into the stories they read.

Selecting and Evaluating Realistic Fiction

When selecting and evaluating realistic fiction books, all the standards of good literature must be met. In addition, the following criteria should be considered.

☐ 1. Can the child identify and relate to the characters or situation as portrayed in the text and illustrations?
☐ 2. Is the content presented honestly and realistically?
☐ 3. Does the child have an opportunity to gain insights and understanding into problems and situations?
☐ 4. Are a variety of cultures and lifestyles represented?
☐ 5. Are the characters and actions plausible?
☐ 6. Is there a hopeful, positive, and mature approach for dealing with a problem or situation?
☐ 7. Is there enough information to allow the child to draw his or her own conclusions?

Suggested Realistic Fiction

Armstrong, William. *Sounder*. Illustrated by James Barkley. Harper & Row, 1969.

Blume, Judy. *Superfudge*. Dutton, 1980.

———. *Blubber*. Bradbury, 1974.

———. *Are You There, God? It's Me, Margaret*. Bradbury, 1970.

Bunting, Eve. *How Many Days to America?* Illustrated by Beth Peck. Clarion/T & F, 1988.

Burch, Robert. *Christmas with Ida Early*. Viking, 1983.

Cameron, Eleanor. *Julia's Magic*. Illustrated by Gail Owen. Dutton, 1984.

Celbulash, Mel. *Ruth Marini, Dodger Ace*. Lerner, 1983.

Cleary, Beverly. *Ramona Forever*. Illustrated by Alan Tiegreen. Morrow, 1984.

———. *Dear Mr. Henshaw*. Illustrated by Paul O. Zelinsky. Morrow, 1983.

Clymer, Eleanor. *The Horse in the Attic*. Illustrated by Ted Lewin. Bradbury, 1983.

Danziger, Paula. *Divorce Express*. Delacorte, 1982.

de Paola, Tomie. *Nana Upstairs, Nana Downstairs*. Putnam, 1983.

Estes, Eleanor. *The Hundred Dresses*. Illustrated by Louis Slobodkin. Harcourt Brace Jovanovich, 1944.

Fox, Paula. *One-Eyed Cat*. Bradbury, 1984.

Giff, Patricia Reilly. *Kids of Polk Street Series*. 12 titles. Dell, 1985.

Harper, Anita. *It's Not Fair*. Illustrated by Susan Hellard. Putnam, 1986.

Hazen, Barbara Shook. *Tight Times*. Viking, 1979.

Lloyd, Alexander. *The El Dorado Adventure*. Dutton, 1987.

Lowry, Lois. *Rabble Starkey*. Houghton Mifflin, 1987.

Mark, Jan. *Handles*. Atheneum, 1985.

Martin, Bill Jr., and John Archambault. *Knots on a Counting Rope*. Illustrated by Ted Rand. Holt, Rinehart & Winston, 1987.

Paterson, Katherine. *Park's Quest*. Lodestar, 1988.

————. *The Great Gilly Hopkins*. Thomas Y. Crowell, 1978.

————. *Bridge to Terabithia*. Illustrated by Donna Diamond. Thomas Y. Crowell, 1977.

Pittman, Helena Clare. *The Gift of the Willows*. Pittman, 1988.

Schick, Eleanor. *City in the Winter*. Macmillan, 1982.

Smith, Janice Lee. *The Show and Tell War and Other Sources About Adam Joshua*. Illustrated by Dick Gackenbach. Harper & Row, 1988.

Sperry, Armstrong. *Call It Courage*. Macmillan, 1960.

Stoltz, Mary. *The Explorer of Barkham Street*. Illustrated by Emily A. McCully. Harper & Row, 1985.

Voigt, Cynthia. *Dicey's Song*. Atheneum, 1983.

Voirst, Judith. *Alexander and the Terrible, Horrible, No Good, Very Bad Day*. Illustrated by Ray Cruz. Atheneum, 1972.

————. *The Tenth Good Thing About Barney*. Illustrated by Erik Blegvad. Atheneum, 1971.

Zolotow, Charlotte. *The Hating Book*. Illustrated by Ben Shecter. Harper & Row, 1971.

HISTORICAL FICTION

Time travel is possible. Children can be transported through the centuries to another age. They can become part of the past, taking part in long-ago events and meeting people who, though different in many ways, are fundamentally like them. Children don't need a time capsule or a magic carpet for this adventure. They simply need books that are rich in history and vivid in detail and that artfully combine fact and fiction—that is, books that are classified as historical fiction.

Historical fiction is a realistic story set in the past. By reconstructing life in another time, these stories allow the reader to vicariously experience past events. In writing historical fiction, the author chooses a specific time in which to set the story. Then he or she must become extremely familiar with that period by researching the setting, both place and time, using a variety of sources from newspapers to diaries and from interviews to books. The details of life, such as food, clothing, and transportation, must be portrayed naturally in order to bring the past to life in a realistic, believable manner. The elements of time and setting are an important influence on the central plot and characters. In addition, the author must establish a tone that holds the reader's attention.

There are different types of historical fiction stories. One type uses fictional characters, but does not refer to known people or to any recorded historical event. *Caddie Woodlawn*, by Carol Ryrie Brink, is an example of this type of historical fiction. Through Caddie, a twelve-year-old fictional character, Brink takes the reader back to the Wisconsin frontier in 1864. No real people or actual historical events are identified in this story, yet the reader gets a feeling for life on a farm in the 1800s.

Another type of historical fiction involves actual people and recorded events. Esther Forbes's *Johnny Tremain* demonstrates this type of historical fiction. Johnny, Paul Revere's apprentice, lives through the prerevolutionary days and early wartime in Boston. Both a real person (Paul Revere) and a recorded event (the Revolutionary War) are vividly and accurately portrayed in this story.

The greatest value of historical fiction is that it allows the reader to experience the past. What more exciting way could children learn about George Washington and his times than through Phoebe's experiences in Judith Berry Griffin's *Phoebe and the General*? Children can become America's first settlers as they share in the adventures of Constance in Patricia Clapp's *Constance: A Story of Early Plymouth*. By reading this book, they will be able to imagine what it was like to stand on the deck of the *Mayflower* and view America, their new home. Through historical fiction, children gain perspectives about life and can learn to see the way in which past events shape the present and the future.

Historical fiction also allows children to gain an understanding of their heritage—the values and beliefs of the people who lived before them. For example, *The Winter When Time Was Frozen*, by Els Pelgrom, provides the reader with realistic examples of values and beliefs held by the Germans and the Dutch during World War II.

Historical fiction also gives readers the unique opportunity to gain additional perspectives. Through the main character, they learn to recognize and identify with the feelings of others. In *Save Queen of Sheba*, by Louise Moeri, King David realizes what it means to the Sioux Indians to have white settlers on their land.

Throughout history, people have learned to overcome problems, work out differences, accept change, and learn alternative ways of handling situations. Historical fiction provides the vehicle through which children can benefit from past experiences. Through their vicarious journeys, children may be better equipped to cope with the everyday realities of life.

Selecting and Evaluating Historical Fiction

As with any other literature, when selecting and evaluating historical fiction, the standards of good literature must be met. In addition, the following special criteria are important.

☐ 1. Are past events depicted accurately and authentically?
☐ 2. Are the details of the times portrayed accurately and authentically?
☐ 3. Do the characters reflect the values of the times?
☐ 4. Is the plot consistent with the times?
☐ 5. Is the language appropriate to the times, yet interesting to present-day readers?
☐ 6. Does the theme provide insight into and understanding of past events?
☐ 7. Does the story provide a perspective of the way in which the past affects the present and the future?
☐ 8. Are fact and fiction blended in an interesting manner?
☐ 9. Is the past brought to life?

Suggested Historical Fiction

Bergman, Tamar. *The Boy from Over There*. Translated by Hillel Holkin. Houghton Mifflin, 1988.

Blos, Joan. *A Gathering of Days: A New England Girl's Journal 1830–1832*. Scribner's, 1979.

Brett, Jan. *First Dog*. Harcourt Brace Jovanovich, 1988.

Brink, Carol Ryrie. *Caddie Woodlawn*. Illustrated by Trina Schart Hyman. Macmillan, 1935.

Clapp, Patricia. *Constance: A Story of Early Plymouth*. Lothrop, 1968.

Dalgliesh, Alice. *The Courage of Sarah Noble*. Illustrated by Leonard Weisgard. Scribner's, 1954.

DeAngeli, Marguerite. *The Door in the Wall*. Doubleday, 1949.

Forbes, Esther. *Johnny Tremain*. Illustrated by Lynd Ward. Houghton Mifflin, 1943.

Fox, Paula. *The Slave Dancer*. Illustrated by Eros Keith. Bradbury, 1973.

Griffin, Judith Berry. *Phoebe and the General*. Dutton, 1981.

Hendershot, Judith. *In Coal Country*. Illustrated by Thomas B. Allen. Knopf, 1987.

Henry, Joanne Landers. *Log Cabin in the Woods*. Illustrated by Joyce Andy Zarins. Four Winds, 1988.

Johnson, Tony. *Yonder*. Illustrated by Lloyd Bloom. Dial Books, 1988.

Lasky, Kathryn. *The Bone Wars*. Morrow, 1988.

MacLachlan, Patricia. *Sarah, Plain and Tall*. Harper & Row, 1985.

Moeri, Louise. *Save Queen of Sheba*. Dutton, 1981.

O'Dell, Scott. *Island of the Blue Dolphin*. Houghton Mifflin, 1960.

Osborne, Chester G. *The Memory String*. Atheneum, 1984.

Pelgrom, Els. *The Winter When Time Was Frozen*. Rudnik, 1980.

Rappaport, Doreen. *Trouble at the Mines*. Illustrated by Joan Sandin. Thomas Y. Crowell, 1987.

Sebestyen, Ouida. *On Fire*. Atlantic, 1985.

Speare, Elizabeth George. *The Sign of the Beaver*. Houghton Mifflin, 1983.

———. *The Witch of Blackbird Pond*. Houghton Mifflin, 1958.

Turner, Ann. *Dakota Dugout*. Illustrated by Ronald Himler. Macmillan, 1985.

von Tscharner, Renata, and Ronald Lee Fleming. *New Providence*. Illustrated by Denis Orloff. Gulliver/Harcourt Brace Jovanovich, 1987.

White, Ruth. *Sweet Creek Holler*. Farrar, Straus & Giroux, 1988.

Wilder, Laura Ingalls. *Little House in the Big Woods*, and any other of the Little House series. Illustrated by Garth Williams. Harper & Row, 1932.

———. *Little House* series. Harper & Row.

Yep, Laurence. *Mountain Light*. Harper & Row, 1985.

Yolen, Jane. *Children of the War*. Viking, 1984.

FANTASY/SCIENCE FICTION

In the world of literary fantasy, anything can happen and the impossible becomes believable. In a world of talking beasts and underground kingdoms, of secret immortality and mysterious wizards, children learn to make sense out of their own lives.

When searching for a definition for fantasy, one phrase is constantly repeated: "Fantasy is the willing suspension of disbelief." Fantasy allows the reader to explore the past, the future, and worlds that coexist in the present. It combines the elements of the impossible and the possible to make the incredible appear credible.

Fantasy books take on many forms, such as stories of enchantment, humorous tales, stories in which animals and toys are personified, and science fiction tales. The common thread that sets fantasy apart from realistic fiction is the blending of the fantastic with realistic detail. Good fantasy weaves at least one element of the impossible in a framework of reality, while realistic fiction may include a situation that only seems improbable.

The elements of literature—setting, characterization, and theme—are important in creating fantasy. Time is another important element. Fantasy may be set in the distant past, the future, or the present. A story may take place in strange new worlds—as in C. S. Lewis's *The Lion, the Witch, and the Wardrobe* or Eleanor Cameron's *The Wonderful Flight to the Mushroom Planet*—that make the strange seem familiar or in realistic surroundings that make the familiar seem strange—as in Mary Norton's *The Borrowers*. Fantasy carries the reader to a setting that is beyond real-life constraints. The characters—whether animate or inanimate, human or animal—possess qualities and experience situations that children can identify with. For example, the animals in *Charlotte's Web*, by E. B. White, and the toys in *The Velveteen Rabbit*, by Margery Williams, feel and express love, hate, joy, and sadness with the same intensity as human characters. Fantasy depends on the ability to honestly convey emotion and portray the human condition, leading the reader to new insights and understanding. The theme is often quite serious, involving social and political issues, or universal, such as human values, emotions, and motivation. The battle between good and evil, greed versus unselfishness, and the meaning of life and death are common fantasy themes.

Within the story, however, regardless of the setting, characters, plot, or theme, well-written fantasy must be consistent. The images, language, experiences, and details must combine to make the plot, characters, and setting logical and believable. After reading fantasy, children often feel as if they have been to wherever the book is set; the settings and the characters become real to them. In fact, they often wish that what they have just read were real.

Fantasy helps children deal with their lives and gives them new ways to look at old problems. As fantasy stretches their imaginations, children become more creative in their ideas and problem-solving techniques, a vital part of the divergent thinking process. They learn to be more accepting, and more open-minded as they analyze different viewpoints, and more spontaneous. And finally, as fantasy makes the impossible seem possible, they dare to dream.

Science fiction is an important subgenre of fantasy and, because of its importance and value to the world of literature, it deserves special attention and analysis. The main factor in determining whether a piece of literature is science fiction or pure fantasy is whether scientific laws or principles are stressed. In science fiction, the scientific world, with its technological advances and possibilities, is of paramount importance. Good science fiction contains the same elements that are intrinsic to good fantasy. It must center around well-defined characters involved in human conflicts or problems. The setting, though often another place and time, must seem possible within a framework of realistic detail. The details contain many scientific truths and possibilities, while the conflict and solution rely on scientific content.

Science fiction looks at life and explores possibilities. As technology advances by leaps and bounds, what was science fiction years ago is today's reality. Jules Verne, for example, wrote of atomic submarines and rockets that journeyed into space. He didn't write works of realistic fiction. His books were considered science fiction when they were written over one-hundred years ago! Science fiction writers work within the context of scientific laws, yet they allow their imaginations to challenge reality. For example, André Norton and Dorothy Madlee's *Star Ka'at* allows children to imagine the rescue of all the earth's cats, as a superior breed of cat sweeps down on earth, before the world destroys itself.

Science fiction allows children to hypothesize about the future by imagining that certain events, conditions, or findings exist. In Jill Paton Walsh's *The Green Book*, for example, a family and others escape earth on a spaceship before "the disaster" occurs.

Science fiction paves the way for "a brave new world" by pointing out how the past and the present affect the future and by helping explain often-incomprehensible technological advances. A good example of this concept is H. M. Hoover's *This Time of Darkness*, in which pollution and the uncertain quality of the outside atmosphere force people to live in underground domed cities for protection.

Human relationships, conflict, and solutions to problems and fears can also be explored through science fiction. In *The Fallen Spaceman*, by Lee Harding, children are vividly drawn into the friendship of Tyro, from outer space, and Eric, an earthling. Even though Eric is initially frightened by the creature from outer space, he is able to overcome his fear.

Science fiction challenges children to believe and confirm that they can achieve almost anything their minds can conceive. It enables them to evaluate how they might live their lives, what types of changes would have to be made, and helps them come to terms with moral and ethical issues: How would they colonize other planets? Who would rule? How would they determine who is to live there? How could they prevent today's problems from occurring in the new world? What would the quality of life be like? How would they deal with other civilizations? Science fiction stimulates the imagination, asking children to think creatively, to open themselves to all possibilities.

Selecting and Evaluating Fantasy/Science Fiction

Good works of fantasy, as with other genres, must meet the standards of good literature. In addition, the following criteria should be considered.

☐ 1. Is the setting authentic and integral to the story?
☐ 2. Is the language appropriate and consistent? Does it add credibility to the fantasy?
☐ 3. Is the plot creative, believable, and ingenious?
☐ 4. Does the story blend fantasy with reality, making that which is impossible seem possible?
☐ 5. Are the details consistent with the plot, setting, characters, and viewpoint?

6. Is the element of time authentically represented?
7. Are the details so vivid that the reader becomes one with the story?
8. Are emotions conveyed honestly? Is the human condition portrayed honestly?
9. Is the reader led into new insights and understandings?
10. Does the story contain worthwhile themes?
11. In works of science fiction, does the story contain scientific laws, principles, and technology that give plausibility to the situations and solutions?

Suggested Fantasy/Science Fiction

Fantasy

Alexander, Lloyd. *The Beggar Queen*. Dutton, 1984.

———. *Westmark*. Dutton, 1981.

Andersen, Hans Christian. *The Emperor's New Clothes*. Retold by Anne Rockwell. Harper & Row, 1982.

Baum, L. Frank. *The Wizard of Oz*. Illustrated by W. W. Denslow. Reilly, 1956.

Bond, Michael. *A Bear Called Paddington*. Illustrated by Peggy Fortnum. Houghton Mifflin, 1960.

Carroll, Lewis. *Alice's Adventures in Wonderland*. Illustrated by John Tenniel. Macmillan, 1963.

Cooper, Susan. *Silver on the Tree*. Atheneum, 1977.

———. *The Grey King*. Atheneum, 1975.

Dahl, Roald. *Charlie and the Chocolate Factory*. Illustrated by Joseph Schindelman. Knopf, 1973.

———. *James and the Giant Peach*. Illustrated by Nancy Burdert. Knopf, 1961.

Ernst, Lisa Campbell. *When Bluebell Sang*. Bradbury, 1989.

Garden, Graeme. *The Skylighters*. Illustrated by Neil Canning. Oxford, 1988.

Grahame, Kenneth. *The Wind in the Willows*. Illustrated by E. H. Shepard. Scribner's, 1908.

Hunter, Mollie. *The Mermaid Summer*. Charlotte Zolotow/Harper & Row, 1988.

Kipling, Rudyard. *Just So Stories*. Doubleday, 1952.

LeGuin, Ursula K. *The Farthest Shore*. Illustrated by Gail Garraty. Atheneum, 1972.

———. *The Tombs of Atuan*. Illustrated by Gail Garraty. Atheneum, 1971.

Lewis, C. S. *The Lion, the Witch, and the Wardrobe*. Illustrated by Pauline Baynes. Macmillan, 1950.

McCaffrey, Anne. *Catwings*. Illustrated by S. D. Schindler. Orchard Books/Watts, 1988.

———. *Dragondrums*. Illustrated by Fred Marcellino. Atheneum, 1979.

———. *Dragonsinger*. Atheneum, 1977.

———. *Dragonsong*. Illustrated by Laura Lydecker. Atheneum, 1976.

McPhail, David. *Emma's Vacation*. Dutton, 1987.

Milne, A. A. *Winnie the Pooh*. Illustrated by Ernest H. Shepard. Dutton, 1954.

Norton, Mary. *The Borrowers*. Illustrated by Beth and Joe Krush. Harcourt Brace Jovanovich, 1953.

Tolkien, J. R. R. *The Hobbit*. Houghton Mifflin, 1938.

Travers, Pamela L. *Mary Poppins*. Illustrated by Mary Shepard. Harcourt Brace Jovanovich, 1962.

White, E. B. *Charlotte's Web*. Illustrated by Garth Williams. Harper & Row, 1952.

Williams, Margery. *The Velveteen Rabbit*. Illustrated by Ilse Plume. Godine, 1982.

Winthrop, Elizabeth. *The Castle in the Attic*. Holiday House, 1985.

Science Fiction

Beatty, Jerome Jr. *Matthew Looney and the Space Pirates*. Illustrated by Gahan Wilson. Young Scott, 1972.

Cameron, Eleanor. *The Court of the Stone Children*. Dutton, 1973.

———. *The Wonderful Flight to the Mushroom Planet*. Illustrated by Robert Henneberger. Little, Brown, 1954.

Christopher, John. *The City of Gold and Lead*. Macmillan, 1967.

Engdahl, Sylvia Louise. *Enchantress from the Stars*. Illustrated by Rodney Shackell. Atheneum, 1970.

Etra, Jonathon, and Stephanie Spinner. *Aliens for Breakfast*. Illustrated by Steve Bjorkmann. Random House, 1988.

Harding, Lee. *The Fallen Spaceman*. Illustrations by John and Ian Schoenherr. Harper & Row, 1980.

Hoover, H. M. *This Time of Darkness*. Viking, 1980.

Key, Alexander. *The Forgotten Door*. Westminster, 1965.

L'Engle, Madeleine. *A Swiftly Tilting Planet*. Farrar, Straus & Giroux, 1978.

———. *A Wrinkle In Time*. Farrar, Straus & Giroux, 1962.

MacGregor, Ellen. *Miss Pickerell Goes to Mars*. Illustrated by Paul Galdone. McGraw-Hill, 1951.

Norton, Andre, and Dorothy Madlee. *Star Ka'at*. Walker, 1976.

Nostlinger, Christine. *Konrad*. Watts, 1977.

Robenstein, Gillian. *Space Demons*. Dial Books, 1988.

Slobodkin, Louis. *The Space Ship Under the Apple Tree.* Macmillan, 1952.

Slote, Alfred. *My Robot Buddy*. Lippincott, 1975.

Walsh, Jill Paton. *The Green Book*. Illustrated by Lloyd Bloom. Farrar, Straus & Giroux, 1982.

Williams, Jay, and Raymond Abrashkin. *Danny Dunn and the Anti-Gravity Paint*. Illustrated by Ezra Jack Keats. McGraw-Hill, 1964.

TRADITIONAL LITERATURE

They are the tales of our youth; the tales of wicked witches, beautiful princesses, and fearless heroes. They have captured the magic of childhood, the belief that anything is possible. They have sheltered our dreams and provided cherished moments of enchantment, wonder, and hope. They are the works of literature rooted in humanity: folktales, fables, myths, and legends.

Traditional literature has formed the foundation for modern literature. Its origins can be traced to the origins of humanity itself. Stories were passed orally from generation to generation, each culture making the stories their own. Timeless and universal themes dealt with peoples' needs to understand themselves, the world around them, and their place in the world. Many tales were written in response to the times and mirrored the feelings people had regarding social castes and the struggles of the poor. Kindness, patience, and hard work were seen as qualities that would, in time, be rewarded; good would eventually triumph over evil and the power of love would prevail. Traditional literature reflects society, providing insight into the human condition and representing the good, the bad, the strengths, and the flaws in all of us.

Types of Traditional Literature

Folktales. Folktales include epics, ballads, folk songs, and legends. They relate the adventures, both plausible and implausible, of humans and animals. Often, the situations and characters are based on historical people and places and draw from a people's religious beliefs, customs, and values. Folktales are classified into various subtypes, such as cumulative tales, *pourquoi*, or "why," tales, humorous tales, beast tales, magic and wonder tales, and realistic tales. The most popular folktale, especially with children, is the fairy tale; this is a folktale for the child in all of us.

Basically, folktales share certain characteristics. They are usually written in a simple, direct manner. The characters, plot, and setting are established in just a few lines, as in this introduction to *The Princess and the Pea*.

> Once upon a time there was a prince who wanted to
> marry a princess but she would have to be a real one.
> He traveled around the world looking for her; but
> every time he met a princess there was always some-
> thing amiss. There were plenty of princesses but not
> one of them was quite to his taste. Something was
> always the matter; they just weren't real princesses . . .

The plot is often simple, filled with fast-paced action, and includes repetition. Humor, rhyme, and repetition can be enjoyed in such tales as *Henny Penny* or *The Pancake* as children join in during the refrains or practice repeating alliterative words and phrases. Situations and other elements are also repeated, usually in threes; often there are three children, three wishes, three chances, and so on. The conclusion usually immediately follows the story's climax. For example, as Sleeping Beauty is kissed by the prince, the kingdom awakens, all is restored as it once was, and they live happily ever after.

The settings are vague—"Once upon a time in a faraway land . . ."—allowing the reader to imagine that the action could happen any place and at any time. The characters are often stereotypes—the good and beautiful princess, the cruel and powerful stepmother, the poor, hard-working, virtuous hero. Often the characters possess special qualities that lead to the denouement.

Folktales appeal to children's sense of justice. In *The Old Traveler*, kindness is rewarded while greed is not. In the end, good triumphs over evil. Folktales also help resolve moral issues. In *Jack and the Beanstalk* greed is depicted as an undesirable quality or in *Cinderella* unselfishness is rewarded while selfishness brings unhappiness.

Many of life's lessons are also learned through folktales. In *Budulinek*, for example, a small boy learns to obey his granny and never open the door to strangers. In *The Husband Who Was to Mind the House*, the husband learned that his wife's job is not nearly as easy as he thought. And, from *The Fisherman and the Sea*, we learn to appreciate what we have.

As with other forms of traditional literature, folktales provide stimulation for artistic expression. Children are often motivated to illustrate, dramatize, or write a creative piece based on the plot, setting, or characters. And as they become involved in these activities, they can better relate to the characters and gain an understanding of languages, dialects, and customs.

The following criteria should be used in selecting and evaluating folktales.

☐ 1. Is the plot suspenseful and fast moving?
☐ 2. Is the setting timeless, one that can occur anywhere or any time?
☐ 3. Is the sequence of events easy to follow?
☐ 4. Is a problem described in a simple and direct fashion?
☐ 5. Can a child identify with the characters?
☐ 6. Does the conclusion immediately follow the climax and reflect a logical outcome?
☐ 7. Is there repetition, either of responses or of situations?
☐ 8. Is it entertaining?
☐ 9. Does the story provide an outlet for the expression of feelings?
☐ 10. Does the story express universal values?

Fables. According to legend, Aesop was a slave who lived in sixth-century Greece. Although little is known of Aesop, the tales long synonymous with his name have entertained us for centuries and have given us reason to pause and ponder. Fables are brief tales that, in the end, startle us with truth that is so simple, yet often so difficult to ascertain in everyday life.

Fables are based on human nature, and although their characters are often animals, the animals personify humankind. The characters are usually one-dimensional; that is, the fox is always clever, the mouse always small and rather weak. Unlike fairy tales in which the poor, unsung hero wins the hand of the beautiful maiden, the characters in fables basically remain the same. However, as the fable unfolds, each character learns, as does the reader, a valuable lesson in life. Everything revolves around the moral, which is the rationale for the fable's existence.

A knowledge of fables should be included as a prerequisite for cultural literacy since their influence is so pervasive. How often have we caught ourselves repeating a lesson from a fable as encouragement to ourselves or others, such as "necessity is the mother of invention" ("The Crow and the Pitcher") or "slowly but surely" ("The Tortoise and the Hare")? How often have we strived to keep our priorities firmly established by reminding ourselves that "precious things are for those who prize them" ("The Cock and the Jewel") or "do not pretend to be something you are not" ("The Ass in the Lion's Skin")?

Fables encourage children to reflect on the strengths and weaknesses all humans possess, and they clarify their understanding of human motivation and human nature. From "The Fox and the Grapes," for example, children can better understand the term *sour grapes*; from "The Two Bags," they realize how easily they see the faults of others yet fail to see their own shortcomings. Children and adults love fables and naturally relate to them on various levels. For children, however, the fable provides a simple, interesting plot, situations with which they can identify, and a message that can be internalized.

The following criteria should be used in selecting and evaluating fables.

- ❑ 1. Is there a message or a moral, whether implied or stated?
- ❑ 2. Does the fable contain few characters, each reflecting one main quality?
- ❑ 3. Are any characters, animate or inanimate, personified?
- ❑ 4. Is there a brief, though interesting, plot?
- ❑ 5. Does the story reflect human strengths, weaknesses, and imperfections?

Myths and Legends. In the beginning, humans told stories to explain what was then incomprehensible and to make sense out of the wonders they beheld. They told stories to reassure themselves that light would follow the darkness, that spring would follow winter, and that everything in life had its own special reason for being. These stories were passed orally from generation to generation and were shared by cultures who adapted them to reflect their own beliefs, values, and customs.

Yet, regardless of the culture, and although the characters and names varied, the themes remained constant. They acquaint us with past times, and yet help raise a consciousness concerning our own lives. They reflect the struggle between good and evil, as in "Theseus" who slew the cruel Minotaur, and strengthen our conviction that goodness will be rewarded, as in "Baucis and Philemon." Stories such as "Persephone and Demeter," which explain why we have the four seasons, or "Pandora," which explains the evils of the world and the existence of hope, relate the origins of life and provide a rationale for certain natural phenomena. Myths and legends also help the readers understand common human traits and the way in which these traits affect them. Myths relating the jealousy of Hera, the curiosity of Pandora, the vanity of Narcissus, the greed of King Midas, and the bravery of Hercules, for example, illustrate fundamental qualities with which we can all identify. Furthermore, myths allow the readers to compare cultures and understand their customs. For example, "Isis and Osiris" explains why Egyptians embalmed their dead and put the bodies beneath towering pyramids.

As we read mythology, it is interesting to note that almost every aspect of life has been affected by the myths. Our language is filled with words and phrases that had their origins in mythology, such as tantalize, narcissism, or "opening Pandora's box." We can drive a Mercury or an Aries, we can visit a physician and see a caduceus, and we can look to the heavens and find that the planets are named for gods and goddesses. Mars, the Red Planet, for example, was aptly named for the Roman god of war.

Legends differ from myths in several fundamental ways. Often legends have a more historical basis. King Arthur may have ruled Britain long ago, although the legend may be hyperbole. There may have been a Robin Hood, and most certainly there was a Sheriff of Nottingham! While the influence of the gods and goddesses may be felt in some legends, the main focus is on the hero and his adventures. Legends also provide background into incidents that might have happened, such as the Trojan War or the disappearance of Atlantis.

The heroes usually exemplify those qualities cherished by the cultures in which they lived. The heroes of traditional literature represent countries in every corner of the globe and include such legendary characters as: Odysseus of Greece, Aeneas of Rome, and El Cid of Spain. As legends were passed from generation to generation, the deeds of their heroes became more astounding, their wisdom deeper, and their courage limitless. As a result of these legends, we tend to set standards by which we measure our own accomplishments and establish our own ideas and ideals.

The following criteria will aid in the selection and evaluation of myths and legends.

☐ 1. Does the tale reflect the customs, values, and beliefs of the culture from which it originated?
☐ 2. Is there an explanation for natural phenomena, the origins of life, or human behavior?
☐ 3. Are the origins of social or religious customs explained?
☐ 4. Does the tale contain action, suspense, and conflict?
☐ 5. Is the story entertaining without requiring a prior knowledge of mythological or legendary characters and events?
☐ 6. Is the setting appropriate for the plot?
☐ 7. Will the tale help the reader better understand human vulnerabilities and strengths?
☐ 8. Does the story provide lessons for life?
☐ 9. Does it stimulate the reader's imagination?

Suggested Traditional Literature

Folktales

Aardema, Verna. *Why Mosquitoes Buzz in People's Ears*. Illustrated by Leo and Diane Dillon. Dial Books, 1975.

Aiken, Joan. *Past Eight O'Clock*. Illustrated by Jan Pienkowski. Viking Kestrel, 1987.

Andersen, Hans Christian. *The Complete Book of Fairy Tales and Stories*. Translated by Erik Christian Haugaard. Doubleday, 1974.

Brett, Jan. *Goldilocks and the Three Bears*. Dodd, Mead, 1987.

Bierhorst, John, ed. *The Naked Bear*. Illustrated by Dirk Zimmer. Morrow, 1987.

Brittain, Bill. *Dr. Dredd's Wagon of Wonders*. Drawings by Andrew Glass. Harper & Row, 1987.

Brown, Marcia. *Stone Soup*. Scribner's, 1947.

Cauley, Lorinda Bryan. *Jack and the Beanstalk*. Putnam, 1983.

Cooper, Susan. *The Silver Can*. Illustrated by Warwick Hutton. Atheneum, 1983.

d'Aulaire, Ingri, and Edgar d'Aulaire, ed. and illus. *East of the Sun and West of the Moon*. Viking, 1969.

DeArmond, Dale. *The Seal Oil Lamp*. Little, Brown, 1988.

Galdone, Paul. *The Little Red Hen*. Seabury, 1974.

———. *The Three Little Pigs*. Seabury, 1970.

————. *Henny Penny*. Seabury, 1968.

Grimm Brothers. *Little Red Riding Hood*. Illustrated by Trina Schart Hyman. Holiday House, 1983.

————. *Hansel and Gretel*. Translated by Charles Scribner, Jr. Illustrated by Adrienne Adams. Scribner's, 1975.

Lester, Julius, reteller. *The Tales of Uncle Remus*. Illustrated by Jerry Pinkney. Dial Books, 1987.

Nygren, Tord. *The Fiddler and His Brothers*. Morrow, 1987.

Opie, Iona, and Peter Opie. *The Classic Fairy Tales*. Oxford, 1974.

Perrault, Charles. *Cinderella*. Illustrated by Marcia Brown. Scribner's, 1954.

Steptoe, John. *Mufaro's Beautiful Daughters*. Lothrop, 1987.

Stobbs, William. *The House that Jack Built*. Oxford, 1983.

Zemach, Harve. *Too Much Noise, An Italian Tale*. Illustrated by Margot Zemach. Holt, Rinehart & Winston, 1967.

Zemach, Margot. *The Three Little Pigs*. Farrar, Straus & Giroux, 1988.

Fables

Aesop. *Aesop's Fables*. Illustrated by Heidi Holder. Viking, 1981.

————. *The Lion and the Mouse*. Illustrated by Ed Young. Doubleday, 1980.

Brown, Marcia. *Once a Mouse*. Scribner's, 1961.

Galdone, Paul. *Androcles and the Lion*. McGraw-Hill, 1970.

Hague, Michael. *Aesop's Fables*. Holt, Rinehart & Winston, 1985.

La Fontaine, Jean. *The Fables of La Fontaine*. Adapted and Illustrated by Richard Scarry. Doubleday, 1963.

Lionni, Leo. *Frederick*. Pantheon, 1967.

McGovern, Ann. *Hee Haw*. Illustrated by Eric von Schmidt. Houghton Mifflin, 1969.

Paxton, Tom, reteller. *Aesop's Fables*. Illustrated by Robert Rayevosky. Morrow, 1988.

Rackham, Arthur. *Aesop's Fables*. Watts, 1968.

Myths and Legends

Asimov, Isaac. *Words from Myths*. Illustrated by William Barss. Houghton Mifflin, 1961.

Chant, Joy. *The High Kings*. Illustrated by George Sharp. Bantam, 1983.

Colum, Padraic. *The Children's Homer: The Adventures of Odysseus and the Tale of Troy*. Illustrated by Willy Pogany. Macmillan, 1962.

Creswick, Paul. *Robin Hood*. Illustrated by N. C. Wyeth. Scribner's, 1984.

d'Aulaire, Ingri, and Edgar d'Aulaire. *Book of Greek Myths*. Doubleday, 1962.

de Paola, Tomie. *The Legend of the Indian Paintbrush*. Putnam, 1988.

Gates, Doris. *The Golden God: Apollo*. Illustrated by Constantinos CoConis. Viking Press, 1973.

Goble, Paul. *Her Seven Brothers*. Bradbury, 1988.

Green, Roger Lancelyn. *A Book of Myths*. Illustrated by Joan Kiddell-Monroe. Dutton, 1965.

Hamilton, Virginia. *In the Beginning: Creation Stories from Around the World*. Illustrated by Barry Moser. Harcourt Brace Jovanovich, 1988.

Hazeltine, Alice. *Hero Tales from Many Lands*. Abingdon Press, 1961.

Hoover, H. M. *The Dawn Palace: The Story of Medea*. Dutton, 1988.

Osborne, Mary Pope. *Favorite Greek Myths*. Illustration by Troy Howell. Scholastic Hardcover, 1989.

McDermott, Gerald. *Musicians of the Sun: A Myth of Ancient Mexico*. Delacorte, 1988.

Melling, O. R. *The Singing Song*. Viking Kestrel, 1987.

Switzer, Ellen, and Costas. *Greek Myths: Gods, Heroes, and Monsters*. Photographs by Costas. Atheneum, 1988.

POETRY

Poetry has several very different characteristics from the other genres. For example, poetry includes a distinctive manipulation of words. The words must be carefully selected to convey beautiful sounds and images, as well as meaning. Well-written poetry appeals to the senses and the emotions. Poetry must be read and reread to children in order for them to hear and feel what the poet is saying and to gain the most from the genre.

Poems, like pictures, convey different meanings to different people. As Siddie Joe Johnson (1967) so descriptively wrote:

> Poetry is a story, a song, a picture. Poetry is the first time you hold a firefly in your hand. . . . Poetry is magic. Poetry is what happens every day to everybody. Poetry is sunlight through a window with leaves moving just outside. . . . Poetry is remembering yesterday and looking ahead to tomorrow and tomorrow and tomorrow. Poetry is something your heart understands but sometimes your mind does not. . . . Poetry is you. And me. And all the people we know, all the people everywhere. Poetry is the nothingness of spider webs and seafoam. Poetry is everything! Yes everything!

Nursery rhymes are often children's introduction to poetry. Just as they enjoy the singing quality, melody, and movement of the word patterns contained in nursery rhymes, they will also enjoy these qualities in the poetry they read later. Poetry for children has particular elements that are appealing to them, such as rhythm, rhyme, sound patterns, imagery, figurative language, and repetition. Robert Louis Stevenson's "Windy Nights" conveys many of these elements:

Windy Nights
Whenever the moon and stars are set,
    Whenever the wind is high,
All night long in the dark and wet,
    A man goes riding by.
Late in the night when the fires are out,
Why does he gallop and gallop about?

Whenever the trees are crying aloud,
    And ships are tossed at sea,
By, on the highway, low and loud,
    By at the gallop goes he:
By at the gallop he goes, and then
By he comes back at the gallop again.

As children read or hear "Windy Nights," they can feel the elements of rhythm or movement of the words. They can hear the rhyming words and sound patterns as they read phrases like "Late in the night when the fires are out, why does he gallop and gallop about?" Repetition is another appealing element in this poem; note the phrase "at the gallop."

The images of sight, sound, smell, touch, or taste naturally occur as the lines of Robert Frost's "Stopping by Woods on a Snowy Evening" unfold:

The only other sound's the sweep
Of easy wind and downy flake
The woods are lovely, dark and deep
But I have promises to keep . . .

Figurative language is best described as a combination of simile and metaphor. A simile compares one thing with another, and a metaphor refers to an object or idea as if it were another object. Alfred Noyes, "The Highwayman," provides a good example of figurative language in the following lines:

The moon was a ghostly galleon tossed upon the
cloudy sea.
The road was a ribbon of moonlight over the purple
moor,
And the highwayman came riding—
Riding—riding.

Poetry can take on many different forms. Although it is not
important for young children to analyze the form of every poem
being read, they will enjoy investigating different forms, particularly as they begin writing poetry. Some children may enjoy the
challenge of writing a complex haiku while others enjoy creating
rhyme. The most enjoyable poetry forms for children include
limericks, haiku, bio-poems, clerihews, diamontes, cinquains,
and free verse. Descriptions and examples of each of these forms
can be found in Chapter 5 in the "Alternatives to the Book
Report" section.

Selecting and Evaluating Poetry

When selecting and evaluating poetry for children, it is important to choose poetry that they can understand and appreciate.
The previously mentioned elements of good poetry must also be
considered. The following questions may serve as a guide when
selecting and evaluating poetry for children.

☐ 1. Are sensory images of sight, smell, taste, hearing, and
touching created?
☐ 2. Does the poem contain figurative and alliterative language?
☐ 3. Is adequate and interesting repetition provided?
☐ 4. Does the poem flow in a natural and rhythmic manner?
☐ 5. Is the language and speech appropriate for the child's
understanding?
☐ 6. Are the words manipulated in an appealing manner to contribute to the meaning of the poem?
☐ 7. Does the poem appeal appropriately to a child's emotions?
☐ 8. Does the poem appeal to a child's sense of humor?
☐ 9. Is there a quality of imagination so a child perceives something in a new way?
☐ 10. Does the poem have a purpose?

Suggested Poetry Books

Atwood, Ann. *Haiku: The Mood of the Earth.* Scribner's, 1971.

Behn, Harry, trans. *More Cricket Songs: Japanese Haiku.* Harcourt Brace Jovanovich, 1971.

Coatsworth, Elizabeth. *Poems.* Illustrated by Vee Guthrie. Macmillan, 1958.

Farjeon, Eleanor. *Eleanor Farjeon's Poems for Children.* Lippincott, 1985.

Field, Rachel. *Poems.* Macmillan, 1964.

Fisher, Aileen. *Feathered Ones and Furry.* Illustrated by Eric Carle. Thomas Y. Crowell, 1971.

Frost, Robert. *Stopping by Woods on a Snowy Evening.* Illustrated by Susan Jeffers. Dutton, 1978.

Hopkins, Lee Bennett. *Pass the Poetry, Please!* Harper & Row, 1987.

Johnson, Siddie Joe. *Poetry Is.* Atheneum, 1967.

Larrick, Nancy, ed. *Bring Me All Your Dreams.* Photographs by Larry Mulvehill. M. Evans, 1980.

Lear, Edward. *The Complete Nonsense Book.* Dodd, Mead, 1946.

Lenski, Lois. *Sing a Song of People.* Illustrated by Giles Laroche. Little, Brown, 1987.

Livingston, Myra Cohn. *I Like You, If You Like Me.* McElderry Books, 1987.

Longfellow, Henry Wadsworth. *Hiawatha.* Illustrated by Susan Jeffers. Dial Books, 1983.

McCord, David. *Far and Few: Rhymes of the Never Was and Always Is.* Illustrated by Henry B. Kane. Little, Brown, 1952.

Noyes, Alfred. *The Highwayman.* Illustrated by Charles Keeping. Oxford, 1981.

Silverstein, Shel. *A Light in the Attic.* Harper & Row, 1981.

——. *Where the Sidewalk Ends: Poems and Drawings.* Harper & Row, 1974.

Stevenson, Robert Lewis. *A Child's Garden of Verses.* Illustrated by Brian Wildsmith. Oxford, 1966.

Thayer, Earnest L. *Casey at the Bat.* Illustrated by Patricia Polacco. Putnam, 1988.

INFORMATIONAL BOOKS

Curiosity is a natural phenomenon of childhood that is whetted and satisfied as children read informational books. Discoveries about our expanding world await children as they leaf through the pages of informational books. Through these books children can explore on their own and search for answers to questions such as "What makes a clock tick? What do hamsters like to eat? Where did I come from? What makes popcorn pop?" Informational books play a crucial role in the total learning process. The right book at the right time has far-reaching consequences and can be a tremendous motivating force in a child's life.

Informational books make up one of the fastest growing and demanding markets for children's books today. From simple concept books for young children to more complex books for adults, informational books provide the reader with accurate, up-to-date, significant facts on a variety of topics. This genre requires authors to be well versed in the subject and to express the information in a fresh, vivid, engrossing manner.

These books allow children to increase their knowledge about subjects they hear about on television or read about in the newspaper. After reading about a city's pollution problems, for example, children may choose to read *Lives at Stake: The Science and Politics of Environmental Health* by Laurence Pringle, which deals with the many problems confronting and threatening our environment.

From learning how to cook to making a kite to taking care of a pet, informational books provide children with the instructions necessary to accomplish new tasks. *The Fun of Cooking* by Jill Krementz teaches children how to safely use a variety of cooking tools and equipment and how to select nutritional foods. The Practical Puffin Series teaches how to make a kite. And Alvin and Virginia Silverstein's *Hamsters: All About Them* tells what to feed a pet hamster. No matter what their interest, children can find an informational book to help them in their desire to learn.

Isaac Asimov's *The Birth of the United States 1763–1816* or John Loeper's *Going to School in 1876* can bring the school's curriculum to life. Children can experience and understand history through the artistry of authors who are able to weave together events in a way that will captivate their readers. Informational books cover topics and concepts in all areas of the curriculum, providing children with a resource that not only supplements basal texts but also enhances and expands understanding.

Through informational books, children can develop higher-order thinking skills and critical reading abilities. As they read several books on the same subject, but by different authors, they can compare the treatment of the subject as they contrast and evaluate the contents of the books. For example, they may compare Sara Stein's *About Dying* and Herbert Zim and Sonia Bleeker's *Life and Death* and discover that the authors approach death from different perspectives, which will encourage them to formulate their own perspectives about death. In addition, they may analyze the relevancy, objectivity, and accuracy of the material. When children compare the contents of books on certain subjects, they must be aware of the importance of the copyright date. For example, comparing information in a book written in 1980 about space travel with a book written in 1988 would not be fair.

Children can become inspired as they read about the achievements of others. A budding young artist may be inspired by reading Piero Ventura's *Great Painters*. Young girls may strive for a particular career after reading *What Can She Be? A Newscaster*, by Gloria and Esther Goldreich, which portrays women in a variety of significant occupations. As they read about various careers, children can learn more about the realities of a profession that are often obscured by television and movies.

Finally, children may develop an interest or a hobby. Miriam Cooper's *Snap! Photography* or Edward E. Davis's *In the Dark, a Beginner's Guide to Developing and Printing Black and White Negatives* are two of the many books that could encourage a child's interest in photography and help develop a lifelong hobby.

Informational books are essential resources for children to tap when searching for facts, comparing perspectives, seeking new ideas, or developing theories. No matter what the subject, informational books are available to encourage children to broaden their knowledge and sustain their natural curiosity.

Selecting and Evaluating Informational Books
The following criteria should be considered when selecting and evaluating informational books.

☐ 1. Is accurate information presented?
☐ 2. Is the information up-to-date?
☐ 3. Are the most relevant and significant facts for the subject being presented?
☐ 4. Does the book reflect the work of an author who is qualified to write on the subject being presented?

☐ 5. Is the information presented without relying on anthropomorphism?

☐ 6. Is the book stereotypic of race, ethnicity, or sex?

☐ 7. Does the book distinguish the difference between fact and theory?

☐ 8. Are different points of view, when appropriate, or controversial subjects presented?

☐ 9. Does the book encourage the reader to become involved, when appropriate, by observing, collecting data, and experimenting?

☐ 10. Are the illustrations accurate and useful?

☐ 11. Is the reader encouraged to pursue the subject further?

☐ 12. Is the text written in an interesting, compelling, and straightforward style?

Suggested Informational Books

Aaseng, Nate. *Meat Eating Animals*. Illustrated by Alcuin C. Dornisch. Lerner, 1987.

Ancona, George. *Turtle Watch*. Macmillan, 1987.

Arnold, Caroline. *Walk on the Great Barrier Reef*. Photos by Arthur Arnold. Carolrhoda, 1988.

———. *Koala*. Photographs by Richard Hewett. Morrow, 1987.

———. *Trapped in Tar, Fossils from the Ice Age*. Photos by Richard Hewett. Clarion, 1987.

Asimov, Issac. *The Birth of the United States 1763–1816*. Houghton Mifflin, 1974.

Barrett, Norman S. *Pandas*. Watts, 1988.

Boyne, Walter. *The Smithsonian Book of Flight for Young People*. Atheneum, 1988.

Cooper, Miriam. *Snap! Photography*. Messner, 1981.

Davis, Edward E. *Into the Dark, a Beginner's Guide to Developing and Printing Black and White Negatives*. Atheneum, 1979.

Fisher, Leonard Everett. *Calendar Art*. Four Winds Press, 1979.

Giblin, James Cross. *Let There Be Light*. Thomas Y. Crowell, 1988.

Goldreich, Gloria, and Esther Goldreich. *What Can She Be? A Newscaster*. Photos by Robert Ipcar. Lothrop, 1973.

Hackwell, W. John. *Signs, Letters, Words*. Scribner's, 1987.

Heller, Ruth. *Animals Born Alive and Well*. Grosset & Dunlap, 1982.

Hirschi, Ron. *Who Lives in the Forest?* Photographs by Galen Burrell. Dodd, Mead, 1987.

Jeffries, David. *The Jet Age: From the First Jet Fighters to Swing-Wing Bombers*. Illustrated by Terry Hadler, Ron Jobson, and Michael Roffe. Watts, 1988.

Krementz, Jill. *The Fun of Cooking*. Knopf, 1985.

Lampton, Christopher. *Stars and Planets*. Illustrated by Ron Miller. Doubleday, 1988.

Loeper, John J. *Going to School in 1876*. Atheneum, 1984.

Miller, Jonathan. *The Human Body*. Designed by David Pelham. Viking, 1983.

Newnham, Jack. *Kites*. Penguin, Practical Puffin Series, 1977.

Norsgaard, E. Jaediker. *How to Raise Butterflies*. Photographs by Campbell Norsgaard. Dodd, Mead, 1988.

Patent, Dorothy. *Whales, Giants of the Deep*. Holiday House, 1987.

———. *Farm Animals*. Photographs by William Munoz. Holiday House, 1984.

———. *Spider Magic*. Holiday House, 1982.

Patterson, Francine. *Koko's Kitten*. Photographs by Ronald H. Cohn. Scholastic Hardcover, 1985.

Pringle, Laurence. *Lives at Stake: The Science and Politics of Environmental Health*. Macmillan, 1980.

Ride, Sally. *To Space and Back*. Lothrop, 1986.

Rogasky, Barbara. *Smoke and Ashes: The Story of the Holocaust*. Holiday House, 1988.

Rogers, Jean. *The Secret Moose*. Illustrated by Jim Fowler. Greenwillow, 1985.

Schwartz, David. *How Much Is a Million?* Scholastic, 1985.

Silverstein, Alvin, and Virginia B. Silverstein. *Hamsters: All About Them*. Photographs by Frederick Breda. Lippincott, 1976.

Simon, Seymour. *Icebergs and Glaciers*. Morrow, 1987.

Smallman, Claire. *Outside-In*. Barron's, 1986.

Stein, Sara Bonnett. *About Dying*. Photographs by Dick Frank. Walker, 1974.

Ventura, Piero. *Great Painters*. Putnam, 1984.

Wharton, Anthony. *Discovering Seabirds*. Watts, 1987.

Zim, Herbert, and Sonia Bleeker. *Life and Death*. Illustrated by Rene Martin. Morrow, 1974.

BIOGRAPHIES

Children learn! Children wonder! Children fantasize! Children pretend! Children *also* seek out truth and reality. By reading a biography, children can step into someone else's shoes and walk through their lives, sharing their accomplishments and failures, loves and hates, strengths and frailties, joys and sorrows. A good biography offers accurate, rich, and vivid details of another person's life and contributes to a better understanding of that person and his or her affect on society.

Until recently, biographies were written primarily about national heroes, mainly men. Today, however, the subject is no longer determined by race, gender, or social position. Today's biographies are concerned with people who have made significant contributions in a wide range of areas. For example, more biographies are now being written about contemporary figures involved in areas such as sports and entertainment.

Authors of biographies have three main elements to consider. First, the author must "know" the subject well and offer a substantial amount of pertinent information. Books, interviews, letters, diaries, newspapers, and accounts of what the subject is credited with saying are just a few of the resources that can provide an accurate picture of the person. Second, the author must consider history and the subject's place in history. The author must have a sense of how the subject affected, and was affected by, the time and place in which he or she lived. An understanding of significant events that influenced the course of history is also vital. Third, the author must then be able to combine the two elements described with good literature. To make an impact, the biography must bring the subject to life in an exciting fashion.

Biographies written for children have always been more fictionalized than those written for adults. Although the emphasis is on authentic facts, authors have the freedom to dramatize certain events to make the reading more interesting. Care is taken in fictionalized biographies to eliminate bias and to accurately represent the subject and the period in which the subject lived. The elements of the story such as dialogue, setting, and situations can be embellished or invented by the author *only* if they do not violate the authenticity of the subject's life.

One of the greatest values of children's biographies is that by reading about other people, children are often inspired to set goals for their own lives. They gain insight into the qualities and dedication that lead to achievement and a perspective on how these achievements have influenced others. One of the best examples can be found in Catherine Owen Peare's *The Helen Keller Story*, which dramatically demonstrates how a person can triumph over physical handicaps and inspire others through her courage and tenacity.

Biographies also allow children to become familiar with the

lives and times of prominent world figures, past and present, and to develop an understanding of the circumstances and events that may have contributed to their accomplishments. *The Life and Words of John F. Kennedy*, by James Wood, and Gertrude Norman's *A Man Called Washington* provide detailed accounts of the historical forces that shaped the experiences and accomplishments of these men.

In our world, there is much political unrest. George Sullivan's *Sadat: The Man Who Changed Mid-East History* provides an excellent portrait of the successful effort of two warring cultures, Israel and Egypt, to convert their swords to plows and attain a true peace. As a result, the reader is afforded an additional dimension to consider as he or she evaluates current problems and conflicts.

Biographies can provide insights into different cultures and races. Ed Clayton's *Martin Luther King: The Peaceful Warrior* helps children better understand the antagonism between races. As children come face to face with prejudice, it is hoped that they will grow in compassion and strive to shape a society in which differences are accepted and appreciated.

By reading biographies, children are exposed to a variety of careers, from astronaut to zoologist and everything in between. June Behrens's *Sally Ride, Astronaut: An American First* and Ernest Raboff's *Pablo Picasso* are just two examples of books that provide children with accurate information concerning all aspects of a career and encourage further investigation.

Reading more contemporary biographies allows children to enjoy a sense that they are sharing the lives of popular celebrities. Reading Harold and Geraldine Woods's *Bill Cosby: Making America Laugh and Learn*, for example, will foster an appreciation for the way Bill Cosby overcame many setbacks to become a success in the entertainment world and a role model in his commitment to education. In addition to stars of the stage and screen, many children also relate to sports heroes. *Jose Canseco: Baseball's 40–40 Man* by Nathan Aaseng describes what it is like to be a star baseball player and gives shape to the dreams of those Little Leaguers who have similar aspirations.

Biographies are a unique genre that provide something for everyone. A biography can be found to fit virtually any child's needs and interests. Biographies allow the reader to take part in historical events, witness great discoveries, and walk beside those men and women who have impacted the past, the present, and even the future. Their stories provide inspiration and reconfirm our own hopes, goals, and ideals.

Selecting and Evaluating Biographies

When selecting and evaluating biographies, consider the following criteria, as well as all the standards of good literature.

- ☐ 1. Are the person and setting depicted in an authentic and accurate manner?
- ☐ 2. Is a balance provided between the requirement for accuracy and the requirement for the book to hold the reader's interests?
- ☐ 3. Do rich and vivid details about a *worthy* subject allow for a better understanding of that person's role or contribution(s) to humankind?
- ☐ 4. Is the information presented in such a way that the subject seems alive and real?
- ☐ 5. Is the representation of the subject honest? Does it include shortcomings and virtues and avoid unnecessary ridicule or acclaim?
- ☐ 6. Does the book omit significant information that may distort the subject's life?
- ☐ 7. Do the text and the illustrations seem to have been researched?
- ☐ 8. Do the dialogue and quotations add depth to the reader's understanding of the subject?
- ☐ 9. Does the book provide a historical perspective?
- ☐ 10. Are experiences or information provided that expand the reader's awareness of the possibilities available in his or her own life?

Suggested Biographies

Aaseng, Nathan. *Jose Canseco: Baseball's 40–40 Man.* Lerner, 1989.

Aliki (Brandenberg). *The Many Lives of Benjamin Franklin.* Prentice-Hall, 1977.

Behrens, June. *Sally Ride, Astronaut: An American First.* Children's Press, 1984.

Burchard, Marshall. *Sports Hero: Ron Guidry.* Putnam, 1981.

Clayton, Ed. *Martin Luther King: The Peaceful Warrior*, 3rd ed. Illustrated by David Hodges. Prentice-Hall, 1968.

Cone, Molly. *Leonard Bernstein*. Illustrated by Robert Glaster. Thomas Y. Crowell, 1970.

de Paola, Tomie. *The Art Lesson*. Putnam, 1989.

Faber, Doris. *Eleanor Roosevelt, First Lady of the World*. Illustrated by Donna Ruff. Viking Kestrel, 1985.

Freedman, Russell. *Lincoln: A Photo Biography*. Clarion/T&F, 1987.

Fritz, Jean. *Traitor: The Case of Benedict Arnold*. Putnam, 1981.

————. *And Then What Happened, Paul Revere?* Illustrated by Margot Tomes. Coward-McCann, 1973.

Jones, Hettie. *Big Star Fallin' Mama: Five Women in Black Music*. Viking, 1974.

Lauber, Patricia. *Lost Star: The Story of Amelia Earhart*. Scholastic, 1988.

Norman, Gertrude. *A Man Called Washington*. Illustrated by James Caraway. Putnam, 1960.

Peare, Catherine Owen. *The Helen Keller Story*. Thomas Y. Crowell, 1965.

Raboff, Ernest. *Pablo Picasso*. Doubleday, 1968.

Sills, Leslie. *Inspirations: Stories About Women Artists*. Whitman, 1989.

Stanley, Diane, and Peter Vennema. *Shaka: King of the Zulus*. Illustrated by Diane Stanley. Morrow, 1988.

Sullivan, George. *Sadat: The Man Who Changed Mid-East History*. Walker, 1981.

Wood, James Playstead. *The Life and Words of John F. Kennedy*. Scholastic, 1966.

Woods, Harold, and Geraldine Woods. *Bill Cosby: Making America Laugh and Learn*. Dillan Press, 1983.

7
Analyzing Elements

Rebecca Lukens (1986) defines literature as "a significant truth expressed in appropriate elements and memorable language." As children select their own reading material, they must develop an understanding of the elements of good literature. In the process, they will become more adept at evaluating and selecting the best possible children's literature.

This chapter describes the elements that constitute good literature: characterization, plot, setting, theme, and point of view. Following the description of each element are activities that will help children analyze that element in meaningful and interesting ways. Some activities will be more appropriate or applicable to some genres than to others. Many of the activities outlined in Chapter 5, "Extending and Sharing Literature," can also be adapted to help children understand the elements of literature.

CHARACTERIZATION

Developing strong, believable characters is a very important element of good literature. Authors build and reveal their characters in many ways: through the character's thoughts, conversations, actions, and behaviors; through narration; and through the thoughts of other characters.

Characters should be as lifelike as possible, and they should develop as the story unfolds. Winnie, in *Tuck Everlasting* by Natalie Babbitt, is an example of a lifelike character who develops from a girl afraid to venture out of her yard to a mature, adventuresome young lady.

Characters should also be memorable. For example, children easily identify with and understand the needs of Frances the badger in Russell Hoban's *Bedtime for Frances*, as she goes through the typical ritual of postponing the final good night to her parents. Children will remember Frances as they go through their own good-night escapades. Many fantasy characters are memorable because of their unusual behavior or because they live in unique worlds. Two good examples are Charlotte the loyal spider and Wilbur the wonderful pig in E. B. White's *Charlotte's Web*. Both characters are vividly portrayed, and they stay in the reader's memory long after the specifics of the story are forgotten.

The characters' actions should be appropriate for their age and culture. Alexander's behavior in Judith Viorst's *Alexander and the Terrible, Horrible, No Good, Very Bad Day* is appropriate for his age and culture. Alexander is upset because he doesn't get a surprise in his breakfast cereal and because he can't get the colorful sneakers he wants. This behavior would be inappropriate for Tom Sawyer in Mark Twain's *The Adventures of Tom Sawyer*.

Characters should also be multifaceted, just as people are. Laura, the main character in Laura Ingalls Wilder's *The Little House* series, is a good example of how a character assumes many good qualities such as courage and honesty. Yet she also becomes frightened, angry, and jealous. This helps the reader identify with these human qualities and also realize that everyone is not perfect—even in books!

The following activities help children analyze characterization as an element of good literature.

1. Discuss what is meant by the term *physical characteristics*. Select a book that is familiar to all your students. Ask them to generate a list of physical characteristics for one of the main characters. Encourage students to imagine what this character might look like if each characteristic were exaggerated in some way. Explain that a *caricature* is a picture in which specific details are exaggerated. Caricatures frequently highlight the subject's likes, interests, and hobbies. Students can then create their own caricatures for this book and others that they read independently. Allow enough time for students to share and compare their drawings and to discuss the ways in which the author helped them "see" the characters.

2. Too often, readers focus on a character's physical attributes, ignoring the qualities below the skin that shape the character's attitudes and actions. To help students gain a deeper under-

standing of a character, introduce the concept of a *continuum*. A continuum will encourage students to analyze the character's inner qualities as they determine where on the continuum their character would fall. You can use the following continuum or students may want to create their own. It is important for students to realize that most people fall somewhere between the two extremes; this middle area results in our humanness and individuality. Characters in books should emulate people, and except in certain genres such as folktales, they should be as multifaceted as the people we meet each day.

3. Characters are revealed in many ways, through their actions and conversations, the author's narration, and the comments of other characters. To help familiarize students with

Title of book _____

Name of character _____

friendly	_____	unfriendly
happy	_____	sad
popular	_____	unpopular
wise	_____	foolish
content	_____	discontent
outgoing	_____	shy
unselfish	_____	selfish
sociable	_____	unsociable
ambitious	_____	lazy
neat	_____	untidy
mature	_____	immature
honest	_____	dishonest
brave	_____	cowardly
kind	_____	cruel

these techniques, have them analyze a character in a selected book and look for examples of how each technique enhanced their understanding of the character. The following chart can be used in this analysis. Ask students to list various qualities of the character and provide examples of those techniques that helped them understand the character.

Title of book: _____ The Story of Ferdinand _____

Author: _____ Munro Leaf _____

Name of character: Ferdinand _____

Qualities	Actions	Conversation	Narration	Comments of Others
subdued	sat and smelled flowers	Ferdinand said, "I like it better here where I can sit quietly and smell the flowers."	He liked to just sit quietly and smell the flowers.	Mother said, "Why don't you run and play with the other bulls and skip and butt your head?"
big and strong			As the years went by, Ferdinand grew until he was big and strong.	Five men saw him and they all shouted with joy. Here was the largest and fiercest bull of all.

As an alternative, have students list the name of a major character in a large circle in the middle of the page. Ask them to list characteristics or qualities of this major character in smaller circles. Then have them draw lines from the larger circle to the smaller ones. Next to each quality, on the lines that they have just drawn, have the students give examples of an action, conversation, narration, or comment that helped determine that quality. Have students identify which technique was used and place it in parentheses above the circle. For example, based on *Miss Nelson Is Missing*:

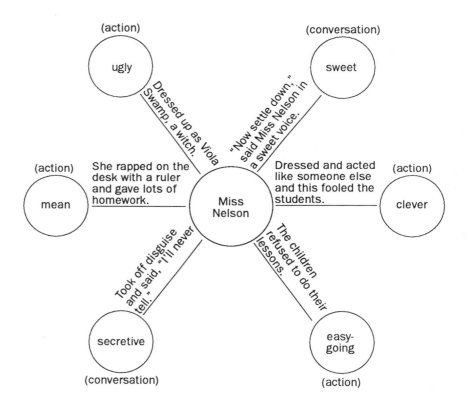

4. People's perceptions of one another are based on many factors. One important determinant is the way a person relates to others and the relationships that he or she forms. Sociograms have been used to better understand these relationships. (A sociogram is a chart that is used to plot the structure of interper-

sonal relationships in a group situation.) Sociograms can also help readers better understand the characters in books.

Have students create a sociogram for the book they are reading. Sociograms can be developed in several ways. In one type, the name of the main character is placed in a large circle in the center of the page. Smaller circles are placed around the larger circle to represent other characters in the book. Arrows are drawn from the larger circle to the smaller ones. These arrows contain the main character's perceptions of each of the other characters. Arrows are then drawn from the smaller circles back to the larger circle. These arrows contain the other characters' perceptions of the main character. For example, based on Frances Burnett's *The Secret Garden*:

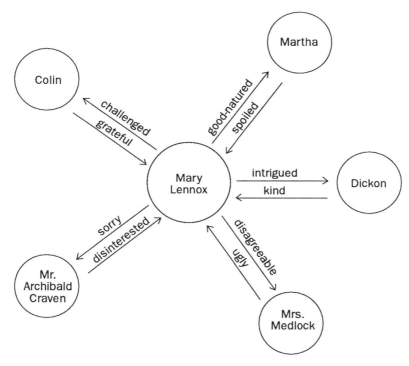

Another kind of sociogram focuses on the various types of relationships that exist between the main character and the other characters in the book. The name of the main character is placed in a large circle in the center of the page. Smaller circles, containing the names of the other characters, are drawn around the larger circle. One line is drawn from the larger circle to each of the smaller circles. This line contains a description of the relationship between the two characters. For example, based on *The Little House in the Big Woods*:

5. An interview technique can also help students gain better insights into a character. Ask each student to identify a specific character in a selected book, and create a list of questions to ask that character. These questions can explore the character's motivation, actions, feelings, and attitudes. For example, if Charlotte from *Charlotte's Web* were to be interviewed, she might be asked: "How did you get the idea for the words you wrote on the web?" "What other ideas did you have for saving Wilbur? What are your feelings about Templeton?"

Next, ask one student to assume the role of the interviewer, and ask the student who wrote the questions to become the character and answer them. If two (or more) students read the same book, one of them may "become" the character being interviewed, while the remaining student prepares and conducts the interview. This activity will compel students to analyze the character in order to answer the questions insightfully.

6. Generally, in most types of genres, effective characterization is based on the inclusion of dynamic characters who change and develop as the story unfolds. Children readily identify with, and appreciate, the way characters change as they are impacted by the events of the story. To help students gain a stronger sense of this change, ask them to analyze characters through a histogram.

Lined paper or graph paper, if possible, can be used to create a histogram. The following paragraphs describe two types of histograms. In one type, the students plot intervals from 1 to 10 on a vertical axis in the left-hand margin of the paper. On the bottom of the page, on a horizontal axis, they list various qualities of a selected character. Then on a scale of 1 to 10 (10 being the highest), they evaluate the degree to which the character displayed each quality at the beginning, middle, and end of the story. Three different lines—each a different color or three different types of lines (i.e., straight lines, lines formed from dashes, or lines formed from dashes and circles)—can be used to plot the qualities as they are exhibited during each of the time frames. Then the students can relate, either artistically, verbally, or in writing, how their impressions and personal feelings about the character changed at various points throughout the story. For example, the histogram on page 136 is an analysis of Winnie in *Tuck Everlasting.*

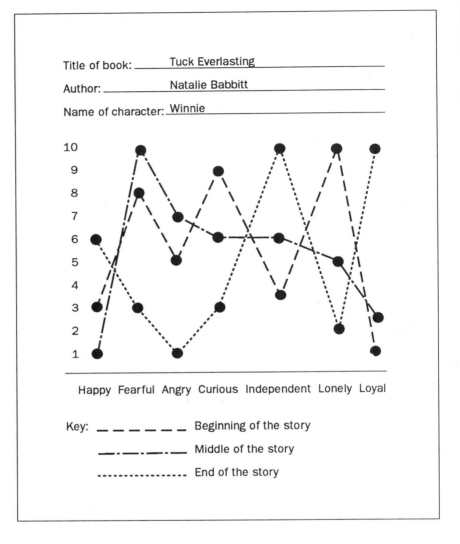

In another histogram, students use a graph with similar markings for the vertical axis. However, on the horizontal axis they list various events from the story in chronological order. Each student then selects a specific quality exhibited by the character being analyzed and graphs, on a scale of 1 to 10 (10 being the highest), the degree to which the quality is affected by specific situations and events. When all events have been plotted, the students analyze the results to determine why certain

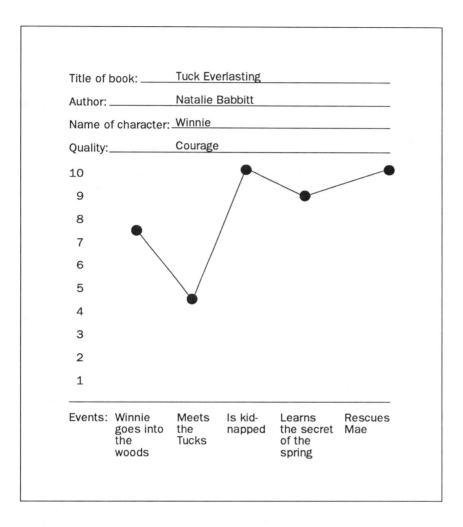

Title of book: _____ Tuck Everlasting _____

Author: _____ Natalie Babbitt _____

Name of character: Winnie _____

Quality: _____ Courage _____

10			●		●
9				●	
8					
7	●				
6					
5					
4		●			
3					
2					
1					

Events: Winnie goes into the woods | Meets the Tucks | Is kidnapped | Learns the secret of the spring | Rescues Mae

events had the effect they had. For example, the histogram above illustrates how Winnie's courage is affected.

PLOT

When evaluating any book, a major concern is whether the book tells a good story. In other words, does the book have a good plot? If the plot is well developed, the reader will have a difficult time putting the book down; if the plot is not well developed, the reader will lose interest. The plot, therefore, is what keeps the reader involved.

The plot involves developing a plan of action that usually follows a certain sequence or order of events. Children's books are usually presented in a linear manner because children have difficulty following more than one plot at a time. Plots may be simple or complex. Younger children are satisfied with simple plots, whereas more mature children enjoy more complex plots.

Good children's books usually have fast-moving, exciting plots, and the climax is usually easy to identify and followed by a quick conclusion. The excitement usually occurs when there is some type of conflict or struggle. These conflicts may seem real to many children because they may be encountering similar problems in their lives. For example, Sam, in *Sam, Bangs and Moonshine*, by Evaline Ness, does not intend to cause any problems with her fibs and lies; yet her lies do cause problems and almost cost the life of a friend. The children reading this story will probably carry something away about the hazards of not telling the truth. Thus, when children read stories with well-developed conflicts, they may be able to better understand their own conflicts and problems.

The following activities will help children analyze plot as an element of good literature.

1. Encourage students to analyze a newspaper article to identify the type of information included. Their analysis should uncover the fact that articles answer the questions *who*, *what*, *where*, *when*, *why*, and *how*. Encourage them to analyze the plot of a story in a similar fashion. Using this information, students can create a literary newspaper by writing articles based on the plots of their favorite stories. They can create a catchy headline, such as "Fountain of Youth Discovered" (*Tuck Everlasting*), draw or photograph illustrations, and write captions for pictures.

2. Students can read an entire book in a half-hour! Select a paperback version of an interesting children's book. The book should have chapters or definite divisions. Tear the book apart by chapter or by division and number each section chronologically. Give each child one section and allow sufficient time for the section to be read. When everyone has finished reading, seat the students in a circle in numerical order. Allow each one a specific amount of time (i.e., three minutes) to summarize his or her section. When they have finished this activity, the entire story will be uncovered.

Lead a discussion on the advantages and disadvantages of reading a book in this manner. We hope that this activity will foster the students' desire to read the entire book.

3. From a book that the entire class has read, either independently or in class, select specific incidents or parts of the plot. Write each incident on a different index card. Distribute one card to each student. Ask each student to read his or her card aloud. Then ask the students to put the cards in the correct chronological order. As the plot unfolds, be prepared for a heated debate!

As an alternative, have students create a time line. Ask each student to select a specific incident from a book that everyone has read. Students can summarize the incident in words or illustrations or both on 8½-by-11-inch pieces of construction paper. Allow time for them to share their work, and then have them determine the correct sequence of events. Display the time line. If several students select the same incident, simply cluster their work on the time line.

4. The conflicts in a book and the ways in which they are dealt with or solved are crucial to the plot. In literature, there are four main types of conflict: person versus nature, person versus self, person versus society, and person versus person. Select a book, and have a class discussion of the types of conflict in the book. It is not unusual for several types of conflict to be included in one selection.

Select one of the conflicts, and have students prepare and present a monologue to express their feelings as the character involved. This monologue should include the thoughts that went through their minds as they decided how to deal with the situation(s). Have younger children tape their monologues rather than write them.

Have students select a conflict in their lives that parallels a conflict from one of the books they have read. Lead students in the steps of Creative Problem Solving (see "Creative Problem Solving," Chapter 15) to select and plan a solution to the conflict.

5. The sequence of happenings in a story—the plot—follows different patterns. At some point, usually toward the end of the story, the action reaches a peak or climax. Some stories do not have a climax, instead the events follow one another in an interesting way and increasingly involve the reader with the

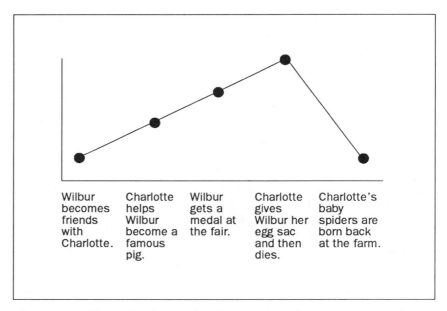

| Wilbur becomes friends with Charlotte. | Charlotte helps Wilbur become a famous pig. | Wilbur gets a medal at the fair. | Charlotte gives Wilbur her egg sac and then dies. | Charlotte's baby spiders are born back at the farm. |

characters. Have students plot the events of a story to see where, or if, the story has a definite climax. The figure above illustrates this kind of event plotting, based on *Charlotte's Web*:

6. Discuss how just one happening in life can completely change the course of events. Make this relevant to content being studied. For example, if the Pilgrims had landed on the west coast of North America instead of on the east coast, what things in our country or our lives might have been different? After this discussion, ask students to read a story and select a specific plot line or incident that they would like to change. Have them write a synopsis of the change and an explanation of how this would affect the entire outcome of the story.

SETTING

The setting of a story is the time and place in which the story occurs. The setting is important in helping create a mood for the reader. A story may take place in the past, present, or future. If a specific time or geographic location is used, however, it must be presented accurately. This is especially important for historical fiction. For example, in Joan Blos's *A Gathering of Days*, the setting is a small New Hampshire farm in the 1830s. The author vividly portrays collecting nuts, tasting maple syrup tapped from maple trees, and preparing a cold remedy in a kettle over open flames. Without the description of these events, the reader would be unable to envision an unfamiliar historical period.

Setting is more important in some stories than in others. Sometimes the setting is so important that neither the plot nor the characters can fully be developed without it. At other times, however, the setting simply provides a background. For example, in Kenneth Grahame's *The Wind In the Willows*, the vivid descriptions of the river and the changing seasons play a major role in helping the reader get a sense of the story and what is going on with the animals. However, in *The Three Billy Goats Gruff* and in many other fairytales, the opening line, "Once upon a time . . ." establishes the background. The reader understands that the story happened somewhere, sometime, usually long ago in some far-away never-never land.

The following activities will help children analyze setting as an element of good literature.

1. Students can focus on the setting by creating a different type of acrostic. Have students write the name or location of a setting from a selected book or story. Ask them to describe one aspect of the setting, for each letter of the name or location. As an example, let's use the town of Treegap from *Tuck Everlasting*:

T ranquil
R emote
E nigmatic
E ternal
G entle
A ustere
P rivate

2. Allow students to focus on the details an author uses to establish the setting by having them list the details of the place, time, and mood of a story. Since these three factors can change within a story, students will have to focus on one specific place, time, and mood. Their findings can be recorded on a chart like the one on page 142.

Title of book: _Alexander and the Terrible, Horrible, No_

_____ _Good, Very Bad Day_ _____

Author: _____ _Judith Viorst_ _____

Place: _Father's office_	Time: _End of day_	Mood: _Restless_
Desk	Picking up father	Knocked books off desk
Books		Fooled around with phone
Father working		Spilled ink and played with copy machine

3. Locate pictures that represent the time and place of a selected story. Use these pictures to stimulate a discussion of life at that time: "What types of clothing did the people wear?" "What were the main forms of transportation?" "What do the expressions on the people's faces tell you about the times?" "How did children spend their time?" Following this discussion, have students compare, in written, oral, or artistic form, life today with life at that time. You can extend this activity by having students research the specific time and place to discover how accurate or inaccurate their perceptions, based on the illustrations, were.

4. Good literature is like good art in that it affects the reader in a personal way. Have students create a collage or poem to express the mood a specific book conveyed. If students select the same book, it will be interesting to discuss the various ways in which individuals were affected by the story and the reasons for the discrepancies in their interpretations of the mood established.

5. Illustrations can be very important to a story because they often extend the text by adding an extra dimension to the

mood established. Select a story that includes vivid description as well as illustrations. Read a specific segment of the story, and ask students to orally list the story clues that most encouraged a mental picture. Then have them illustrate the same scene based on the clues mentioned. Allow time for students to compare their own illustrations with one another as well as with the illustrations included in the story.

6. Book illustrators use a variety of media to convey their impressions, such as woodcuts, collages, watercolors, crayons, and ink. Display examples of each medium to give students the background they will need to compare artistic media. Select several versions of the same story. Folktales are especially appropriate since so many versions of the same stories have been written. Allow students to study the illustrations from the different versions. Ask them to give a one- or two-word reaction to each medium used and encourage them to give reflective responses such as "detailed," "delicate," "realistic." Then ask questions such as: "Which illustrations did you prefer and why?" "Which illustrations seemed to best convey the mood of the story?" "Which illustrations added additional dimension to the story? Explain." "How do illustrations contribute to the mood of a story?" "How do the various media affect mood?" Allow time for students to experiment with the media as they illustrate scenes from a favorite story or from a story they have written.

7. In good literature, the author selects a time period and makes the details of the story accurate and consistent with that period. Select a specific story that is set in an earlier time. Have students select a specific event from the story and rewrite it as if the story were taking place in a very different time and location. For example, what if the setting of *Caddie Woodlawn* were New York City in the 1960s instead of the Wisconsin wilderness in the 1860s? "What dangers might she face rather than Indian raids?" "What leisure activity might she take part in?" "In what ways would Caddie be different if she lived in a different time?" Remind students of the importance of language usage and vocabulary in keeping with the setting.

8. Create a literary time line by stringing a clothesline across the room. As students complete a story, have them fill out the following Literary Time Line Card. The first completed card can be placed anywhere on the line. Additional cards should be

placed in appropriate locations in relation to the times indicated on the other cards. This time line will allow students to become familiar with and gain insight into the past and present and help them formulate their own impressions of life in the future.

LITERARY TIME LINE CARD

Title:_____

Author: _____

Setting: Time _____ Place _____

Impressions (Brief explanation of what life is like at that

time and place): _____

_____

_____

_____

_____

Illustration (Photograph, picture, or your own drawing to

illustrate the setting):

THEME

The theme of the story ties together the plot, characters, and setting. A story's theme is its message. It is a feeling, an idea, a meaning that the author wants to convey about life, values, beliefs, society, or human behavior. Often, themes deal with understanding oneself and others. Elizabeth Speare's *The Witch of Blackbird Pond* deals with prejudice and the determination of two children to listen to their own hearts rather than the preconceived and misguided notions of the adults around them. *Call It Courage*, by Armstrong Sperry, is an excellent example of a theme that focuses on dealing with a problem, regardless of the difficulty; Mafatu's search for courage leads him to danger and the unknown.

Some themes are timeless, like the friendship in *Charlotte's Web*, and their messages are as appropriate now as they were when the stories were written. Other themes are more contemporary. Often, the theme is stated directly. At other times, it is implied, and the reader must interpret the message based on his or her frame of reference. This implied theme is generally more effective and makes a more lasting impression. Stories for young children contain themes, just as stories for older children illustrate specific ideas. Often a theme will touch a nerve in the reader, causing him or her to question, analyze, and reevaluate his or her values. And perhaps, the message that readers take with them will help them become more caring individuals who are capable of improving the quality of their own lives and the lives of others.

The following activities will help children analyze theme as an element of good literature.

1. Often, the theme of a story is stated directly, as in Aesop's Fables. Read several of these fables to the class and discuss the themes of each. Have each student select one theme, and relate, either through written, oral, or artistic expression, a time when this theme had significance in his or her life. For example, after reading "The Tortoise and the Hare" and discussing the themes of "overconfidence" and "persistence can be more important than speed," a student might relate a time when she didn't think she had a chance of achieving a certain goal, yet she kept at it and ultimately found success.

2. Authors write for many purposes: to persuade or change perceptions; to relate an incident in their own lives; to provide insight into human behaviors, virtues, and faults; to share a philosophy. At the same time, they entertain us through the events and characters they create. Hans Christian Andersen's tales are excellent sources for examining the author's purpose and his message or theme.

Assign students, either individually or in groups, to read selected tales by Andersen. "The Ugly Duckling, and "The Tinder Box" are examples of his biographical stories. "The Emperor's New Clothes" and "The Red Shoes" illustrate human behavior. Andersen shares his philosophies in "The Fir Tree" and "The Little Match Girl." As students read these and other Andersen stories, have them identify and discuss the main theme. Ask students to find one quote in the story that best sums up the theme. Then have them illustrate the quote. Display the pictures in the classroom.

"It does not matter that one has been born in the hen yard as long as one has lain in a swan's egg."

3. Gather lyrics of folk songs, especially those made popular in the 1960s such as "If I Had a Hammer" or "Blowing in the Wind." Choral read the lyrics with students and discuss the theme of each song. Have students identify stories that might contain similar themes.

4. Select a specific theme, and depending on the level of the students, either read them selected books or assign specific

books that deal with this theme. Have students respond orally to the book in the following ways: emotionally, interpretively, critically, and evaluatively. As you encourage students to respond in these four ways, they will become more involved in the story. Emotional responses allow them to vent their feelings about a particular story, plot, or character by becoming involved vicariously. Their responses can be either verbal or nonverbal. In interpretive responses, students make inferences about motivation, events, the style of the text, and illustrations. Critical responses are ". . . a category of responses in which the reader judges the general literary quality of the story or reacts specifically to language, style, or characterization" (Sutherland and Arbuthnot, 1986). Finally, in evaluative responses, students make some type of judgment; they may evaluate various elements of literature or the entire story and the way in which it affected them. For example, based on *Alexander and the Terrible, Horrible, No Good, Very Bad Day*, students might respond by saying:

> "I could feel Alexander's frustration when his mother yelled at him for hitting the boy who pushed him into the mud." (Emotional response)

> "Alexander always said he wanted to move to Australia but I think he just said that for attention." (Interpretive response)

> "The pictures in the story are black and white and this type of picture allowed me to focus on the details." (Critical response)

> "I think Alexander was spoiled because he refused to wear the white sneakers." (Evaluative response)

At the end of the activity, have students compare the way the different books dealt with similar themes. Ask questions that will result in emotional, interpretive, critical, and evaluative responses.

5. Allow students to make an anthropomorphic connection as they become the theme of a story. For example, after reading a book that deals with prejudice, such as *The Witch of Blackbird*

Pond, allow them to look at prejudice from a different perspective as they *become prejudice*. Have them ascertain what prejudice might look like (its form and color), feel like, smell like, or taste like. Have students write about their life as *prejudice*. Encourage them to use the story and the feelings the story evokes to help them with this activity.

POINT OF VIEW

The interpretation of an event or experience can change drastically when described by different people, because their points of view vary due to their different values, cultures, experiences, and perspectives. Consider how Beverly Cleary's *Ramona Quimby, Age 8* might change if the story were told from an adult's point of view rather than from the viewpoint of a seven- or eight-year-old child.

An author has several options when deciding on the story's point of view. He or she can choose a first or third person's point of view, an objective point of view in which the actions speak for themselves, or a limited omniscient point of view in which the experience of one character is highlighted but the author may be all-knowing about the other characters. Although there doesn't seem to be a preference in children's literature regarding the author's choice of point of view, certain genres appear to favor one viewpoint over another. For example, realistic fiction tends to favor first person because it allows children to easily empathize or identify with characters.

The following activities will help children analyze point of view as an element of good literature.

1. A story's point of view is responsible for the way in which the reader sees the characters, the events, and theme. Have students read a book that is written in either first or third person. Then ask them to select one of the characters, and determine how the reader would be affected if the book were written from that character's point of view. Have students choose one small event and rewrite it from this new point of view. For example, if "Cinderella" were written from the viewpoint of one of the stepsisters, it might read as follows:

> Everyone always felt sorry for Cinderella. She looked so lovely and so angelic people thought she could do no wrong. But the Cinderella the public saw was very

different from the way she actually was. When our mother married Cinderella's father, we tried to be nice to her. We wanted to help her with the chores, but everytime we tried to help she played tricks on us and teased us until we cried. After years of taking this abuse, we decided that it was time to teach Cinderella a lesson. . . .

2. Involve students in a discussion based on questions dealing with point of view. The questions are speculative; there should be no right or wrong answers. Students should be able to cite specific portions of the selection to defend their responses: For example, if *Tuck Everlasting* were written from the stranger's point of view, how would he or she describe the value of the spring? If *Charlotte's Web* were written from Templeton's point of view, what would he suggest they do to save Wilbur's life?

3. Encourage students to select a specific incident that is perceived as negative by the character. Have students discuss how the situation can be looked at in a more positive way. For example, in *Alexander and the Terrible, Horrible, No Good, Very Bad Day*, Alexander realizes that his mother forgot to pack a dessert with his lunch. Perhaps a different character would see this as a positive occurrence: it might prevent Alexander from getting a cavity and gaining weight!

4. Select a book that the entire class has read. Have the class decide on a specific incident. Then have each student write a Dear Diary entry from the point of view of one of the characters. Allow time for students to compare their diary entries, and then discuss the way in which point of view changes their perceptions of certain characters and even of the story's theme.

5. Have students create a comic that illustrates the way in which two different characters from the same story perceive a certain situation. For example, in *Sylvester and the Magic Pebble*, Sylvester is turned into a rock. This event greatly saddens the lion who is about to pounce on Sylvester and Sylvester's parents because they lose someone they love. (See p. 150 for an illustration of these characters.)

"Where has our poor Sylvester gone?"

"I'm hungry."

EVALUATING GENRES AND THEIR ELEMENTS

Once students are familiar with the various genres and the literary elements that constitute good literature, they should be given activities that will cause them to synthesize and apply these understandings. *Synthesis activities* require students to evaluate selected works based on their knowledge of the elements of literature, their understanding of the different genres, and their ability to discern and apply the criteria for selecting good literature. These activities will help them become educated readers who are more adroit at selecting books that represent the best in children's literature. The following activities are designed to further this end.

Literary Evaluation

In this activity, students become the evaluators as they "grade" the books they have completed. Evaluation can be based on the way in which the specific literary elements were used to develop the story. Encourage students to use the criteria checklists for each genre given in Chapter 6 to aid them in their evaluation. A Literary Evaluation can take the following form:

LITERARY EVALUATION

Date of evaluation: _____

Title being evaluated: _____

Author: _____

Genre: _____

Literary Element	Grade	Comments
Characterization:	☐	_____
		_____
Plot:	☐	_____
		_____
Theme:	☐	_____
		_____
Setting:	☐	_____
		_____
Point of view:	☐	_____
		_____
Overall evaluation:	☐	_____
_____		_____

Name of evaluator: _____

– –

Evaluation Guide

5 = Outstanding   4 = Good   3 = Fair

2 = Needs improvement   1 = Poor (a waste)

PLOT

Name: _____

Genre: _____

Title: _____

Author: _____

Plot: Very briefly, tell what the story was about.

_____

_____

_____

How would you characterize the plot? (fast-paced, little

action, etc.) _____

CHARACTERIZATION

Name: _____

Genre: _____

Title: _____

Author: _____

Characterization: Describe the story's main character.

_____

_____

What helped you understand this character the most?

_____

_____

Retrieval Charts

After students have completed a book, have them fill out four cards, one each on characterization, plot, setting, and theme. (Examples for characterization and plot cards are on page 152.) Each card should ask for the student's name, genre of the book, the title, and the author. In addition, each card should ask questions that help the students analyze the way in which each literary element developed the story.

After students have filled out all four cards, tape them onto the appropriate square on the retrieval chart (as shown) that is posted in the classroom. Periodically, discuss the cards within each genre to see how the literary elements are developed. What commonalities can they find? Were the literary elements not developed as completely in some books within the same genre?

RETRIEVAL CHART

	Folktales	Realistic Fiction	Historical Fiction	Fantasy/ Science Fiction	Bio-graphy
Character-ization					
Plot					
Setting					
Theme					

Literary Log

Encourage students to keep a log of the books they read during the year. This Literary Log can take many forms, based on the students' level. More advanced students might divide a notebook into sections according to genre and place their log in the appropriate section. However, an analysis of genre is not appropriate for primary students. They need to be exposed to good literature to begin to develop an awareness of genre. Logs should be brief so that they are not viewed as a chore. Before students begin their logs, have them, as a class, list criteria for good literature. Keep this list available in the classroom for future reference. The following Literary Log is an example of an intermediate-level student's assignment.

LITERARY LOG

Name: _____ Date: _____

Title: _____

Author: _____

Genre: _____

General impressions (List five criteria that you think are

important for a good book in this genre to have. Evaluate

this book based on these criteria.):

1. _____

2. _____

3. _____

4. _____

5. _____

General recommendation: _____

_____

The following example is a primary-level log.

LITERARY LOG

Name: _____ Date: _____

Title of book: _____

Author: _____

Genre (circle one): realistic fiction   fantasy   poetry

                       historical fiction   picture book   folktale

I (liked) (did not like) (circle one) the book because:

_____

_____

_____

The Pulitzer Prize

Have your class come up with a name for the prize for a special book competition. Books will be competing for Best Realistic Fiction, Best Picture Book, Best Biography, and so on. The following steps will help your competition go smoothly:

1. Set aside a day at the end of the year for the awards. Allow students to design a special plaque or trophy that will be awarded to the winning selections.
2. Throughout the year, have students nominate their favorite selection within each genre. To nominate a book, the student must complete a Nomination Form (see page 156) to explain why the selection is an outstanding contribution to the genre and to children's literature.
3. Set a date by which all nominations must be made (approximately four weeks before the awards assembly). Read all nomination forms to the class and compile lists of the nominees by genre.
4. Allow time for a class discussion in which students discuss the merits of each nominee.

NOMINATION FORM

Title: _____

Author: _____

Genre: _____

In fifty words or less, explain how this book is an outstanding

example of its genre: _____

_____

_____

_____

_____

_____

_____

_____

What one thing about this book impresses you most?

_____

_____

Student's name: _____ Date: _____

5. Conduct an election in which students vote, by secret ballot, for the books (one per genre) of their choice.
6. Select a student to be the Master of Ceremony at the awards ceremony and choose those students who best championed each winner to accept the award.
7. Display winning books and their awards, as well as the other nominated books, in the classroom so that students have an opportunity to read these outstanding selections.

SUGGESTED BOOKS FOR CHILDREN

Allard, Harry, and James Marshal. *Miss Nelson Is Missing*. Illustrated by James Marshal. Houghton Mifflin, 1977.

Andersen, Hans Christian. *The Complete Book of Fairy Tales and Stories*. Illustrated by Erik Haugaard. Doubleday, 1974.

Aesop. *Aesop's Fables*. Illustrated by Heidi Holder. Viking, 1981.

Babbitt, Natalie. *Tuck Everlasting*. Farrar, Straus & Giroux, 1975.

Blos, Joan. *A Gathering of Days: A New England Girl's Journal, 1830–32*. Scribner's, 1979.

Brink, Carol Ryrie. *Caddie Woodlawn*. Illustrated by Kate Seredy. Macmillan, 1936.

Burnett, Frances H. *The Secret Garden*. Illustrated by Tasha Tudor. Lippincott, 1936.

Cleary, Beverly. *Ramona Quimby, Age 8*. Illustrated by Alan Tiegreen. Morrow, 1981.

Galdone, Paul. *The Three Billy Goats Gruff*. Clarion, 1973.

Grahame, Kenneth. *The Wind in the Willows*. Illustrated by E. H. Shepard. Scribner's, 1940.

Hoban, Russell. *Bedtime for Frances*. Illustrated by Garth Williams. Harper & Row, 1960.

Leaf, Munro. *The Story of Ferdinand*. Illustrated by Robert Lawson. Puffin, 1977.

Ness, Evaline. *Sam, Bangs & Moonshine*. Holt, Rinehart & Winston, 1966.

Speare, Elizabeth. *The Witch of Blackbird Pond*. Houghton Mifflin, 1958.

Sperry, Armstrong. *Call It Courage*. Macmillan, 1968.

Steig, William. *Sylvester and the Magic Pebble*. Windmill, 1969.

Twain, Mark (pseud. Samuel Clemens). *The Adventures of Tom Sawyer*. Harper & Row, 1876.

Viorst, Judith. *Alexander and the Terrible, Horrible, No Good, Very Bad Day*. Illustrated by Ray Cruz. Atheneum, 1972.

White, E. B. *Charlotte's Web*. Illustrated by Garth Williams. Windmill, 1969.

Wilder, Laura Ingalls. *The Little House Series*. Illustrated by Garth Williams. Harper & Row, 1953.

———. *Little House in the Big Woods*. Illustrated by Garth Williams. Harper & Row, 1932.

REFERENCES

Lukens, Rebecca. *A Critical Handbook of Children's Literature*. Glenview, Ill.: Scott, Foresman, 1986.

Parnes, Sidney J. "Guiding Creative Action." *The Gifted Child Quarterly* 21 (1977): 460–472.

Sutherland, Zena, and May Hill Arbuthnot. *Children and Books*, 7th ed. Glenview, Ill.: Scott, Foresman, 1986.

8

Involving Students in Selecting Genres

Children and adults can get into a reading rut by selecting books from one or two genres and neglecting the wonderful offerings of other genres. Often, they select books out of habit rather than by conscious choice. A concerted effort must be made to familiarize students with a variety of genres. The activities offered in this chapter encourage students to read books that represent different genres. Once they are familiar with every genre, we hope that they will be motivated to choose from the many literary offerings available and expand their horizons.

INTEREST INVENTORIES

It is important to understand why children read and what they read in order to select materials that will motivate them to want to read. Research indicates that children and adults read for two major reasons: (1) to gather information, and (2) for enjoyment. First, however, the person must be motivated to read. For some, this motivation occurs naturally. Motivation to read a particular book usually stems from an interest in the subject matter. For example, before a student reads a biography of Abraham Lincoln, he or she must have a need for, or an interest in, gathering information about Lincoln or the student must enjoy finding out what kind of a man Lincoln was, what kind of president he was, or what life was like during that time.

In the past, there was much concern over matching student reading levels with the readability level of books as determined by formulas such as those developed by Dale and Chall (1948), Spache (1966), or Fry (1977). However, research has found that many other factors, including interest and maturation, determine a student's ability to read a book. Therefore, there is no need to be overly concerned with readability because students will select the books that they can and want to read. Instead, the concern should be to provide students with as many opportunities as possible to be involved with books.

Although some generalities can be drawn from the research studies such as the types of books a particular-age child might like better or the types of books that girls might prefer, it is important to find out the subjects that most interest individual students. Without looking at individual interests, a teacher may overlook the fact that a first-grade girl is interested in baseball— a topic that research indicates is generally of interest to older boys. In addition, by being aware of the subjects that most interest the students, a teacher can be more effective in selecting books for the read-aloud and silent reading programs and in assisting individual students who seem reluctant to select books on their own.

There are several ways to determine the reading interests of children. The simplest way is through informal conversation. Ask questions: "What do you like to read about?" "Do you have any hobbies?" When working with a number of children, however, some way of recording the information, such as the Interest Inventory on page 162, is usually needed. On this form, students answer questions about their favorite TV shows, hobbies, sports, and so on. Older students can write in their own answers, and adults can help younger children read the form and fill in the answers.

MONTHLY TOPICS

Each month, explore a particular topic of interest to the students. Have all students read at least one selection based on that topic from a book that is representative of an assigned genre. For example, if the topic is baseball, students might read the following:

Poetry: *Casey at the Bat*, by Ernest L. Thayer
Realistic fiction: *Here Comes the Strikeout*, by Leonard Kessler
Biography: *Hank Aaron*, by Bill Gertman
Informational: Basic *Baseball Strategy*, by S. H. Freeman

At the end of the month, allow time for the students to react to the selection they read, and compile a "baseball anthology."

INTEREST INVENTORY

1. My name is ———————————————————

2. My address is ——————————————————

3. My phone number is ————————————————

4. I have ———— sisters and ———— brothers.

5. I like to read books about ————————————

6. The best book I have ever read is ——————————

7. I would like to know more about ——————————

8. I already know a lot about ————————————

9. Some interesting places I have visited are ——————

10. Places that I would like to visit are ————————

11. I like to collect ——————————————————

12. My favorite TV show is —————————————

13. When I have free time, I like to ————————

14. My favorite sport is —————————————

15. The person I most admire is————————————

16. When I grow up, I want to be a ————————

17. The thing I worry about most is ————————

18. The thing I do best is ————————————

19. The area in which I need the most help is —————

20. My favorite animal is ————————————

Circle *Yes* or *No*.

I enjoy reading.	Yes	No
I have a library card.	Yes	No
I like for someone to read to me.	Yes	No
I get books from the school library.	Yes	No
I like to get books as gifts.	Yes	No
I read a newspaper every day.	Yes	No
I subscribe to at least one magazine.	Yes	No

CURRENT EVENTS

This activity is similar to the monthly topic activity described earlier, however, the topic selection is based on current events. Allow time for the students to discuss major issues facing their city or state or the world. Have them vote on the topic they would most like to learn about. Once students have completed their readings, conduct a discussion in which they debate the merits of the type of genre they used in learning about the topic.

AUTHOR, AUTHOR

Many well-known authors have written books in several genres. Divide students into groups, and have each group select an author from a list of those who have written across the genres, such as Isaac Asimov, Judith Viorst, or Herbert Zim. Have groups read and discuss several of the author's books. (Make sure that the books chosen are not all in the same genre.) Encourage students to discuss their opinions and reactions to the books, which ones they preferred, and why. Each group is then responsible for planning a short skit in which the author and some of his or her works are introduced to the class.

CALENDAR OF GENRES

Divide the class into eight groups, one for each genre: realistic fiction, historical fiction, fantasy/science fiction, traditional literature (folktales, fables, myths and legends), poetry, informational books, biographies, and picture books. Each group is responsible for developing activities for one month that will involve the class in that group's genre. For example, October might be "fantasy month" and December might be "poetry month." Activities should include decorating the room or bulletin board, providing the class library with books representative of the genre, planning the month's read-aloud program, preparing an annotated bibliography of the group's favorite selections, and preparing a culminating activity that will familiarize the class with favorite selections from the genre. This last activity can take any form. Try monologues from various selections, role-playing of scenes from different selections, or a game show.

GENRE UNITS

Develop units in which students read a variety of selections within a genre. Then design activities to foster an appreciation for and enjoyment of the genre and to help students understand the elements and characteristics specific to that genre. To help you with your unit planning, we've provided three such units: traditional literature (folktales), traditional literature (mythology), and poetry. To give students variety, the format and the resulting products of each unit are quite different. In addition to fostering growth in reading, these activities will further objectives within other content areas such as writing, language arts, and social studies. This activity is most appropriate for students in the intermediate grades, although students in the primary grades may be introduced to the genres and their elements.

Traditional Literature—Folktales

Objectives. On completion of this unit, students will
- list the characteristics of a folktale in terms of characterization, plot, setting, and point of view
- analyze folktales for other commonalities
- create a folktale based on their knowledge of the genre's ingredients

Procedure

1. Assign each student a different folktale.

2. Distribute the Folktale worksheet on page 165; allow sufficient time for students to read their story and complete the worksheet. Note: With lower-level students, read aloud several of the folktales and discuss the questions from the worksheet.

3. Put the following elements on the chalkboard, and discuss each one according to the tales the students have read and analyzed:

Setting—where and when
Characters/characterization
Plot
Purpose of the tale
Point of view
Common features

4. Once every student has had an opportunity to add a few features of his or her selection to the chalkboard, encourage the class to form generalizations regarding the elements of folktales. The following generalizations might be elicited.

   a. Setting—Where: In a land far, far away; a land that is part of the real world, no matter how strange. When: Once upon a time, long, long ago.

FOLKTALES

Title of folktale: _____

1. List the main character in the story and describe his or her physical appearance.

   _____

2. Describe the main character's personality and other qualities that can't be seen in a picture.

   _____

   _____

3. When did the story take place?

   _____

4. Where did the story take place?

   _____

5. Briefly explain the plot of the story.

   _____

   _____

6. What message do you think the story is trying to give?

   _____

   _____

7. From whose point of view is the story being told?

   _____

8. What magical happenings, chants, etc., were described?

   _____

   _____

9. What was the first line of the story? Copy it.

   _____

   _____

10. How did the story end (happily, sadly, etc.)? Explain.

    _____

    _____

11. In your opinion, why has this story continued to be a favorite of children for over a hundred years?

    _____

    _____

b. Characters/characterization: Characters usually are good or evil; rich or poor (and the poor often become rich). Characters have human faults and desires and often exhibit qualities similar to our own and to those of people we know.

c. Plot: The plot is more important than the characters. It is filled with action and holds the reader's interest.

d. Point of view: Told in third person, the teller is omniscient.

e. Commonalities: Things happen in threes—three wishes, three chances. Often include elements of magic: a magical chant, a magical character, magical objects.

5. Encourage students, either individually or in groups, to create their own folktales. Review the formula that has made folktales such popular, well-loved stories. The tale can be an updated version of an older tale (Space-Age Cinderella), or it can feature a new plot with characters from older tales, or it can be an entirely new tale.

Traditional Literature—Mythology

Objectives. On completion of this unit, students will

- understand the way in which mythological characters share characteristics of people everywhere
- be able to evaluate the influence of mythology on their lives
- become aware of the elements of mythological stories and the purposes for which they were written
- create a myth based on knowledge of the elements of mythological stories

Procedure. Have students compile the activities they complete into a mythological booklet for future reference.

1. Before students can analyze mythological characters, they must first be able to identify them. Have students fill in a chart similar to the one on page 167 with the names of the major and some minor Greek or Roman gods and goddesses, along with their "titles." You may wish to extend the activity to include the identification of mythological characters from other countries and other Greek or Roman mythological characters and deities.

2. Read several myths aloud. List the main characters in each myth on the board. Ask students to suggest words that best describe the characters listed. Involve students in a discussion comparing the characters in mythology with people they know today.

GODS AND GODDESSES

Greek Name	Roman Name	Title
Zeus	Jupiter	King of all the gods
Poseidon	Neptune	God of the sea

3. "Zeus was at times extreme in both his punishments and rewards." Have students write a paper defending this statement. Encourage them to cite specific examples. Have each student choose one additional mythological character. Ask them to list the character's main qualities and then cite specific examples that led them to their conclusions.

4. Read the following myths aloud, and then have students complete and discuss the questions that follow:

   a. "Daedalus and Icarus"

   Why was Daedalus imprisoned?

   What inspired Daedalus's escape plan?

   What does this story tell you about the desire to fly?

   Look at a map of Europe. What body of water was named for one of the characters in this story?

   b. "Pandora"

   What was Pandora's main fault?

   What happenings in life does this myth help explain?

   Do you agree that "hope" is the most wonderful gift of all? Explain.

   What does the phrase "You've opened a Pandora's box" mean?

   Tell about the time you or someone you know opened a "Pandora's box."

   c. "Phaëton and the Chariot of the Sun"

   How did the ancients explain day and night?

What landforms does this myth help to explain?

What quality did Phaëton possess that almost destroyed the earth?

What other qualities are equally destructive? Why?

5. Have students read at least two myths. Ask them to summarize each myth and analyze its purpose. Was the purpose to explain a natural phenomenon? human qualities?

6. Have students read the following stories (or read them aloud to the class). After reading each pair of stories, complete and discuss the questions that follow:

a. "Odin and Mimir" and "King Midas"

What does the story of Odin and Mimir tell us about the importance of wisdom?

Is wisdom easily achieved? Explain.

Which do you think is more important—wealth or wisdom? Why?

How would you describe King Midas at the beginning of the story? at the end of the story? What caused him to change?

What do you think was the main message he learned?

What is your definition of wisdom?

b. "Arachne" and "Prometheus"

What was Arachne's main fault?

Do you agree with her punishment? Why or why not?

If you were Athena, how would you have punished her?

Why was Prometheus punished?

Do you agree with his punishment? Why or why not?

Of Arachne and Prometheus, whose actions can you defend more easily? Explain.

7. Nowhere in our culture is mythology's influence more greatly felt than in our language. Have students copy the following list of mythological characters and the derived words that appear in our language today (shown in parentheses beside the character's name).

Arachne (arachnid)   Gaea (geography, geology)
Atlas (an atlas)   Hydra (hydrant)
Brontes (brontosaurus)   Hygeia (hygiene)
Ceres (cereal)   Iris (iridescent, iris)
Chaos (chaos, chaotic)   Janus (January)
Furies (fury, furious)   Mars (martial)

Midas (the Midas touch)   Pan (panacea, panic)
Muses (museum)   Tantalus (tantalize)
Narcissus (narcissim)   Titans (titanic)

Ask the students to tell a little about the mythological character and then define the word in parentheses. Make sure that they are able to make a connection between the word and the character. Here is an example:

Arachne was a proud Greek girl who was foolish and challenged the goddess Athena to a weaving contest. Because of Arachne's pride, Athena turned her into a spider so that she could weave forever.

An *arachnid* is a classification of arthropods. Spiders are included in this classification.

8. Have students complete the chart on pages 170–171 to help them create their own myths.

BE A MYTH MAKER!

1. Select two myths. List the main characters of each myth, and below the names include one or two words that best describe the character. Decide what the purpose of each myth might be (i.e., to explain a happening in nature).

Title: _____

Main characters: _____

Qualities: _____

Purpose: _____

Title: _____

Main characters: _____

Qualities: _____

Purpose: _____

2. Make a list of ten happenings in nature that you would like to explain. (For example: Why do we have hurricanes? Why do stars shine? Why do rainbows disappear?)

_____   _____

_____   _____

_____   _____

_____   _____

_____   _____

3. Choose one happening from the list as the basis for your own myth. Decide how the ancients might have explained this happening and write a short summary below.

_____

_____

_____

_____

4. Based on your knowledge of their talents and qualities, what mythological characters would best fit into this story? List the characters with a brief explanation of their part in the myth.

_____

_____

_____

_____

What additional characters would you create? What talents or qualities would they possess?

_____

_____

5. Write your own myth to explain the happening you selected.

6. Illustrate your myth and share it with others.

Poetry

Objectives. On completion of this unit, students will
- gain an enjoyment and appreciation for poetry, both old and new
- distinguish the various devices used in poetry
- examine the purpose(s) of various poems
- analyze poems for mood and tone
- evaluate the works of traditional and contemporary poets

Materials. We used the following poems in the activities procedures described in this unit. However, based on availability, teacher preference, and student interest, other poems can easily be substituted to meet the unit's objectives.

"Annabel Lee," by Edgar Allan Poe
"The Arrow and the Song," by Henry Wadsworth Longfellow
"Casey at the Bat," by Ernest L. Thayer
"Daffodils," by William Wordsworth
"Eldorado," by Edgar Allan Poe
"Father William," by Lewis Carroll
"If," by Rudyard Kipling
"Little Orphan Annie," by James W. Riley
"Lost," by Carl Sandburg
"The New Colossus," by Emma Lazarus
"O Captain! My Captain!" by Walt Whitman
"Old Ironsides," by Oliver Wendell Holmes
"Poor Old Lady," author unknown
"The Road Not Taken," by Robert Frost
"The Rum Tum Tugger," by T. S. Eliot
"Sea Fever," by John Masefield
"Silver," by Walter De la Mare
"Stopping by Woods on a Snowy Evening," by Robert Frost
"The Village Blacksmith," by Henry Wadsworth Longfellow
"Wind Song," by Carl Sandburg

Procedure.
1. Introduction
   a. Choral read several poems; include the sublime as well as the ridiculous (i.e., "If," "Father William," and "Poor Old Lady"). Allow students to simply enjoy each poem.
   b. Discuss the question: "Which of these can be considered poems?" Students should realize that all of the selections are poems, yet they cover a wide spectrum in terms of content, style, and mood.

c. In "Wind Song," Carl Sandburg described poetry as "a series of explanations of life, fading off into horizons, too swift for explanations." Allow students time to discuss this quote as well as to write and share their own definition of a poem.

2. Devices used in poetry. Students can better understand and appreciate poetry if they recognize the devices poets use to convey their thoughts.

a. Furnish each student with a copy of the worksheet, "Devices Used in Poetry" (page 174). Discuss the devices described. Ask students to create their own examples to illustrate each device.

b. Choral read the following poems and analyze them for each of the devices listed: "The Arrow and the Song," "Eldorado," "Lost," "Daffodils," and "Silver."

c. Ask students what the main differences are between poetry and prose?

3. Purposes of poetry

a. Discuss the question: "For what reasons are poems written?" Possible responses include to tell a story, to offer insight, to create a feeling, to capture a special mood or moment, to entertain.

b. Choral read and discuss the purpose(s) behind the following poems: "The Rum Tum Tugger," "Little Orphan Annie," "The Village Blacksmith," and "Old Ironsides." Encourage students to use the worksheet "Purposes of Poetry" (page 175) to aid in their analysis of each poem. You may divide the students into four groups, each analyzing a different poem, or you may have each student analyze all four poems.

4. Experiencing mood from poetry

a. Depending on the poem and the reader's interpretation, poems can leave the reader with a variety of feelings that cover the entire scope of emotions. Allow students time to read the following poems: "Casey at the Bat," "The New Colossus," and "Sea Fever."

b. Have students relate, either verbally or in written form, the mood each of these poems produced. As a result of what the individual brings with him or her (background, experiences, etc.), it will be interesting to compare and contrast the way in which each poem affected each student.

DEVICES USED IN POETRY

1. Rhythm — Regular patterning of sounds.

2. Alliteration — Repetition of the same first letter or consonant sound, such as "snowy summits old in story."

3. Euphone — Succession of light harmonious syllables that have a pleasing sound, such as "the splendor falls on castle walls."

4. Blank or free verse — Lines that do not rhyme.

5. Simile — Comparison of two unlike objects or ideas, using the words *like* or *as*, for example, "couched in his kennel, like a log, with paws of silver, sleeps the dog."

6. Metaphor — Comparison of two unlike objects or ideas, without using the words *like* or *as*, such as "The road was a ribbon of moonlight."

7. Personification — Giving human characteristics to objects or ideas that are not human; for example, "Slowly, silently, now the moon Walks the night in her silver shoon."

8. Rhyme — When the endings of words are alike in sound (poems may have "end rhyme" in which the last words of lines rhyme, or "internal rhyme" in which a word in the middle of the line rhymes with a word at the end of the line).

9. Repetition — Deliberate repeating of a key word.

10. Onomatopoeia — Forming or putting together words to resemble the sounds made by the thing signified.

A good poem

• sounds good rhythmically

• uses devices such as alliteration and onomatopoeia effectively

• employs vivid images by using devices such as metaphors, similies, and personification

• offers insights into meaningful ideas

• is imaginative

• draws the reader back again and again

PURPOSES OF POETRY

Directions: Use the following criteria to help you better understand the poem you are analyzing.

1. Does the poem entertain? If so, how?

2. Does the poem tell a story? If so, explain the story.

3. Does the poem teach a lesson? If so, describe this lesson in your own words.

4. Does the poem describe a certain person, place, or time? If so, what does it describe?

5. Does the poem create a certain feeling? If so, how does the poem make you feel?

6. What facts about the poet, if any, help you better understand the poem?

---

5. Poems that tell a story and more
   a. "The Road Not Taken" is an excellent poem to use in analyzing the devices and purposes of poetry.

   Choral read the poem and discuss any vocabulary that students might find troublesome.

   Discuss the poem, stanza by stanza, to best understand what Frost is trying to relate.

   Discuss why Frost might have written the poem. To what might he have been referring when he wrote, "Two roads diverged in a wood, and I—I took the one less traveled by, And that has made all the difference"?

   Allow students to relate times when they had to make a choice and how they feel about the choices they made.

   Discuss the question: "What feeling or mood does the poem evoke?" Encourage students to identify what most prompted this feeling.

   Now that students have a better feeling for the poem, have them again do a choral reading of "The Road Not Taken."

b. Divide students into groups, and allow each group to analyze one of the following poems: "Stopping by Woods on a Snowy Evening," "Annabel Lee," or "O Captain! My Captain!" Encourage them to use both worksheets in analyzing the poem. Have biographical material on each poet available to aid in their analysis. When each group has completed their analysis, allow the members to lead the rest of the groups in a discussion of the poem they have just studied.

6. Sketch of a poet

a. Who are the men and women behind the lines of verse that cause us to laugh, to cry, to wonder, and to dream? Allow students time to peruse a wide variety of poetry books. Encourage each student to skim through these books until he or she finds a poem that says something special. The following list of poets should be available for students to read. While this list does not include all the great poets, it does include some of the best-known American and British poets of the past and present. Ask students which poets they would like to see added to the list.

Stephen Vincent Benét	John Masefield
Robert Browning	Rod McKuen
William Cullen Bryant	Edna St. Vincent Millay
Robert Burns	A. A. Milne
Lord Byron	Ogden Nash
Lewis Carroll	Alfred Noyes
Samuel Taylor Coleridge	Edgar Allan Poe
e. e. cummings	James W. Riley
Walter De la Mare	Carl Sandburg
Emily Dickinson	William Shakespeare
T. S. Eliot	Percy Bysshe Shelley
Ralph Waldo Emerson	Shel Silverstein
Eugene Field	Robert Louis Stevenson
Robert Frost	Sara Teasdale
Oliver Wendell Holmes	Alfred Lord Tennyson
Julie Ward Howe	Ernest L. Thayer
Joyce Kilmer	Walt Whitman
Rudyard Kipling	John G. Whittier
Emma Lazarus	William Wordsworth
Vachel Lindsay	William Butler Yeats
Henry Wadsworth Longfellow	

b. Assign students individual research on the poet selected. Research should cover a variety of materials from encyclopedias, biographies, reference books such as Kunitz's *Twentieth Century Authors* (if applicable), and magazines. Motivate students to prepare an *original* presentation that will introduce his or her poet to the class. Students may even wish to dress up as their poet. The presentation should include a reading of the poem that initially stimulated the student to research the poet. Ask students to make a copy of their poem, and then combine these poems into an anthology of "Classroom Favorites."

SUGGESTED BOOKS FOR CHILDREN

Arbuthnot, May Hill, ed. *Time for Poetry*, 4th ed. Scott, Foresman, 1976.

Asimov, Isaac. *Fantastic Voyage II: Destination Brain*. Doubleday, 1987.

———. *Words from the Myths*. Illustrated by William Barss. Houghton Mifflin, 1961.

Coatsworth, Elizabeth. *Poems*. Illustrated by Vee Guthrie. Macmillan, 1958.

Cole, William. *Oh, That's Ridiculous*. Illustrated by Tomi Ungerer. Viking, 1988.

d'Aulaire, Ingri, and Edgar d'Aulaire. *Norse Gods and Giants*. Doubleday, 1967.

———. *Book of Greek Myths*. Doubleday, 1962.

Farjeon, Eleanor. *Eleanor Farjeon's Poems for Children*. Lippincott, 1951, 1985.

Farmer, Penelope. *Daedalus and Icarus*. Illustrated by Chris Conner. Harcourt Brace Jovanovich, 1972.

Field, Rachel. *Poems*. Macmillan, 1964.

Fleishman, Paul. *Joyful Noise*. Illustrated by Eric Beddows. Zolotow/Harper & Row, 1988.

Freeman, S. H. *Basic Baseball Strategy*. Illustrated by Leonard Kessler. Doubleday, 1965.

Frost, Robert. *Birches*. Illustrated by Ed Young. Holt, Rinehart & Winston, 1988.

Gertman, Bill. *Hank Aaron*. Grosset, 1973.

Green, Roger Lancelyn. *A Book of Myths*. Illustrated by Joan Kiddell-Monroe. Dutton, 1965.

Hawthorne, Nathaniel. *The Golden Touch*. Illustrated by Paul Galdone. McGraw-Hill, 1959.

Kessler, Leonard. *Here Comes the Strikeout*. Harper & Row, 1965.

Little, Lessie Jones. *Children of Long Ago*. Illustrated by Jan Spivey Gilchrist. Philomel, 1988.

Livingston, Myra Cohn, ed. *Poems for Mothers*. Illustrated by Deborah Kogan Ray. Holiday House, 1988.

Morrison, Lillian, ed. *Rhythm Road: Poems to Move to*. Lothrop, 1988.

Pollack, Merrill. *Phaëton*. Illustrated by William Hoffmann. Lippincott, 1966.

Thayer, Ernest L. *Casey at the Bat*. Illustrated by Patricia Polacco. Putnam, 1988.

Viorst, Judith. *If I Were in Charge of the World and Other Worries: Poems for Children and Their Parents*. Illustrated by Lynne Cherry. Atheneum, 1982.

————. *The Tenth Good Thing About Barney*. Illustrated by Erik Blegvad. Atheneum, 1971.

Zim, Herbert. *The New Moon*. Morrow, 1980.

Zim, Herbert, and Sonia Bleeker. *Life and Death*. Illustrated by René Martin. Morrow, 1970.

REFERENCES

Dale, Edgar, and Jeanne S. Chall. "A Formula for Predicting Readability: Instructions." *Educational Research Bulletin 27*, no. 2 (1948): 37–54.

————. "A Formula for Predicting Readability." *Educational Research Bulletin 27*, no. 1 (1947): 11–20.

Fry, Edward. "Fry's Readability Graph: Clarifications, Validity, and Extension to Level 17." *Journal of Reading 21* (December 1977): 249.

Kunitz, Stanley. *Twentieth Century Authors*. N.Y.: H. W. Wilson and Co., 1955.

Spache, George D. *Good Reading for Poor Readers*, 6th ed. Champaign, Ill.: Garrard Press, 1966.

CONNECTIONS

Affective Response to Literature

Literature for Critical and Creative Thinking

The Reading-Writing Connection: Writing Process Approach Language Experience Approach

Literature and the Curriculum — A Thematic Approach

LITERATURE AND THE READING PROGRAM

Strategies for Reading

Literature and the Basal Reading Program: Extending the Basal Literature-Based Materials

A Model for Literature-Based Reading Programs

Using the Library

Reaching Beyond the Classroom: Parent Involvement

THE LITERATURE CONNECTION

DEVELOPING INTEREST IN READING

The Read-Aloud Program

Shared Reading

Sustained Silent Reading

Storytelling

Extending and Sharing Literature

GENRES AND ELEMENTS

Exploring Genres: Picture Books, Realistic Fiction, Historical Fiction, Fantasy/Science Fiction, Traditional Literature, Poetry, Informational Books, Biographies

Analyzing Elements: Characterization, Plot, Setting, Theme, Point of View, Evaluating Genres and Their Elements

Involving Students in Selecting Genres

P A R T   T H R E E

LITERATURE
AND THE
READING PROGRAM

Becoming a Nation of Readers (Anderson et al., 1985), a national report on reading research and practices, confirmed that 70 percent of children's reading instruction time is spent on seatwork such as skill sheets and workbooks. Further, students were actively involved in actual reading for an average of only seven minutes of the regular classroom reading time.

These findings and the results of similar research appear to have made an impression on the educational community. In reviewing the current educational trends in teaching reading, and in perusing new educational publications, we have noticed that conventional methods of reading instruction are being challenged. Today's reading curriculum puts real books by real writers into the students' hands. In many areas of the country, the reading of trade books has become the core of the reading curriculum. In many other areas, trade books are being used to supplement the more conventional reading program.

As literature becomes an integral part of classroom reading, the benefits to students are tremendous. Perhaps

181

the greatest benefit is that good literature in the classroom can foster a lifetime love of reading. Often, children who previously disliked reading become immersed in reading a good book and discover that reading can be pleasurable. Although children have no control over the subject matter when they read basals, they can make their own selections when trade books are adopted. Good literature has been written on almost every conceivable topic, and a child can usually find a book that matches his or her interests and needs.

Good literature also provides a model for oral and written language. Because of the constraints usually imposed on the basal, the beauty of our language is often lost. As children read good literature, they can hear the poetry of the words and become aware of the magic that is created by the right word choice.

Too often, in teaching reading, we emphasize, and isolate, the skills needed for effective reading. While practice in reading is necessary, as is skill development, many skills can be learned as the book is read rather than in a structured, isolated lesson. Learning in this way is more meaningful, and the children retain the skills more readily. Research has shown, for example, that using literature has a positive effect on vocabulary development and comprehension (Cohen, 1968).

Good literature allows the reader to vicariously experience the story and empathize with the characters. As they read, children learn about other people, about themselves, and about life. They discover that others have often experienced similar joys, sorrows, and fears, and they gain insight into solving their problems and dealing with their own world.

Finally, and perhaps the most viable reason for using literature in the classroom, is that it works! Children love it! Teachers love it! Bader, Veatch, and Eldredge (1987) reported that "the use of children's literature to teach children had a strong effect upon student's achievement and interest in reading—much greater than the traditional methods used to teach children how to read."

Part III of *The Literature Connection*, "Literature and the

Reading Program," focuses on some of the most commonly asked questions regarding the use of literature in the reading program: What literature-based strategies can be used to foster the reading process and the development of reading skills? How can literature be used to supplement the basal reading textbooks already being used? How can literature be used as the core of the reading curriculum? What type of evaluative measures can be adapted to a literature-based reading program? What changes will have to be made in classroom organization to accommodate a literature-based reading program? How can students become more familiar with the library, and how can a classroom library be organized? How can parents be encouraged to read with their children and make the reading of good literature an important part of their home life?

REFERENCES

Anderson, R. C. et al. *Becoming a Nation of Readers*. Washington, D.C.: National Institute of Education, 1985.

Bader, L., J. Veatch, and J. L. Eldredge. "Trade Books or Basal Readers?" *Reading Improvement 24* (Summer 1987): 62–68.

Cohen, D. "The Effect of Literature on Vocabulary and Reading Achievement." *Elementary English 45* (1968): 209–213, 217.

9

Strategies
for
Reading

While students do make gains in such reading skills as vocabulary development and comprehension through the reading of literature (Cohen, 1968; Bader, Veatch, and Eldredge, 1987), it is imperative to develop strategies based on the literature being read that will guide students in the reading process and will develop and strengthen their reading skills.

There has been a conceptual shift in the way many researchers and teachers think about reading, which gives students a much more active role in the learning and reading comprehension process. This shift is reflected in changes from packaged programs to experiences with books and from concentration on isolated skills to practical reading and writing activities.

Yet, improvements in higher-level reading skills cannot come about simply by an emphasis on reading instruction in isolation from the other work students do in school. To foster higher-level literacy skills is to place a new and special emphasis on thoughtful, critical elaboration of ideas and understandings drawn from the material students read and from what they already know. (*Reading Report Card*, 1985)

Many strategies actively involve students in the reading process, causing them to interact with the material in a thoughtful and meaningful way. Such strategies include metacognition, directed reading, modeling, story mapping, reciprocal teaching, and questioning. This chapter defines each strategy and provides specific examples of their applications based on H. A. Rey's classic children's story *Curious George*. The activities described have been used successfully with children and can be adapted in the classroom to any appropriate work of literature.

METACOGNITION

Metacognition is a general term that refers to "thinking about thinking" (Garner, Wagner, & Smith, 1983). Although the term *metacognition* is fairly new, the skills necessary for successful reading and thinking have been known for a long time. As students become aware of the processes implicit in reading and problem solving, they will become more aware of the skills necessary to satisfy a specific learning situation. Questions such as "What makes a person a good reader?" or "What do you do when you are reading and get to a word that you do not know?" will help students identify and analyze the skills needed in the reading process. When asked a comprehension question based on a reading, students should be taught to analyze the question to determine what thinking skills are necessary; for example, "Is the answer provided in the text?" "Do I need to use my own background knowledge and ideas, or will I have to make inferences or deductions based on the information and clues provided?"

As students complete, either orally or in written form, the following questions based on *Curious George*, you can help them analyze the questions to determine the thought processes necessary for arriving at the answers.

1. "Why do you think the monkey in this story is named Curious George?" Ask the students: "Is the answer stated in the story?" (Yes, we are told George is quite curious. "This is George. He lived in Africa. He was very happy. But he had one fault. He was too curious.")

2. "Do you think the zoo was a good place for Curious George?" Since the answer is not stated in the story, ask the students questions such as: "What will you have to know to answer this question?" (what a zoo is like; a recollection of past experiences in which they have visited a zoo; values concerning whether animals should be allowed to roam free or be kept in zoos) and "Are there any clues in the story that will help you answer the question?" (Yes, George looks happy at the zoo; the zoo looks safe and might protect him from wandering off and getting into trouble.)

In addition to being able to identify the processes or skills needed to complete a task, students must also be able to determine whether they are using these skills correctly and whether the task is being performed correctly. Cooper, Warncke, and Shipman (1988) mention four strategies readers can follow to "monitor" their ability to comprehend what they have read. Each strategy can be followed at regular intervals throughout the reading: (1) summarize (tell what has been read), (2) clarify (ask "Is this clear?" If the meaning is unclear, reread the part that is confusing, discuss the section with someone else, look up any unknown words, etc.), (3) question (ask a question to determine understanding), and (4) predict (hypothesize what might happen next).

Involving students in these and similar exercises will help them become aware of the different thought processes and strategies needed for successful reading, determine which is most appropriate to a particular situation or question, and monitor their reading comprehension.

DIRECTED READING

Directed reading is a strategy used to guide students through the reading of a specific selection by means of five stages: (1) providing background information, (2) setting the purpose for reading, (3) reading the selection, (4) discussing the selection, and (5) developing skills. Story units incorporating these stages can be developed or purchased from a variety of publishing companies.

An Example of Directed Reading

The following story unit, based on *Curious George*, contains activities that illustrate ways of developing the five stages of directed reading in order to enhance reading enjoyment and to foster the growth of reading skills. A brief explanation of the stages of directed reading and the ways in which each is reinforced within the story unit follows this section.

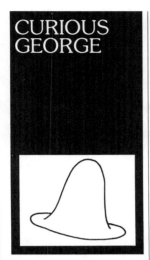

CURIOUS GEORGE

Author
H. A. Rey

Illustrator
H. A. Rey

Publisher
Houghton Mifflin Publishers, 1941

Pages	Grade Level
48	K–3

Other Books by Rey
Curious George Rides a Bike; Curious George Takes a Job; Curious George Gets a Medal; Curious George Flies a Kite; Curious George Learns the Alphabet

Summary
George is a funny little monkey who is always very curious. As a result of his curiosity, he gets into a lot of trouble.

Introduction
George's curiosity gets him into a lot of trouble. Has your curiosity ever gotten you into trouble? How?

Key Vocabulary
Write these words on the chalkboard and choral read them:

curious	monkey	yellow	hat
balloons	fireman	zoo	prison

Key Vocabulary Instruction
Color Stand Up
Tell all the children wearing yellow to stand up and pronounce the first word, all children wearing red to pronounce the second word, and so on. As a finale, tell all children who like monkeys to stand up and pronounce all eight vocabulary words.

Discussion Questions

1 Why do you think the monkey in this story is named "Curious George"? (because he was always curious about things)

2 How did the man in the yellow hat catch Curious George? (Curious George wanted to look at the hat, and when he did, the man caught him)

3 Where did the man with the yellow hat take the monkey after he caught him? (on a little boat and then to a big ship)

4 What happened to Curious George because of his curiosity while he was on the big ship? (he fell overboard)

5 Why do you think the firemen took Curious George to jail? (because George had fooled them and there really wasn't any fire)

6 How did Curious George get out of jail? (answers may vary)

7 What do you think would have happened to Curious George if he hadn't escaped from jail? (answers may vary)

8 Where did the man in the yellow hat finally take Curious George? (to a zoo) Do you think this was a good place for Curious George? Why or why not? (answers may vary)

CURIOUS GEORGE

Bulletin Board
Using cutout letters, put the caption "CURIOUS GEORGE'S
FRIENDS AT THE ZOO" on the bulletin board. Using the pattern
below, cut hats out of yellow construction paper. Have children cut
out pictures of other animals that might be in the zoo with Curious
George and put these animals on the yellow hats. Have them label
the pictures with appropriate names of animals. Adhere the yellow
hats to the bulletin board.

CURIOUS GEORGE

Name _____ Date _____

Directions

Help Curious George find the words that are hidden in the balloon below. When you find the word in the balloon, circle it. The first one is done for you.

Hidden Words

CURIOUS	HAT	ZOO	MONKEY
BALLOONS	PRISON	YELLOW	FIREMAN

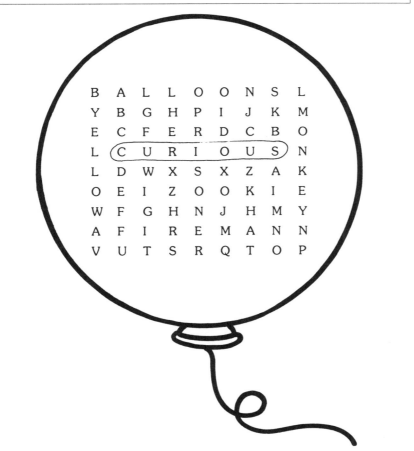

CURIOUS
GEORGE

Name _____ Date _____

Directions
Pretend that Curious George held onto the balloons and
sailed across the countryside instead of the city. In the space
below, draw a picture that includes what Curious George
would have seen as he held onto the balloons and sailed high
over the countryside. In your picture, you might include such
things as those in the box.

Curious George hanging onto the balloons	flowers
people around their houses and in the fields	blue skies
fields with grass	trees
animals in the fields	cars on the roads
fences around the fields	houses
roads in between the fields	fluffy clouds

CURIOUS
GEORGE

ACTIVITY
SHEET 3

Name _____ Date _____

Directions
Pretend that Curious George did not escape from the jail
and needed some advice about what to do. In the space
below, write Curious George a letter to tell him what you
think he should do.

_____ (Date)

Dear Curious George, (Greeting)

(Body) _____

_____

_____

_____

_____

_____

_____

Your Friend, (Closing)

_____ (Signature)

Additional Activities

1 Read the book *Curious George Takes a Job*. Compare and contrast all the things that happen to George in this book with all the things that happen to George in *Curious George*. Discuss suggestions for George to help him avoid all the trouble he gets into.

2 On the chalkboard, list "Description Words" such as curiosity, cuteness, niceness, foolishness, and so on. In another column, write "Recipe Words" such as mix, bake, dip, toss, squeeze, stir, dash, pour, cup, teaspoon, tablespoon, and sprinkle. Tell the children to use these words to write a recipe describing Curious George. The following example may be helpful to get started:

Curious George Casserole

2 cups of curiosity
2 tablespoons of silliness
a dash of foolishness

Mix all the above ingredients together. Mix in a little cuteness and sprinkle with cleverness. Bake for 20 minutes in a 350° oven and you will have a Curious George Casserole.

---

3 On a map or globe point out Africa, the continent where Curious George lived. Discuss the necessity for traveling on a boat if the man in the yellow hat was to bring Curious George to a zoo in the United States. Discuss the various routes the boat may have taken. List different places that Curious George may have passed on his way to the zoo. This would also be a good time to introduce the other six continents and identify their locations.

4 Invite a fire fighter to come into the classroom to discuss fire safety rules. In addition, discuss the instructions for properly reporting a fire and the dangers involved in falsely reporting a fire.

5 Encourage the children to use encyclopedias, books, or magazines to find out important facts about monkeys: where they live, what they eat, what different kinds of monkeys exist, and so on. After the children have recorded the information they have found on monkeys, provide a time to discuss their findings.

6 Tell the children that Curious George loves bananas and he would like to share the following favorite banana recipe with his friends:

George's Banana Pops

Put half of a banana on a popsicle stick. Dip into a mixture of one-half lemon juice and one-half water. Roll banana in crushed Grape Nuts, place on wax paper, and freeze.

Stages of Directed Reading

Providing Background Information. Students are provided with vocabulary and concepts that facilitate their understanding of the text. Activities, such as "Color Stand Up," encourage the learning of specific vocabulary, while "Additional Activities" encourages students to discover more about monkeys, thereby gaining a greater understanding of the main character. Vocabulary and concept development can also be enhanced as students create a semantic map of a concept or issue related to this story.

```
            Space    Underwater
                        \  /
   Scientists      Explorers          Cats    Monkeys
          \       /                      \    /
        People  —                          Animals
                    ( Curious )      /
                                     —  Exciting
               /        \
    Exploring unknown         \
         /    \                  Adventure
   Trouble   Rewarding
```

Setting the Purpose for Reading. This is often referred to as prereading; statements and questions are designed to motivate reading and to provide a purpose for reading, thereby increasing comprehension. For example, students may be instructed to "read to find out . . ." or they may be asked, "Based on the illustrations (or title), what do you think this story will be about?" In the "Introduction" of the story unit, students are asked to read to find out how Curious George's curiosity got him into trouble.

Reading the Selection. The selection is read, either orally or silently, based on student ages and abilities. If the selection is read orally with young children, a Big Book can be used so that students can choral read.

Big Books can easily be made by simply copying the text onto blank sheets of paper approximately 25 by 15 inches. Individual students or pairs of students can then be assigned pages to illustrate, or original illustrations from the book can be enlarged and posted into place. Pages can then be sequenced into the correct order and bound together using a heavy-duty stapler, metal rings, or heavy stitching. (For more information, see the section "Making Big Books" in Chapter 2.)

Discussing the Selection. Discussion can be oral or written and can take many forms. For example, students may be given the questions before the discussion so that they can formulate their answers, or the questions may simply be asked and the students have to respond, or a "Shared Inquiry" technique may be used in which the answers are determined by interpretation alone. An example of a Shared Inquiry Question may be, "Was Curious George better off in the city or in the jungle?" Shared Inquiry often results in a stimulating discussion as students cite specific portions of the story to support their interpretation.

Discussion can take place at any time. Often, it may be necessary to follow a discussion question with related questions until students reach a level of understanding. However, asking too many questions can have negative results and lessen motivation. The discussion should reflect the purposes set for reading and focus on questions that foster the higher-level thinking skills of analysis, synthesis, and evaluation.

Many activities can be developed to foster greater involvement and comprehension of the story and the story elements (characterization, plot, setting, theme, and point of view). For example, Additional Activity 1 fosters a comparison of plots as students contrast this story with other *Curious George* adventures. Additional Activity 2 helps students gain in-depth understanding of George's qualities.

Developing Skills. Skill development should emphasize a balance among decoding skills, comprehension skills, attitude, and interest. A relationship should exist between the skill being developed and the text. For example, Activity Sheet 1 helps develop visual discrimination skills and word recognition.

Activities should also be designed to integrate various content areas. Activity Sheet 2 stimulates creative thinking and helps develop the concepts of *city* and *country*; Activity Sheet 3 fosters development of writing skills while asking students to problem-solve; Additional Activity 3 is a social studies lesson that helps students become aware of other parts of the world; Additional Activity 4 develops career awareness and safety rules; Additional Activity 5 involves students in research; the Bulletin Board activity helps build vocabulary and develops the concept of zoo animals.

Further reading can be stimulated by suggesting books with a similar theme or topic or books written by the same author.

MODELING

Modeling both encompasses and extends the benefits of reading aloud, while demonstrating to students the thinking processes that are essential to effective reading. These processes include guessing word meanings, using background information, making and changing predictions, becoming emotionally involved, summarizing, and making mental pictures.

In modeling, the teacher reads a selection and verbalizes the mental processes that usually are silent. As he or she models the thinking skills necessary for effective reading, students should begin to identify these skills to help them with their own reading and reading comprehension. A modeling lesson using *Curious George* might take the following form:

TEACHER READS: "This is George. He lived in Africa. He was very happy. But he had one fault. He was too curious."

TEACHER SAYS: "I wonder what *curious* means. Well, I see George eating a banana. Perhaps it means he eats too much." (guessing word meaning)

TEACHER CONTINUES TO READ ABOUT HOW GEORGE MEETS THE MAN IN THE YELLOW HAT:

". . . The man put his hat on the ground, and of course George was curious. He came down from the tree to look at the large yellow hat."

TEACHER SAYS: "Curious must have nothing to do with eating too much. Maybe it means he likes to find out things." (guessing word meaning)

"I wonder what the man looks like. He must be

quite large if he wears such a big hat." (making
mental pictures)

TEACHER CONTINUES TO READ ABOUT HOW GEORGE IS CAUGHT:
". . . The man picked him up quickly and popped
him into a bag. George was caught."

TEACHER SAYS: "Poor George is being kidnapped, he must be so
frightened. I'd scream and kick a hole through the
bag." (becoming emotionally involved)
"George is clever. I bet he'll figure out a way to
escape." (making predictions)

The teacher continues in this manner, reading and modeling
the thinking skills that good readers do automatically. As students become more aware of the processes, they can write down
the different skills being modeled and then model these same
skills as they read orally with a partner.

STORY MAPPING

A story map is "a unified representation of a story based on a
logical organization of events and ideas of central importance to
the story and the interrelationships of these events and ideas"
(Beck and McKeown, 1981). A story map can be used to help
students achieve a mind-set for reading the story or as a framework for discussion following the story. "In story maps, specific
relationships of story elements are made clear. Main ideas and
sequences, comparisons of characters, and cause-effect relationships are some of the features of stories that can be shown
in maps" (Burns, Roe, & Ross, 1988).

Each student can create his or her own map, or a class map
can be developed. For example, in *Curious George*, the story's
events can be mapped using outlines of Africa and the United
States. Or, shapes representing balloons can be cut out and
students can fill each balloon with events from the story. Balloons can then be organized into the correct chronological
order.

To help students become familiar with creating a story map,
ask them "What happened first in the story?" Write their responses on the board and continue until the entire story has
unfolded and the main events have been identified. Students can
then copy or rewrite the items listed onto their story maps.

RECIPROCAL TEACHING

Reciprocal teaching allows students and teachers to change roles. Once students are aware of the strategies of monitoring (namely, summarizing, clarifying, generating questions, and predicting), they take turns being the "teacher" and prepare and ask questions based on a specific reading. During reciprocal teaching, the teacher becomes one of the students and takes an active role in responding to their prompting.

According to Cooper, Warncke, and Shipman (1988), the following steps can be used to help students monitor their reading through reciprocal teaching:

1. Select stories or articles that are at the student's instructional level.
2. Present the four steps of the process to students, showing them how to use each step while they are reading.

Summarize—What did I read? (Tell it.)

Clarify—Was it clear to me? (Read or discuss parts that are unclear.)

Question—What question could a teacher or text ask about this material? (Pose the question.)

Predict—What is likely to happen next (or later) in this text? (Make predictions.)

3. Identify a time for reciprocal reading. Carry out the procedure for fifteen to thirty minutes per session. At the primary levels, use the process once a week; at the intermediate levels use it twice a week.

To introduce the strategy of reciprocal teaching to students, the teacher must first model the procedure, explaining that the students will be taking turns being the teacher and reminding them that they will be using the steps of the monitoring process. The students then read a specific selection, stopping at an appropriate interval depending on their levels. The teacher then models the monitoring process and summarizes, clarifies, questions, and predicts based on the material that has been read. Students and teacher are actively involved in answering the questions generated both in the questioning portion and in the part the teacher wishes to clarify. Once students understand the steps involved, the teacher selects another student to act as the "teacher." Students read another section of the material and the process continues.

In addition to being used as a large group strategy, reciprocal teaching can be used with small groups and with pairs of students. The main objective is to help students focus on what they are reading to ensure that the words they are reading have meaning for them.

QUESTIONING

Asking good questions is one of the most vital aspects of developing comprehension and thinking skills. Good questions should satisfy the following criteria:

1. They should be relevant. Too many questions that simply require students to answer with facts stated in the text will interfere with their enjoyment of the story and do little to enhance comprehension and higher-level thinking. Ask meaningful questions.

2. They should foster higher-level thinking. It is vital that questions be written at the different levels of thinking, as were those developed for *Curious George*. Although literal questions (knowledge and comprehension) are important to ascertain students' understanding of the story, questions should be included that ask students to analyze ("reason that," "what are the causes," "what are the consequences," "examine evidence"), synthesize ("create," "devise," "design"), and evaluate ("what is good/bad," "what do you like best," "judge the evidence"). These higher-order questions are especially important for fostering development in critical and creative thinking.

3. They should help students reach an understanding of an issue or concept. Questions should flow and reflect sense of continuity rather than be isolated. In this way, students will be guided to form their own conclusions and judgments. Students might be asked, for example, to explore the concept of *curiosity* and to decide whether curiosity is a good or bad trait in an individual.

4. They should encourage application of background knowledge, ideas, and experiences. For example, "Where would Curious George be happiest and why?" or "If you were allowed to choose where you would live, where would you want to go and why?" The latter question encourages students to reflect on their own values and interests and then choose criteria to access a multitude of options.

5. After asking a question, students should be given time in which to reflect on the questions and possible responses. A wait time of three to five seconds is generally recommended. Often it will be necessary to rephrase a question based on students' level of understanding.

It is important to remember that these strategies enhance reading comprehension as students become actively involved in the reading process. The strategies are easily adaptable regardless of the type of reading material, basal readers or trade books, and can be used to promote understanding in any of the content areas. Higher-level literacy skills will significantly improve as students are guided to develop them.

REFERENCES

Children
Rey, H. A. *Curious George*. Houghton Mifflin, 1941.

Teacher
Bader, L., J. Veatch, and J. L. Eldredge. "Trade Books or Basal Readers?" Reading Im*provement 24* (Summer 1987): 62–68.

Beck, I. L., and M. G. McKeown. "Developing Questions that Promote Comprehension: The Story Map." *Language Arts 58*, no. 8 (1981): 913–918.

Burns, P., B. Roe, and E. Ross. *Teaching Reading in Today's Elementary Schools*. Boston: Houghton Mifflin, 1988.

Cohen, D. "The Effect of Literature on Vocabulary and Reading Achievement." *Elementary English 45* (1968): 209–213, 217.

Cooper, D. J., E. W. Warnche, and D. A. Shipman. *The What & How of Reading Instruction*, 2nd ed. Columbus: Merrill, 1988.

Garner, R., S. Wagoner, and T. Smith. "Eternalizing Question—Answering Strategies of Good and Poor Comprehenders." *Reading Research Quarterly 18* (4) (Summer 1983): 439–447.

National Assessment of Educational Programs. *Reading Report Card*, Report No. 15-R-01. Princeton, N.J.: Educational Testing Services, 1985.

Rothlein, Liz, and Terri Christman. *Read It Again!* Glenview, Ill.: Scott, Foresman, 1989.

10

Literature and the Basal Reading Program

The basal reader approach to teaching reading is the most widely used approach in U.S. schools today. Most basal reader series consist of a set of graded texts, beginning with a readiness book and continuing with one or two readers for each succeeding grade level through sixth or eighth grade. In addition to the graded texts, the series includes the following:

1. teacher's manuals with detailed lesson plans for directed reading activities (see Chapter 9)
2. workbooks or skill sheets for practicing and reinforcing skills
3. diagnostic and prescriptive materials and activities for assessing progress and meeting curriculum objectives
4. record-keeping systems for systematically recording students' progress
5. supplementary materials such as puppets, Big Books, duplicating masters, parent suggestions, computer programs, and other selected materials

As with any reading program, the basal reading series has advantages and disadvantages. The first major advantage is that the series provides the scope and sequence of skills to be mastered and a systematic way to teach and review these skills. Second, the books are carefully graded in difficulty; that is, the vocabularies are controlled so that students are not confronted with too many unfamiliar words at once. Third, the words are repeated often so that students have the opportunity to fix them in their memories. Fourth, the series offers explicitly detailed teacher's manuals, which contain many valuable suggestions that save much planning time. Finally, the basal reader series covers all areas of reading, including word recognition, comprehension, and oral and silent reading. Thus, overemphasis or underemphasis of any one area can be avoided.

Although the series provides for many aspects of teaching reading, it does have some disadvantages that need to be considered. First, controlling the vocabulary has often left the stories dull and boring, offering little literary merit. A second, closely related disadvantage is that the sentence structure often does not parallel children's normal speech patterns. Third, many of the characters and settings are unfamiliar to the children, who often can't relate to or identify with the stories presented. Fourth, many teachers follow the teacher's manual word for word, without considering the special needs of particular students. Often, teachers believe they must do every activity, even though some may not be appropriate or necessary for their students; thus they misuse time that could be spent on more interesting and appropriate activities. Finally, teachers often believe that the basal series is a complete reading program. As a result, they may not offer the variety of experiences that are essential to a well-balanced reading program such as the one described in Chapter 11. In fact, Bernice Cullinan (1987) reports that even though 80 to 90 percent of the classrooms across the United States use the basal reading series as the core instructional material, no basal was ever intended to be a completely self-contained program.

REFORM MOVEMENT

Educators are recognizing the need to include more children's literature in the classroom reading program. This movement was reinforced by the following explicit recommendations about basal readers and their use reported in The Report Card On *Basal Readers* (1988). (These recommendations, in turn, were based on a study by the Commission on Reading [1985].)

1. Teachers should not be required to use any program they find professionally objectionable.

2. No adoption of any basal should exclude the possibility of teachers' modifying its use or using alternate materials and methods.

3. Publishers should immediately discontinue the practice of revising and censoring selections from children's literature.

4. Publishers should change the way teachers are treated in teachers' manuals of basals. They should be addressed as professionals and should be supported in their exercise of professional judgment.

5. School authorities should establish criteria for reading instructional materials and should not adopt materials that do not meet their criteria.

6. In all aspects of development, selection, and use of basals and alternate methods and materials, the needs and welfare of the students must be placed above all other considerations.

7. School authorities, legislatures, foundations, professional organizations, and others should encourage innovation within and outside basals through funding research and experimental programs in schools.

Publishers are attempting to include more literature selections in the basal readers and to make the language more like normal conversation. Recent editions reflect a trend of introducing characters and settings from various backgrounds and races that include a variety of roles. Although publishers are making favorable progress in including children's literature in the basal series, what has been called the *basalization* of children's literature is often found. That is, the publisher has revised the literature selections to fit their own constraints; as a result, often the original author would not recognize his or her story if a different title were used. Since basal readers form the backbone of most reading classes, it makes sense to extend the basal readers to include real literature. In other words, the answer to developing and maintaining a well-balanced reading program for those using basal readers seems to be a marriage between basal readers and literature.

EXTENDING THE BASAL READING PROGRAM

If the basal reader is to be used as an integral part of the reading program, there is much that can be done in the classroom to extend the basal and provide students with those approaches and strategies that will foster a love of reading, bring good literature to the forefront, and involve students in actual reading a greater percentage of the time.

One of the most frequently expressed complaints is that there is little time, during the reading program, to do anything other than the activities included in the basal. This problem is easily resolved by using pretests and posttests. All students *do not* need to do all the activities suggested in the basal; in fact, the tremendous amount of skill sheets and questions is usually counterproductive in terms of encouraging students to read and fostering a love of reading. Pretests and posttests are excellent diagnostic tools and help provide a profile of student strengths and weaknesses. Rather than teaching the entire class a certain lesson or skill, small groups or individuals can be pulled out, and the other students can be allowed to read independently or work alone or in small groups. This approach also allows time to work on specific skills as they are needed and provides time to hold conferences with individuals, to teach mini-lessons, and to evaluate students' progress.

Many of the basal readers, especially those published recently, include a greater number of selections from classic and contemporary literature. These selections should be used to encourage students to read the entire work as well as other books based on a similar theme or by the same author. Many basals have incorporated strategies such as read-aloud and storytelling into their lessons; yet, reading is still taught and viewed as an isolated skill. Little is done to help students make the connections between reading and the other components of language—namely, writing, listening, and speaking. Nor are connections being made between reading and other content areas. In addition, students are given little opportunity to take an active part in their own education, and few associations are encouraged between reading and real-life purposes, problems, and needs.

The use of thematic units can help alleviate many of these concerns. Many basals group their literary selections thematically. Depending on the year's objectives, appropriate literary selections from the basal can be chosen to augment units of study in content areas such as social studies and science. Even if the basal is not arranged thematically, it doesn't preclude the use of certain works with a thematic lesson.

The following section outlines possible ways of extending a basal selection (*Sarah, Plain and Tall* from *Sometimes I Wonder*, Book 4, Scott, Foresman, 1989) using many of the approaches, activities, and strategies mentioned throughout this book. (See "Thematic Unit: Intermediate Level [Social Studies]," Chapter 17, for related information, books, and activities.) The charts on pages 208 and 209 illustrate a suggested framework for a two-hour reading program that extends the basal.

**DAILY PRIMARY READING SCHEDULE USING THE
BASAL READING PROGRAM**
(Total Time: 2 Hours)

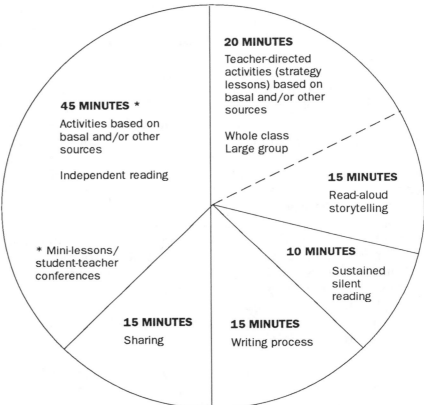

1. Introduction: Have students web a main theme or concept from Patricia MacLachlan's *Sarah, Plain and Tall* (the touching story of a young woman who journeys West to begin a new life in the frontier). Themes might include pioneer life, the westward movement, loneliness, or survival. Encourage students to generate questions and activities that they would like to pursue based on the completed web.

2. Read-Aloud: Read other books or poems dealing with the theme or concept selected. For example, if "pioneer life" were selected, read *Little House on the Prairie* by Laura Ingalls Wilder. If "survival" was selected, read *Julie of the Wolves* by Jean George

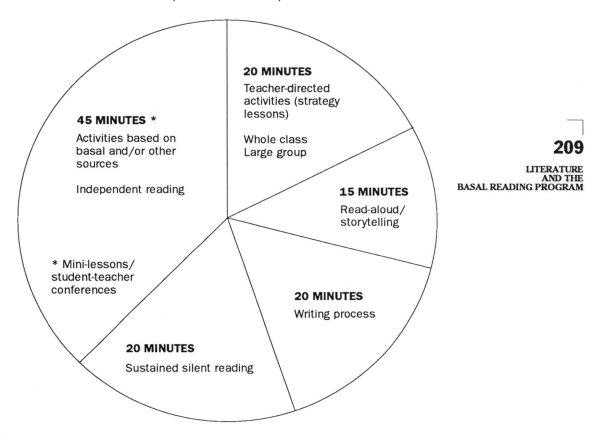

**DAILY INTERMEDIATE READING SCHEDULE USING
THE BASAL READING PROGRAM**
(Total Time: 2 Hours)

20 MINUTES
Teacher-directed
activities (strategy
lessons)

Whole class
Large group

45 MINUTES *
Activities based on
basal and/or other
sources

Independent reading

15 MINUTES
Read-aloud/
storytelling

* Mini-lessons/
student-teacher
conferences

20 MINUTES
Writing process

20 MINUTES
Sustained silent reading

or *Island of the Blue Dolphin* by Scott O'Dell. When reading aloud, model comprehension and critical thinking strategies such as predicting, evaluation, context clues, and so on.

3. Storytelling: Students may want to recreate a favorite scene or chapter from a related book. Groups of students may want to prepare a Reader's Theatre or a Story Theater (see "Alternatives to Storytelling and Extended Activities" in Chapter 4). Scenes from any of the *Little House* series lend themselves especially well to Reader's Theatre since the narrator describes the action while the students read the dialogue.

4. Sustained Silent Reading: Along with your students, bring

in books and other written materials related to the theme or concept selected, materials of a similar genre, or materials written by the same author(s) being studied. Although students have the freedom to select their own reading materials for SSR, they might decide to read one of the related materials if the books are easily accessible.

5. Writing Process: Time should be kept for this very important process. Although topics are selected by students, many may react to something read or discussed in the literature. Students will also be involved in writing throughout the two-hour block. Writing activities are woven throughout the activities portion as well as in mini-lessons and teacher-directed activities.

6. Teacher-Directed Whole-Class/Large-Group Activities (Strategy Lessons): Use a Shared Reading Approach or use this time to present a specific skill the entire class or large group needs. Either activity may be based on the basal selection and appropriate activities from the basal. However, choose only those that *best* meet objectives and student needs.

7. Activities: Have students work independently or in small groups on activities to extend the literature, whether from the basal or other literary source. Activities may be categorized as "required" and "optional" so that students have choices. Include activities that cause students to think critically and creatively and to analyze literary elements or genres, and that are based, in large part, on questions and interests generated by the students.

Time must also be allotted for independent reading, either of the basal or of books related to the concept or theme being explored. Students may read to find answers to questions or to complete specific activities, developed by both students and teachers, or just for the fun of it!

As students work and read independently or in groups, conferences may be held with individual students or "mini-lessons" may be taught to small groups, based on student needs. For example, students might have kept a diary of life on the prairie. Their writing might have indicated a need for knowing how to use quotation marks. The teacher might create a mini-lesson to teach this type of punctuation.

The main goal of the reading program should be to involve students in reading. The more they read and the more they enjoy reading, the more fluent they will become. And as they become more fluent in reading, they will want to read more. It is a circular pattern that can be directly affected by the way reading is approached in the classroom. No matter what materials are used to help achieve the reading objectives, whether literature or basal, students can be involved with language and begin to make connections between reading and aspects of the world they live in.

LITERATURE-BASED MATERIALS

Many publishing companies have risen to the challenge of bringing good literature to students. Literature packages and resource books have been developed to integrate literature with all areas of the curriculum and to extend students' language and thinking skills.

These materials can be used to establish a literature-based reading program as well as to supplement a basal reading program. When selecting material it is vital to choose those books that best meet the goals established based on student needs and interests, as well as the district objectives. In addition, the materials selected should be usable in conjunction with other materials being adopted, should work well within the framework of the curriculum, and should be congruent with the teacher's philosophy.

The following annotated listing represents a sampling of available materials that promote the use of literature in the classroom.

Creative Publications, 788 Palomar Avenue, Sunnyvale, California 94086, (408) 720-1400

Windows on Language and Literature: Child-Centered Activities for Exploring Storybooks. This series is designed around six themes: friendship, home and neighborhood, fears and fantasies, the family, animal adventures, and once upon a time. Each resource book is devoted to one of the themes and contains materials and activities based on eight familiar storybooks. Activities involve children actively; encourage appreciation for books and literature; present a wide variety of listening, speaking, reading, and writing experiences; and enrich the language experience. (PreK–Grade 2)

Curriculum Associates, Inc., 5 Esquire Road, N. Billerica, Massachusetts 01862-2589, (508) 667-8000

Unified Language Series. The components of this Whole Language Program include:

Story Pictures Plus. Classic literature is used to build readiness skills such as story characters, retelling the story, choral rhymes, gross and fine motor skills, comprehension, directional/positional concepts, and so on. Children create a take-home booklet to "read" to their families. Each *Story Pictures Plus* set includes six, full-color, stand-alone story posters with story texts and a teacher guide. (Kindergarten)

Storybooks. Classic literature is used to build oral and written language. Each storybook contains twenty take-apart pages that can stand alone as posters. A teacher guide includes learning materials that build language skills through story-related activities. An activity book is available for home use and for school use to extend the learning unit. (Grade 1)

Willie MacGurkle and Friends (Grade 2), *Rutabaga Ruby and Friends* (Grade 3), *Finnigan and Friends* (Grade 4), and *Tamaranda, New Friends, and New Places* (Grade 5). Humorous characters and amusing rhymes in each level blend with serious activities for oral language and literacy skills development. Each level includes poems that are used as catalysts to reproduce, discuss, and extend sounds, words, and ideas. Teacher guides offer step-by-step lesson plans. Each lesson includes many features such as across-curriculum activities for reading, creative expression, art, science, literature, math, social studies, and so on.

Dale Seymour Publications, P.O. Box 10888, Palo Alto, California 94303-0879, (415) 324-2800

Let 'Em Talk: Oral Language Activities for the Classroom. This teacher handbook focuses on oral language skills using literature-based activities. The book includes activity sheets with poems, fables, folktales, and myths that can be used as models for activities that can be done with any literary selection chosen. Activities include dramatic play, pantomime, improvisation, role-playing, choral reading, Reader's Theatre, storytelling, interviewing, panel discussion, and more. Guidelines are included for getting started in the different aspects of oral language learning, as well as rating sheets for self-evaluation and peer evaluation. (Grades K–8)

Teaching Characterization. A collection of activities based on high-fantasy literature. Activities draw on characterizations in three sets of books: Robin McKinley's *The Blue Sword* and *The Hero and the Crown*, Meredith Ann Pierce's *The Darkangel* and *A Gathering of Gargoyles*, and P. C. Hodgell's *God Stalk* and *Dark of the Moon.* Many of the stimulus sheets can be used to explore characterizations in these books as well as in any literature. All the reproducible sheets contain open-ended writing and discussion activities. (Middle grades and up)

Metaphor: The Language of Magic. This unit of study includes twenty-five stimulus sheets that introduce the metaphor and teach students to recognize metaphors in their reading, interpret them, and develop metaphors of their own. Exemplary use of metaphors in Lloyd Alexander's series, *Chronicles of Prydain* is included. (Middle grades and up)

Educational Impressions, 210 Sixth Avenue, P.O. Box 77, Hawthorne, New Jersey 07507, (201) 423-4666

Circles and Square Pegs. Thematic units help children explore the hopes, fears, dreams, and realities of their lives. Activities and appropriate children's literature focus on units such as dealing with success and failure, insecurity and self-confidence, peer pressure, coping with emotions, prejudice and stereotypes, looking different, handicaps, dissolution of the family, moving and starting over, death and dying. (Middle grades and up)

Good Apple, Box 299, Carthage, Illinois 62321, (217) 357-2794

Famous Fables for Little Troupers. This workbook includes fifteen expanded versions of Aesop's Fables with suggestions for playacting, discussion questions, and lead-ins to improvisation. (Grades K–8)

Mighty Myth. Twelve myths are vividly retold with an instructional guide for classroom discussion and skills activities. (Grades 5–12)

Treasure Hunts. Sixty projects are based on ten classics by authors such as Mark Twain, Robert Louis Stevenson, Lewis Carroll, and Shakespeare. (Grades 4–7)

Good Year Books, Scott, Foresman and Company, 1900 East Lake Avenue, Glenview, Illinois 60025, (312) 729-3000

Fantastic Reading. Seventeen short science fiction and fantasy stories are followed by creative activities and projects that challenge students' imaginations and reinforce writing and study skills. (Grades 5–8)

The Gingerbread Guide. The complete texts for fifteen multicultural folktales are included as well as background concepts, strategies, and activities grouped by age, reproducibles, annotated bibliography, and resource lists. (Ages 3–8)

Read It Again! Imaginative ideas and activities for fifteen popular read-aloud books develop a lifelong love of literature as well as word recognition, general comprehension, and critical thinking skills. Highly motivating activities involve children in music, pantomime, cooking, math, storytelling, and more. (Book 1—Grades K–2; Book 2—Grades 3–5; Book 3—Grades 3–5)

Jamestown Publishers, P.O. Box 9168, Providence, Rhode Island 02940, (401) 351-1915

Sudden Twists and More Twists. Companion volumes feature short stories from around the world. Each story, characterized by unexpected plot twists, is accompanied by reading comprehension exercises. Questions are designed to encourage class discussion and serve as a basis for writing. (Reading level 6; interest level 6–10)

Best Short Stories. Well-known classic and contemporary stories are used to teach comprehension skills and an appreciation and critical understanding of the essential elements of literature. (Middle level—Reading level 6, interest level 10; Advanced level—Reading and interest levels 9–college)

Learning Links, Inc., 2300 Maracus Avenue, New Hyde Park, New York 10042, (516) 437-9071

Novel Ties. Over 125 Novel-Ties study guide titles introduce students to fine literature. Each study guide contains background information, prereading and postreading activities, bibliography of related books, answer key, synopsis, vocabulary skills, chapter-by-chapter format with writing activities, cloze activities, and comprehensive questions. Novel-Ties can be purchased separately or they are available in the following packages, which include books, study guide, and/or activity books:

Topical Ties. Novels focus on a specific theme such as coping with divorce, death and dying, fantasy, friendship, grandparents, the Holocaust, humor, mystery and suspense, Native Americans, and so on.

Author Ties. These are outstanding novels by authors such as Lloyd Alexander, Natalie Babbitt, Judy Blume, Ray Bradbury, Beverly Cleary, Roald Dahl, Katherine Patterson, Mark Twain, and so on.

Series Ties. This is a collection of books by one author who uses many of the same characters in different situations.

Unit Ties. This supplemental reading program is based on a single unit of study such as biography, Greek and Roman myths, poetry, short stories, and folktales. (Intermediate levels)

Primary Ties. This collection, specifically geared to the young readers in grades K–3, focuses on specific themes such as bears, dinosaurs, friends, monsters, science or nature, special days, transportation, and classics.

Historical Ties. This collection fosters an understanding of specific times in history such as westward expansion, the frontier, Colonial America, and the Revolution. (Grade levels depend on the titles selected.)

Novel Units, P.O. Box 1461, Palatine, Illinois 60078, (312) 541-8573
Novel Units. Novel units were developed to expand or extend students' learning and love of reading. Novel units are available for over one-hundred popular pieces of quality children's literature. Each booklet contains a brief story summary, initiating and prereading activities, vocabulary lists, suggested activities to develop vocabulary, predicting questions, comprehension questions, activity sheets to engage students in oral and written exercises to accompany reading, postreading activities, and summarizing activities that encourage students to provide their point of view and feeling on aspects of the story. (Titles are available for grades 1 through 8.)

The Perfection Form Company, 1000 North Second Avenue, Logan, Iowa 51546, (800) 831-4190

Reading Beyond the Basal and *Reading Beyond the Basal Plus.* These teacher guides offer a wide variety of reading, writing, and other learning activities based on a best-selling children's book title. Guides include prereading activities, critical thinking questions, and writing activities, and suggestions for developing oral language and listening skills, art projects, a learning center activity, information about the author, across-the-curriculum activities, annotated bibliography, and more. (*Reading Beyond the Basal*, grades K–4; *Reading Beyond the Basal Plus*, grades 4–6)

Portals to Reading. Each activity book, based on a best-selling children's book, teaches reading skills such as sequencing events, following directions, thinking creatively, and so on. Notes about the novel's author and plot are also included. (Grades 4–8)

Perma-Bound, Vandalia Road, Jacksonville, Illinois 62650, (217) 243-5451

S.O.A.R. (Special Outlooks for Advanced Readers). Designed to motivate academically gifted students to expand their reading and thinking skills, this program provides activities to help teach advanced reading skills and to provide the bridge between basal reading and literature. An integral part of the program is a twenty-page teacher's guide that gives information about the academically gifted child and how best to use literature with this group of children. Units are available for a variety of titles. (Grades 1–7)

M.O.R.E. (Motivational Organizers for Reading Enrichment). This program is designed to help expand students' interest in reading and provide the teacher with a simple structure for managing the classroom's supplemental reading program. Organized into theme units, such as *Books to Make You Giggle and Grin, Solve It— I Dare You,* and *An Ark Full of Animals,* each unit is divided into six sets according to readability and interest levels. (Grades 1–6)

Classroom Favorites. These perennially popular titles have free teaching guides that include plot synopsis, discussion questions, students' activities, objective tests and answers. Over 150 titles are available. (Grade levels depend on titles selected.)

Over five thousand of the most popular titles found in children's literature, many with teacher guides and materials, are also available. LIT-PACS give a grade-by-grade, thematic literature–whole language booklist.

Scholastic, Inc., 730 Broadway, New York, New York 10003, (800) 325-6149

Book Center. This whole-language reading program begins with and builds on the strengths and interests of each student. The material for each grade consists of fifty-six paperback books spanning three reading levels (with multiple copies of four of the titles), a teacher's resource book containing conference papers and a resource and management section, student activity cards (one for each title) providing questions and activities related to each book, a poster, a professional manual describing whole-language teaching strategies, and a teacher's journal describing one teacher's experiences with the program. Work in each *Book Center* involves students in a variety of activities including silent reading, shared reading, oral reading, and writing about their books. The in-service aspect of professional materials includes working with less-confident readers, working with emergent readers, arranging the environment, and applying whole-language principles. (Grades 2–6)

Bridges. Designed as a bridge from basal reading to the reading of literature, *Bridges* includes material for each grade level that contains eighty-five paperback books spanning three reading levels (including thirty-five copies of one title for that grade level, ten copies of each of three titles, and two copies of ten titles, "buddy books"); lesson plans that teach necessary reading skills through the use of literature, extend the literature, and include activities that cut across the curriculum; a writing component; student response logs; and activity cards for each title that include higher-level thinking questions. (Grades 1–6)

Sundance Publishers and Distributors, Newton Road, Littleton, Massachusetts 01460, (508) 486-9201

Leap (Literature Enrichment Activities for Paperbacks). A program designed to increase reading enjoyment by giving students a break from structured skills development. Students work together in small groups to share their appreciation and to reinforce each other's understanding and reading pleasure. LEAP includes prereading exercises to focus students' thinking and get them actively involved in the reading; activities to promote vocabulary development, comprehension skills, and writing skills; postreading questions to initiate class discussions and get students to think critically; extension and enrichment activities to combine reading with art, music, writing, and more. (Grades 2–6)

Lift (Literature Is for Thinking). Great children's literature is used as a catalyst for good thinking as well as for learning the four basic skills of communicating with language: listening, speaking, reading, and writing. By concentrating on a single book considered as a whole, students learn these skills in an integrated way. Each LIFT packet contains activity sheets including one prereading activity, "during reading activities," one postreading activity, a rationale, and a teacher's guide. The program helps students learn to read and interpret a whole book and involves them in writing in a variety of modes on subjects related to the book. LIFT teaches students to gather evidence, make inferences, and solve problems, and helps them understand the process of literary analysis. (Grades 4–8)

Alert Reader Library. Reading skills and reading enjoyment are fostered by giving students an individualized reading program based on quality literature. Challenging questions and exercises foster vocabulary development, good literary and study skills, and help promote basic reading and critical thinking skills. (Grades 2–6)

Sundance also publishes a variety of teaching packets for the kindergarten through third grade "shared reading."

Teacher Created Materials, Inc. 5445 Oceanus Drive, #106, Huntington Beach, California 92649, (714) 891-7895

Literature and Critical Thinking Series. Favorite children's stories reinforce skills in critical thinking, reading, writing, listening, speaking, and imaginative thinking. Each book contains plot summaries and provides imaginative, ready-to-use activity pages based on Bloom's Taxonomy that build skills through story starters, puzzles, art projects, games, creative writing, and more. (Primary, Intermediate, Challenging, and Classic volumes, grades K–6; Activities for Young Learners, grades preK–1; Fairy and Folktales, preK–1; Nursery Rhymes, preK–1)

Troll Associates, 100 Corporate Drive, Mahway, New Jersey 07430, (201) 529-4000
Troll offers paperback editions of highly recommended books of all kinds: classics, historical fiction, biography, mythology, science fiction, modern fantasy, and more. Troll offers single titles as well as groupings of books in special packages.

Troll Big Books: Big Books that feature amusing stories with memorable characters.

SUGGESTED BOOKS FOR CHILDREN
George, Jean. *Julie of the Wolves*. Harper & Row, 1976.
MacLachlan, Patricia. *Sarah, Plain and Tall*. Harper & Row, 1985.
O'Dell, Scott. *Island of the Blue Dolphin*. Dell, 1960.
Wilder, Laura Ingalls. *Little House on the Prairie*. Illustrated by Garth Williams. Harper & Row, 1935.

REFERENCES

Commission on Reading. *Becoming a Nation of Readers: The Report of the Commission on Reading*. Washington, D.C.: National Institute of Education, 1985.
Cullinan, Bernice, ed. *Children's Literature in the Reading Program*. Newark, Del.: International Reading Association, 1987.
Goodman, Kenneth, Patrick Shannon, Yvonne Freeman, and Sharon Murphy. *Report Card On Basal Readers*. Katonah, N.Y.: Richard C. Owen, 1988.
Petty, Walter, Dorothy C. Petty, and Richard T. Salzar. *Experience in Language*. Boston: Allyn & Bacon, 1989.

11

A Model for Literature-Based Reading Programs

A literature-based reading curriculum uses a variety of reading materials and literary genres and adapts a variety of approaches and strategies to these materials to foster the development of language skills. This integration can easily be implemented in any classroom situation.

The Daily Reading Schedule, as shown in the pie charts on pages 223 and 224, is a suggested framework for implementing a balanced, developmentally appropriate reading curriculum in the primary and intermediate grades. The two-hour time frame is realistic since the schedule integrates the communication areas of reading, writing, listening, and speaking. However, remember that the times and divisions serve only as a guide; there must be flexibility. Of paramount importance is sensitivity to the children's needs and interests.

The developmentally appropriate reading program should reflect a balance among large-group, small-group, and individual activities. A balance should also be achieved between teacher-directed activities and student-directed activities.

COMPONENTS OF LITERATURE-BASED PROGRAMS

The following components should be considered in literature-based reading programs.

Teacher-Directed Activities (Strategy Lessons)

You need time to teach specific skills to a group of children or to the entire class. Skills should be introduced and taught only as they are appropriate to the literature being discussed. "In whole language programs, direct instruction is sometimes referred to as strategy lessons. Reading strategy instruction builds upon the prior knowledge and language strengths of the learner, and

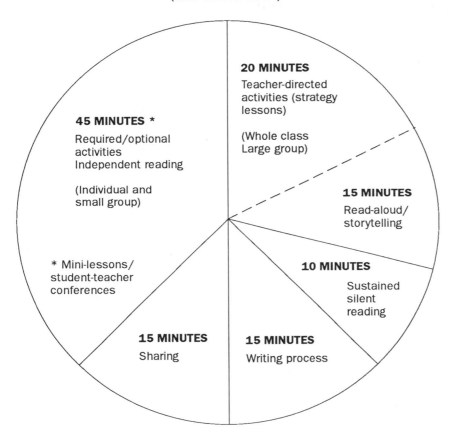

**A DAILY PRIMARY READING SCHEDULE USING A
LITERATURE-BASED CURRICULUM**
(Total Time: 2 Hours)

20 MINUTES
Teacher-directed
activities (strategy
lessons)

(Whole class
Large group)

45 MINUTES *
Required/optional
activities
Independent reading

(Individual and
small group)

15 MINUTES
Read-aloud/
storytelling

10 MINUTES
Sustained
silent
reading

* Mini-lessons/
student-teacher
conferences

15 MINUTES
Sharing

15 MINUTES
Writing process

helps students integrate and become more flexible in their use
of efficient and effective strategies." (Slaughter, 1988) Students
should be actively involved in reading and writing during most
of the time allotted for reading. A smaller percentage of the class
time should be set aside for activities (strategy lessons) that you
direct.

Activities
It is vital that students have the opportunity to initiate their own
activities and take responsibility for completing them. The Daily
Record Sheets on pages 225 and 226 give children an opportunity

A DAILY INTERMEDIATE READING SCHEDULE
USING A LITERATURE-BASED CURRICULUM
(Total Time: 2 Hours)

20 MINUTES
Teacher-directed
activities (strategy
lessons)

(Whole class
Large group)

15 MINUTES
Read-aloud/
storytelling

45 MINUTES *
Required/optional
activities
Independent reading

(Individual and
small group)

* Mini-lessons/
student-teacher
conferences

20 MINUTES
Writing process

20 MINUTES
Sustained silent reading

to record their daily activities and frees you to facilitate learning. As a facilitator, you guide children as they make decisions about their own learning. Allowing children to make decisions, problem solve, and take responsibility for their own learning better prepares them for the work demands of the real world (Schweinhart, 1987).

The activities developed should take into account the importance of the connection between literature and all aspects of life. Concepts from other curriculum content areas such as science, social studies, and math can be integrated with those concepts being stressed through the literature. Art, music, and drama can

DAILY RECORD SHEET: REQUIRED ACTIVITIES

Name: _____

Directions: Fill in the number of each required activity you

complete, the date, and any comments you have.

Required activities:

Activity number: _____ Date: _____

Student comments: _____

_____

_____

Teacher comments: _____

_____

_____

Activity number: _____ Date: _____

Student comments: _____

_____

_____

Teacher comments: _____

_____

_____

Activity number: _____ Date: _____

Student comments: _____

_____

_____

Teacher comments: _____

_____

_____

DAILY RECORD SHEET: OPTIONAL ACTIVITIES

Name: _____

Directions: Fill in the number of each optional activity you

complete, the date, and any comments you have.

Optional activities:

Activity number: _____ Date: _____

Student comments: _____

_____

_____

Teacher comments: _____

_____

_____

Activity number: _____ Date: _____

Student comments: _____

_____

_____

Teacher comments: _____

_____

_____

Activity number: _____ Date: _____

Student comments: _____

_____

_____

Teacher comments: _____

_____

_____

also be enhanced through well-developed activities. For example, students may analyze illustrations, create their own illustrations of selected scenes, compose music to accompany text, dramatize events, and so on. Activities should also encourage students to go back into the book, think critically, problem solve, analyze elements, and better understand the specific genre.

Make sure to allot time for independent reading. Students may read for a specific purpose such as to find answers to questions or to complete activities that you or they have developed. And time must be allotted for students to read for the sheer pleasure of reading.

Student-Teacher Conference

Often, as students work on required or optional activities, either independently or in groups, mini-lessons can be held for those who need a lesson in the development of a specific skill or understanding. Also, this time can be used for individual conferences. The reading conference is a valuable evaluative technique. Through periodic meetings with each student, on a one-to-one basis, you can gather important information concerning the student's interests, attitudes toward reading, and growth in specific reading and thinking skills.

During the conference, make the students feel comfortable and encourage them to express their opinions freely. They should see the conference as a pleasurable experience in which they establish a dialogue with you. The student-teacher conference should include the following elements:

1. A discussion of a selection read by the student. You should be an active part of the discussion; don't just ask questions. The discussion may focus on any element(s) of the selection, concepts, or issues brought up in the selection, the author, or the genre.

2. Questions to assess the student's comprehension of the selection. Ask a few well-focused questions that involve the student in higher-level thinking. If he or she seems to have a problem, you can conduct an additional assessment to evaluate which comprehension skills need remediation.

3. Oral reading in which the student selects a specific part of the selection to read aloud. The section read may be a favorite part,

a part that surprised her, a part that caused him to laugh, and so on.

4. A discussion of the activities that the student has completed or is working on. The discussion can focus on the selection process for Optional Activities, the plan of attack for completing work, the student's interests, and so on.

5. A check of the student's Independent Reading Log to establish his or her choices or interests (see page 46).

6. Recommendations and suggestions. Discuss suggestions for further reading and recommendations for skill development. After each conference, fill in the Conference Log on page 229.

Approaches for Developing Interest in Reading

The Daily Reading Schedule involves students in a combination of approaches and strategies that promote comprehension and skills development. These approaches, which have been discussed in detail in previous sections of the book, include reading aloud (Chapter 1), shared reading (Chapter 2), sustained silent reading (Chapter 3), storytelling (Chapter 4), and language experience and the writing process (Chapter 16). Set aside specific times for SSR, read-aloud, and storytelling and the writing process. However, as indicated on the Daily Reading Schedule, because of time constraints, the read-aloud portion might be part of a whole-group activity, in which you read specific portions of a story as a prerequisite for a specific lesson.

Many of the literature-based strategies that aid in the development of comprehension (see Chapter 9) can be incorporated into the Whole Group Teacher-Directed Activities and into the required and optional activities. The Activities for Extending and Sharing Literature (Chapter 5) can also be incorporated into these two sections. These activities can be adapted to most literary works and can help extend and promote the reading experience and foster skills development in reading, writing, listening, and speaking.

The sample plans that begin on page 230 illustrate ways in which activities and approaches work together to create a reading program in which literature is at the heart of the curriculum.

CONFERENCE LOG

Name of student: _____ Date: _____

Name of book or selection: _____

Rating scale: Rating is on a scale of 1 (poor) to 5 (excellent)

1. Attitude toward reading: 1   2   3   4   5

2. Comprehension skills:

    Overall understanding   1   2   3   4   5

    Context clues   1   2   3   4   5

    Main ideas   1   2   3   4   5

    Analysis/interpretation   1   2   3   4   5

    Inferences   1   2   3   4   5

    Evaluation   1   2   3   4   5

3. Oral reading:

    Fluency   1   2   3   4   5

    Word attack   1   2   3   4   5

    Reading with emotion/expression 1   2   3   4   5

4. Strengths: _____

5. Weaknesses: _____

6. Student reading log:

    Student has read _____ books in _____ weeks.

    Student has selected books from a variety of genres:

    Yes _____ No _____

    Types of books selected: _____

7. Student activities: (comments) _____

8. Suggestions/recommendations to the student:

_____

SAMPLE PLAN FOR A PRIMARY READING SCHEDULE

To implement the Suggested Daily Primary Reading Schedule, the following specific daily activities based on *Corduroy*, by Don Freeman, are provided.

Whole-Group Teacher-Directed Activities (approximately 20 minutes per day): Time schedules may vary from class to class.

Monday:
Materials Needed:
    a copy of the book *Corduroy* by Don Freeman
    a piece of corduroy fabric (green, if possible)
    a note to parents telling them you'd like their child to
        bring a stuffed bear to school and why
Procedures:
1. Prereading: Tell the children that you are going to read a story about a special bear named Corduroy. Tell them to listen as you read the story to see if they can decide how Corduroy got his name.
2. Read-aloud: Read the story orally.
3. Critical thinking: Discuss how Corduroy got his name. Following this discussion, show the children a piece of corduroy, and allow time for them to feel it.
4. Questioning: Ask the following discussion questions:
   a. Where did Corduroy live?
   b. What reasons did Lisa's mother give for not buying the bear?
   c. Why do you think Corduroy waited until the store closed to go looking for his button?
   d. How do you think Corduroy felt when Lisa sewed his button on?
   e. Why was it important to Corduroy for Lisa to buy him?
   f. Do you think this story is true? Why or why not?
5. Parent involvement: Give the children the note for their parents requesting them to bring their stuffed bears to class the next day. Explain to the children what the note says.

Tuesday:

Materials Needed:

> bears brought from home
> copy of the book *Corduroy*
> large pieces of chart paper
> a marker

Procedures:

1. Sharing: Allow time for the children to introduce and share their bears.
2. Read-aloud: Reread *Corduroy*, modeling emotions as you read.
3. Language experience/Skill development: Ask children to retell *Corduroy* in their own words, as you write their sentences on large pieces of chart paper. If students contribute conversation, discuss the use of quotation marks.
4. Shared reading: Once the story is written, reread the story in unison.

Wednesday:

Materials Needed:

> sentence strips (prepared from the sentences dictated on Tuesday) adhered to 12- by 18-inch sheets of paper. Adhere *one* sentence strip per sheet of paper. Tape sheets in correct order along the chalkboard.
> scotch tape or masking tape
> bears brought from home

Procedures:

1. Shared reading: Group the children and their bears together as they choral read the sentences on the large sheets of paper.
2. Skill development: Remove the sheets of paper from the chalkboard and assign one sheet to each child or small group. Tell them to draw an illustration that represents the text written on the sheet of paper.
3. Skill development: When everyone is finished with the illustrations, as a group, tape the story back on the chalkboard in the correct sequence.
4. Shared reading: Choral read the story.

Thursday:
Materials Needed:
> a copy of a Big Book, which you have made using the large sheets from the chalkboard that contain the story of Corduroy (see page 33 for instructions on making Big Books)
>
> small plain pieces of paper taped over all the nouns on each page of the Big Book text
>
> scotch tape or masking tape
>
> children's bears

Procedures:
1. Skill development: Gather the children and their bears together. Explain to the children that you have made a Big Book from the story they wrote and illustrated about Corduroy and that you have covered all the names that represent a person, place, or thing. These words are called nouns. Tell them that they should fill in the word that is covered as you read the story together.
2. Dramatization: Choral read the story, allowing the children to fill in the covered words as you read. Remove the paper covering the word after the children supply the word.
3. Dramatization: Ask the children to think about all the things that Corduroy did in the story. Take turns allowing children to mime something from the story, while others take turns guessing what is being mimed.

Friday:
Materials Needed:
> The Big Book of Corduroy
>
> a copy of *A Pocket for Corduroy*
>
> the bears brought from home
>
> refrigerated roll of sugar cookies (available in the refrigerated sections of most grocery stores)
>
> small circle to cut parts of the cookie (i.e., the top from a bottle)
>
> cookie sheet
>
> oven or toaster oven
>
> pot holders
>
> spatula

Procedures:

1. Shared reading: Choral read the Big Book about Corduroy.
2. Read-aloud: Read *A Pocket for Corduroy* to the class and their guest bears.
3. Critical thinking: Discuss this book and then ask the children to compare and contrast this story with the Corduroy story.
4. Have a party for the children and their bears by serving "Bear Paw Cookies" and juice. To make the cookies: Use already prepared sugar cookie dough. Make one large circle for the paw and five smaller circles for the claws. Place them on the cookie sheet. Attach the five smaller circles to the large circle as illustrated and bake in the oven or toaster oven. Remove the sheet from the oven with a pot holder. Allow cookies to cool. Remove them with a spatula. Each child will then have a giant bear paw cookie.

Required Activities:

1. Make a cassette tape of *Corduroy* (Don Freeman's version), the Big Book version, and *A Pocket for Corduroy*. Provide time for the children to listen to these tapes and follow along in the appropriate book.
2. Cut pieces of paper in the shape of Corduroy. Allow children to use these bear-shaped pieces of paper to write their own story about Corduroy. Provide time for the children to share these stories.
3. Tell the children to pretend that they are Corduroy and that they are still in the department store wishing for someone to take them home. Ask them to create a poster to display beside Corduroy that would convince customers to take Corduroy home with them.
4. Provide students with instruction on how to do a webbing or semantic mapping (see page 331). Then discuss with

them the concept of friendship and how Lisa and Corduroy became friends. Next, assign a webbing or semantic activity on the word *friendship*, to be prepared by each child. Provide a time for the children to share their webbings or mappings.

5. Duplicate and distribute the three activity sheets on pages 236 through 238. Assign no more than one activity sheet per day as a follow-up.

Optional Activities:

1. Provide construction paper, crayons, paints, sample party invitations, and so on. Tell the students to make an invitation for someone (parent, grandparent, neighbor, stuffed bear), inviting them to come to school for the party on Friday. (*Note:* The time, place, and date will need to be provided.)

2. Provide construction paper, pieces of fabric (especially corduroy), glue, buttons, yarn, and tell the students to create their own bear.

3. Collect newspaper advertisements from toy stores, catalogs, and magazines. Provide plain sheets of 8 1/2 by 11-inch white paper. Then ask the students to make an ABC book of their favorite toys. Tell them to put a large *A* and a small *a* on the top of the first page. Then have them find a toy they would like that begins with the letter A, cut it out, and paste it on the *A* page. Have them continue throughout the alphabet. Finally, staple the pages into a book. Children may paste more than one toy on each page. Provide a large envelope for each child working on this project to keep the pages and cutouts together.

4. Provide paper bags, tongue depressors, assortments of cloth or scraps, and glue. Tell students to work in small groups to make puppets representing the characters in *Corduroy* and then present a puppet show to the class.

5. Provide materials for the children to make a new cover for Don Freeman's *Corduroy*. Hang these covers on the bulletin board so that others can see them.

6. Tell the children to design a Corduroy bookmark to use as they read other bear books such as *Beady Bear* and *Bearymore* by Don Freeman or the following:

A Bear Called Paddington, by Michael Bond
Ask Mr. Bear, by Marjorie Flack
Bear by Himself, by Geoffrey Hayes
Bear Hunt, by Anthony Browne
Bear Mouse, by Berniece Freschet
Bear Party, by William Pene DuBois
The Bears' Bazaar, by Michele Cartlidge
The Bears' House, by Marilyn Sachs
The Bear's Toothache, by David McPhail
Brown Bear, Brown Bear, What Do You See? by Bill Martin
Ernest and Celestine, by Gabrielle Vincent
Fix-It, by David McPhail
Ira Sleeps Over, by Bernard Waber
The Three Bears, by Paul Galdone
Winnie the Pooh, by A. A. Milne

235

**A MODEL FOR
LITERATURE-BASED
READING PROGRAMS**

CORDUROY

Name _____ Date _____

Directions
In the picture below, color a space brown if it contains one of the vocabulary words in box 1. Color a space green if it contains a word in box 2. If the space contains a word not found in box 1 or 2, color it red.

ACTIVITY
SHEET 1

Box 1
button   girl   store watchman   eyes

Box 2
bear   overalls bed

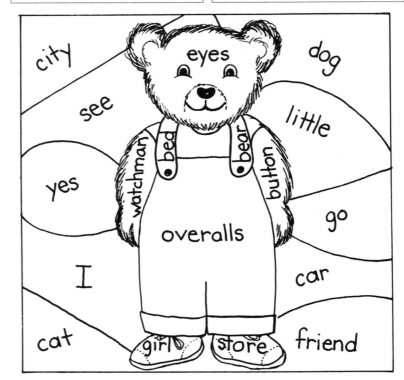

CORDUROY

Name _____ Date _____

ACTIVITY
SHEET 2

Directions
Look at the word at the end of each blank below. Fill in the
blank with a word from the box that best describes it. Use
each word only once.

white	green	little	brown
department	bright	night	small

1 _____ bear   5 _____ girl

2 _____ overalls 6 _____ eyes

3 _____ store   7 _____ bed

4 _____ button   8 _____ watchman

Directions
In the space provided below, draw a picture of one of the phrases you have just
completed.

CORDUROY | Name _____ Date _____

Directions

As you read the story below, fill in the blanks using the vocabulary words in the box. Use each word only once.

bear	store	girl	bed
overalls	button	eyes	watchman

Once upon a time there was a _____ named

Corduroy. He was wearing green _____. He had

very bright _____. Corduroy lived in a department

_____ with other animals and dolls. One day a little

_____ named Lisa came to the store, saw Corduroy,

and wanted to buy him. Her mother said no because she had already spent too

much money and the bear was missing a _____.

That night, Corduroy looked all over the store for a button. He made so much

noise the _____ found him and put him back on his

shelf. The next day, Lisa came in and bought him. She took him home to her

apartment and sewed a button on for him. She also had a _____

for him to sleep in. Now they were both happy and they became very good

friends.

SAMPLE PLAN FOR AN
INTERMEDIATE READING SCHEDULE

This sample plan is based on Katherine Paterson's *Bridge to Terabithia*, a moving tale of friendship and courage as a young boy comes to terms with tragedy.

Teacher-Directed Activities: In most cases, these activities will be completed over a much longer time than indicated. Time schedules will vary from class to class. Besides involving students in the activities listed, give students an opportunity to read *Bridge to Terabithia* in class.

Materials Needed: Each student will need a copy of *Bridge to Terabithia*.

Monday:
Introduction
1. Prereading: Ask students: "What do you think Terabithia might be?" "Where do you suppose Terabithia is located?"
2. Read-aloud: Read Chapter 1 of the book to students.
3. Skill development: Discuss the concept of foreshadowing. Reread the sentence: "He thought later how peculiar it was that here was probably the biggest thing in his life and he had shrugged it off as nothing."
4. Predicting: Ask students: "What do you think Jess might have meant by that statement?" "Why might this be the biggest thing in his life?"
5. Ask students to look for other examples of foreshadowing in Chapter 1. Discuss each and what events might be foreshadowed.

Tuesday:
Shared inquiry: (See Chapter 15, "Thinking Models or Strategies"; for this lesson to be successful, students should have completed Chapter 3.) Involve students in a shared inquiry strategy. As impetus for the discussion, ask them: "Did Jess ask Leslie to race because he didn't think she was a threat or because he felt it was only fair?"

Wednesday:

Setting Analysis

1. Webbing: Collectively, make a web of Terabithia. (See page 331 for more information about webbing.)

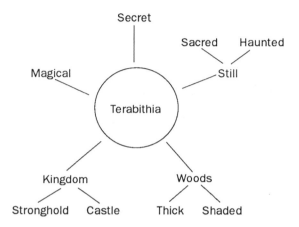

2. Ask students to skim the book, looking for words that they believe best describe Terabithia. Ask them to add these words to the classroom web.
3. Ask: "Which words most effectively help you create a mental picture of Terabithia?" Discuss their selections.
4. As a class, or in smaller groups, create a cinquain, haiku, or an acrostic to describe Terabithia.

Thursday:

Figurative Language

1. Read several examples of similes from *Bridge to Terabithia*, and write them on the board.
2. Ask students what similarities they can find in these examples (i.e., use of the words *as* or *like*, a comparison of two unlike things).
3. Discuss the use of similes and how they affect the images we receive from the written word.
4. Allow time for students to locate similes in the book and to write their favorite ones on the board.

5. Using a few of the similes as models, have students make up their own. For example, "He (Jess) didn't worry about a shirt because once he began running he would be hot as popping grease." What comparisons can students substitute for "popping grease"?
6. Discuss what makes a simile effective (i.e., the comparison fits the setting and mood). Make a list of the criteria for writing good similes and evaluate the ones the students created.

    A similar procedure can be used to enhance the understanding of other types of figurative language such as metaphor, personification, and hyperbole.

Friday:
Theme
1. Explain to students that people deal with death and tragedy in different ways but that they all go through similar stages.
2. As a class, create a story map that illustrates the stages Jess went through from the time he learned that Leslie had died. (See "Story Mapping" in Chapter 9.)
3. Have students research the stages of dealing with death and compare these stages with the map they have developed. (Research can include talks with professionals such as doctors and nurses or talks with those who have had to deal with death.)

Required Activities
1. After reading Chapters 1–6, create a sociogram (as described in "Characterization," in Chapter 7) that illustrates the relationship Jess had with his family and specific friends. After reading Chapters 7–13, create another sociogram. Compare how Jess's relationships changed and give possible reasons for these changes.
2. Create your own Terabithia. Describe it using any form you prefer: poetry, drama, art, music.
3. After completing *Bridge to Terabithia*, complete the following:
   a. In what ways did Jess's life change after meeting Leslie?

b. What lessons did Jess learn from Leslie? Which lesson do you feel is the most valuable? Why do you believe this to be valuable?

c. What did Terabithia represent to Jess? to Leslie?

d. Look at the illustrations. Choose your favorite.
How does the illustration reflect the mood of the story?
How does the illustration reflect details from the story?
What information or feelings did you gain from the illustration that you didn't gain from the text?

4. You are Jess. Write and deliver a eulogy for Leslie.

Optional Activities: Students may contract to complete a certain number of activities or you may decide how many must be completed.

1. Read another book by Katherine Paterson. Compare the two books, based on setting, characters, themes, and your reaction to each.

2. Recreate Terabithia in mural form. (Group activity)

3. Retell one of the conflicts that Jess and Leslie had with Janice. First, explain the conflict from Janice's viewpoint and then from either Jess's or Leslie's.

4. Using a book of quotations, select one on the subject of "friendship" that best reflects the relationship between Leslie and Jess. Illustrate the quotation using the same style as the illustrations in *Bridge to Terabithia.*

5. Listen to the tape "Free to Be You and Me." This was the same song Jess and Leslie sang in music class. Rewrite a verse as if you were one of the book's characters.

EVALUATION OF THE LITERATURE-BASED READING PROGRAM

Evaluation of student achievement in reading has been an issue in educational circles for years. Most school districts and states use standardized tests as a systematic means for evaluating growth in reading skills. Because of the importance and credibility given to test results, these standardized tests often determine the curriculum.

In addition to standardized tests, teacher accountability and student progress are also determined by informal reading inventories, such as *Qualitative Reading Inventory* by Lauren Leslie and JoAnne Caldwell, published by Scott, Foresman. Although standardized tests and informal reading inventories can provide important information, unfortunately, much of what is achieved in a literature-based program cannot be measured using such traditional methods. As a result, advocates of literature-based programs are continually looking for and developing new assessment procedures to reflect the student achievements in all areas of language: reading, writing, listening, and speaking.

Tools of assessment are needed that will focus on process rather than product, concepts rather than rote memorization, and growth in language and attitude. To be a valid measure of student achievement and change, evaluation cannot be consigned to a test or series of tests. Instead, evaluation should be ongoing as teachers observe, analyze, and interact with students (Marek, et al., 1984). These "kidwatching" activities can be categorized to provide a framework for evaluating whole-language education. Students can be observed, analyzed, and interacted with using a combination of the formal and informal procedures illustrated in the following table. In formal procedures, some record of an activity is carried out at regular intervals. Many of the logs and worksheets contained in this book (i.e., Literary Logs, pages 216–217; Retrieval Chart, pages 213–215; Read-Aloud Evaluation Form, page 22; Shared Reading Observation Sheet, page 40; Reading Log, page 63; and Daily Record Sheets, pages 304–305, will be especially helpful as part of the formal evaluation process.

Informal evaluation may occur any time you come into contact with your students. Informal evaluation is not a formal plan or record, although you may note what you learn informally, including names and dates, and use this information at a later time to reinforce the formal evaluation.

FORMAL AND INFORMAL EVALUATION

Activity	Informal	Formal
Observation	Watching and listening as student works alone, in groups, and in whole-class activities.	Keeping anecdotal records
Interaction	Daily conversation with students	Asking planned questions to determine how students perceive concepts, internalize what has been discussed, read, written, and so on. Conducting student-teacher conferences
Analysis	Listening to students and analyzing language skills and needs	Monitoring student compositions and written reactions Listening to student tapes of readings and conversations Monitoring student logs and checklists

One last form of evaluation—self-evaluation—is one of the most important evaluative measures, yet it is often overlooked. Students need to examine their progress as they observe their own actions, assess their interaction with you and with others, and analyze their work. Students should assess the strategies they have used for specific tasks and evaluate their appropriateness and effectiveness. Students should also be encouraged to continually ask questions about their own progress. Questions such as "How did I do?" "How might I have improved?" "What did I understand from reading this book?" "Is the strategy I'm using working?" will focus their attention on their own accomplishments and provide a framework for improvement. Many of the logs and worksheets mentioned involve students in self-evaluation.

To facilitate continued assessment and retrieval of needed information, keep all the materials gathered on each student in individual journals, reading folders, or on cassette tapes. The evaluation information provided through teacher and student observation, interaction, and analysis can be used in conjunction with standardized achievement tests to provide an accurate assessment of student growth and needs in language skills.

ORGANIZING THE CLASSROOM

The organization and arrangement of the classroom is very important to the success of a literature-based reading program. When organizing the classroom, several factors must be considered.

Student Groupings

The room arrangement must be conducive to students working independently, in pairs, in small groups, or in whole-group activities. Workstations or individual desks can accommodate the independent workers, but tables or clusters of desks would best accommodate a small group. Areas of desks or tables or large circle areas are best for whole-group activities.

Furniture Selection

Round tables permit more flexibility than square or rectangular tables, especially in areas where space is a concern. Low shelves can often double as room dividers as well as storage for materials and supplies.

Types of Activities

The noise level of the various activities must be considered when arranging the classroom. There must be a quiet area for activities such as independent reading, conferencing, listening centers, and writing. However, the area where students are storytelling, miming, dramatizing, conducting puppet shows, or creating murals should have a hum of productive noise. Because space allocation is so critical to the success of the literature-based classroom, platform areas or lofts are often created to extend the existing space. This solution also separates quiet and noisy areas. Another way of extending space and accommodating noisy activities is to move them into the patio or hallway area.

Student Work

A designated place needs to be identified for student logs, work folders, and journals so that students know what they are supposed to do with an activity or project when it is being worked on or when it is completed.

Record Keeping

Some form of individual record keeping of the daily activities should be maintained. One simple way to do this is to require students to keep a log of their daily activities (see pages 225–226). In this log, both you and the student react to the work being completed. Another way to keep records is to keep a designated sheet at each center for the student to sign his or her name, the date, and the time he or she enters and leaves the center.

Monitoring Students

Not all activities can be completed at individual desks, therefore the overall organization of who will do what and when is important so that various centers and spaces within the classroom do not become too crowded. For example, if one of the planned activities requires using the listening center and it can only accommodate six students, you have to plan activities so that no more than six students will be at the center at one time and yet all students will have the opportunity to go to the listening center at some time. One way to organize this is to color-code the areas of the room. Then provide colored wristbands (available in most sporting goods stores) to designate where students will go. If the listening center can accommodate six people, then only six wristbands would be the same color as that center. Usually in a literature-based classroom, students can choose among a variety of areas in which to work and among a variety of activities. Therefore, if the listening center is full, the student simply makes another selection and returns to the listening center at a later time.

Maintenance, Distribution, and Storage of Materials and Supplies

Students need to know where and how to obtain necessary materials. Specific areas need to be designated for art supplies, writing materials, audiovisual equipment, and other curriculum materials. There need to be adequate shelves for books, both library books and student-authored books, as well as racks to accommodate big books.

On the very first day of school, establish rules for working in the different areas. Once the rules are established, they should be posted, reviewed, and enforced consistently. For example, if students are in the listening center, they need to learn how to operate the equipment and how to rewind the cassette tape for the next listener(s). You need to make it clear that there are designated places for all equipment and materials to be stored.

Display Area

Bulletin boards and room dividers can be used to display students' work. In addition, students' work can be hung from the ceiling or displayed on doors and walls.

Classroom Library

In a literature-based classroom, perhaps the most important factor is the use of the library and the organization of the classroom library. See Chapter 12 for details on organizing and using the classroom library.

In summary, in a literature-based classroom where students are continually reading, writing, thinking, collaborating, creating, and making choices, the overall success relies on identifying developmentally appropriate activities and then organizing the environment so that it is conducive to learning.

SUGGESTED BOOKS FOR CHILDREN

Bond, Michael. *A Bear Called Paddington.* Illustrated by Peggy Fortnum. Houghton Mifflin, 1960.

Browne, Anthony. *Bear Hunt.* Atheneum, 1980.

Cartlidge, Michele. *The Bears' Bazaar.* Lothrop, 1980.

DuBois, William Pene. *Bear Party.* Viking Press, 1951, 1963.

Flack, Marjorie. *Ask Mr. Bear.* Macmillan, 1968.

Freeman, Don. *A Pocket for Corduroy.* Viking Press, 1978.

———. *Corduroy.* Viking Press, 1968.

———. *Bearymore.* Viking Press, 1957.

———. *Beady Bear.* Viking Press, 1954.

Freschet, Berniece. *Bear Mouse.* Illustrated by Donald Carrick. Scribner's, 1973.

Galdone, Paul. *The Three Bears.* Scholastic, 1973.

Hayes, Geoffrey. *Bear by Himself.* Harper & Row, 1976.

McPhail, David. *Fix-It.* Dutton, 1984.

———. *The Bear's Toothache.* Little, Brown, 1972.

Martin, Bill. *Brown Bear, Brown Bear, What Do You See?* Holt, Rinehart & Winston, 1983.

Milne, A. A. *Winnie-the-Pooh.* Illustrated by Ernest H. Shepard. Dutton, 1926.

Paterson, Katherine. *Bridge to Terabithia.* Illustrated by Donna Diamond. Thomas Y. Crowell, 1977.

Sachs, Marilyn. *The Bears' House.* Illustrated by Louis Glanzman, Doubleday, 1971.

Vincent, Gabrielle. *Ernest and Celestine.* Greenwillow, 1982.

Waber, Bernard. *Ira Sleeps Over.* Houghton Mifflin, 1972.

Wilder, Laura Ingalls. *Little House on the Prairie.* Illustrated by Garth Williams. Harper & Row, 1935.

REFERENCES

Coordinating Council of the National Reading Initiative. *Celebrating the National Reading Initiative.* Sacramento: California State Department of Education, 1988.

Goodman, Kenneth S., Yetta M. Goodman, and Wendy J. Hood, eds. *The Whole Language Evaluation Book.* Portsmouth, N.H.: Heinemann Educational Books, 1989.

Jagger, A. M., and M. T. Smith-Burkey, eds. *Observing the Language Learner.* Newark, Del.: International Reading Association, 1985.

Leslie, Lauren, and JoAnne Caldwell. *Qualitative Reading Inventory.* Glenview, Ill.: Scott, Foresman, 1990.

Marek, A., and D. Howard. "A Kid-Watching Guide. Evaluation for Whole Language Classrooms." Occasional Paper No. 9. Tucson Program in Language and Literacy. Tucson: University of Arizona, 1984.

Schweinhart, Lawrence J. "When the Buck Stops Here." *High/Scope Resources*, Fall 1987, pp. 1, 9–13.

Slaughter, Helen B. "Indirect and Direct Teaching in a Whole Language Program." *The Reading Teacher*, October 1988, pp. 30–34.

**A MODEL FOR
LITERATURE-BASED
READING PROGRAMS**

12

Using the Library

As children's love for literature and for reading grows, they naturally want to read more. What better place to nourish this need than the library. Young children become familiar with the library by visiting with their parents, finding special "treasures" to bring home and read, and listening during Story Hour as librarians and storytellers bring books to life. Unfortunately, all children do not have the same advantages, and many come to school having had little or no contact with libraries.

Any book on literature for children then would be incomplete without a discussion of the library and suggestions to encourage children, parents, and teachers to take advantage of the many quality books, materials, and activities available. The strategies described in this section will help you familiarize students with their local public library and the school library. Suggestions are also included to facilitate the planning and implementation of a classroom library.

THE PUBLIC LIBRARY

The public library is a source of tremendous opportunities for children. In addition to making thousands of books available to them, public libraries host puppet shows, storytelling hours, travel documentaries, guest speakers, movies based on literature, and a vast variety of activities that are designed to educate, inform, and entertain—and all for free!

The following activities will help students, and their parents, become familiar with their local libraries:

1. *It's all happening . . . at the library.* What does your public library offer? Involve students in a "fact-finding mission" to learn what activities and events their local library hosts. Have stu-

dents advertise monthly events through a school newsletter, announcements, and "billboards."

2. *Calendar of events*. Select students each month to create a Calendar of Library Events bulletin board. Select a strategic location for the bulletin board, such as the cafeteria, so that all students will be sure to see it. Copies of the calendar can be sent home for parents as well. Encourage students to evaluate the activities and select those events that they would like to attend.

3. *Library field trip*. Arrange a tour of the local public library. The tour should include an explanation of the organization of the library and procedures for checking out materials. Allow time for children to browse through the aisles of books, searching for those that capture their interest. If a child is having difficulty finding a book, have previously completed interest inventories handy (see page 162) so that you can recommend appropriate materials.

To check out books, students will need their own library card. Most libraries require that parents of minors fill out and sign a special form since the parent is ultimately responsible for anything borrowed from the library. Before the field trip, determine what procedures your library follows, and send parents appropriate forms to be completed if their child does not have a library card.

4. *Scavenger hunt*. Prepare a scavenger hunt (appropriate for your students' abilities) that asks students to locate certain materials in the library. Divide students into teams, and award points for each item, with those items that are more difficult to find being worth more points. At the end of the time limit, determine which group has earned the most points. Allow groups to discuss what they found and how they went about finding each item. A scavenger hunt for grades 3–6 might take the following form:

SCAVENGER HUNT

Directions: You and your team members have 30 minutes to
locate the following items. Find as many of these items as
you can.

A book for young children on colors	2 points
A nonfiction book on space	5 points
A mystery book for children who are your age	5 points
A book with maps of different countries	10 points
A magazine on the subject of science	5 points
A book that gives information about your state	5 points
A volume of a general encyclopedia	3 points
A biography of a famous artist	10 points
A volume of the *Readers' Guide to Periodical Literature*	10 points
A record, filmstrip, or cassette tape on any subject	5 points

Total Possible Points: 60

---

5. *Guest librarians.* Invite local librarians to your classroom
for a "story-sharing session" to introduce students to specific
books, either on a selected theme or that are new to the library.

THE SCHOOL LIBRARY

The school library is another excellent source of good
literature. The library will seem more accessible to students as
they become familiar with its organization and adept at locating
specific works. As students become more comfortable with
using the library, they will visit it more regularly, searching both
for recreational reading materials and for materials to help them
fulfill specific assignments.

The following activities will aid students in using their school libraries:

1. *Library play.* After learning about the organization of the library and the Dewey Decimal Classification System, have students create a play that will introduce other students to the library and to the variety of books that can be found there. For example, they can design sandwich boards decorated with the number of a certain section of books and with pictures representative of that section. Then, as that section, they can tell about themselves in prose or poem. The student introducing section 800–899 might say the following:

For books that take you back in time,
To ages long ago,
The 800 section of the library
Is the place for you to go.

For books on travel to places
You've always wanted to see,
For books on History and Geography,
The 800s is the place to be.

LIBRARY CHECKLIST

Directions: Using the list below, locate those reference works that are available. As you find each of the materials, place a check to the left of the appropriate item. On the line following each resource, indicate its location in the library.

☐ Card catalog _____

☐ Dictionary _____

☐ Encyclopedia _____

☐ Familiar quotations _____

☐ First facts _____

☐ Thesaurus _____

☐ World almanac _____

☐ World atlas _____

☐ *Current Biography Yearbook* _____

☐ *Readers' Guide to Periodical Literature* _____

☐ *Twentieth Century Authors* _____

☐ *Webster's Biographical Dictionary* _____

☐ *Who's Who in America* _____

☐ Newspapers _____

☐ Magazines _____

☐ Microfilm _____

☐ Filmstrips _____

☐ Cassette tapes/records _____

☐ Photograph file _____

2. *Library checklist.* Distribute the checklist on page 256. Have students visit the library to discover which of these items are available. Students can then compare the school library to the local public library to determine which library has more appropriate materials for them, which library has a greater variety of materials, which library is easier to use and why.

3. *Where in the library am I?* Involve students in a library version of hide-and-seek. Hide several objects around the library and give students clues that will help them locate the objects and at the same time become more familiar with the materials in the library. For example:

> If you're searching for an outer-space book,
> This is the place that you should first look.
> (card catalog under "space")

Depending on their ability, students can create their own clues for classmates to solve.

4. *Magical library tour.* Have students develop their own maps of the school library, and then lead a tour of the library, pointing out the special places and materials they've indicated on their maps. Copies of the maps can be distributed to students on the library tour. Special times can be set aside for the tour, and teachers can make tour reservations for their classes or for individual students.

5. *Story hour.* Establish a Story Hour, a read-aloud program in which you select students to read to younger students. Give the reader an opportunity to select the material for the Story Hour, making sure that it is appropriate for the youngsters who will attend. A flier advertising the Story Hour and the book being read can be written and distributed weekly to teachers of the targeted age group. Encourage students to read their own published works as well as the works of well-known authors.

THE CLASSROOM LIBRARY

Children should be surrounded daily by good books. The classroom library is the perfect place to house all types of reading material, from classics to children's own published works, from national periodicals to local newspapers. A room filled with a variety of exciting books and an adult who encourages students to read is the perfect combination for creating an atmosphere that nurtures a love of reading.

The following activities will aid you and your students in organizing a classroom library:

1. *Collecting reading materials*. Materials can be gathered for the classroom library in many ways:

   a. Book fairs: Plan and hold a Book Fair. Many publishing companies, local children's bookstores, and local book companies will help set up and stock a book fair. Consult the yellow pages in the telephone directory for such companies. Often the companies will, based on the percentage of sales, give the school either books or money to purchase books for the classroom library.

      Book fairs can be much more than simply a display of books. They can involve the entire school family: faculty, students, friends, and relatives. For example, invite storytellers (parents, grandparents, etc.), local authors and student authors to speak about books they've written, or "storybook characters" to greet students; display student-created book advertisements, bookcovers, book reviews; provide donated food items that represent certain books or book characters, such as Curious George Frozen Bananas and Babar the Elephant Peanut Butter Cookies.

   b. Encourage parents and relatives to donate books and magazines. Place a sticker inside each book with the name of the person who donated the book and the person in whose name the book was donated. In this way, the book will serve as a lasting tribute.

THIS BOOK IS DONATED IN HONOR OF

_____

By _____

Date _____

c. Organize a traveling library in which classrooms can share books. Each classroom can select a variety of books from their collection to be included in the traveling library. These books can be kept in a large plastic bin to allow for easy access and ease in transport. Label each book in the traveling library with a classroom-identification mark and put a cardholder in the back of the book, so that the book can be checked out just as in the regular library. Members of the participating classrooms should establish rules for the traveling library.

d. Most public libraries allow classroom teachers to check out a substantial number of books at one time. Take advantage of this, so that you can add to the classroom library every few weeks.

e. Collect a variety of reading materials from various sources. Brochures can be collected from travel and governmental agencies. Student volunteers can take turns bringing in the daily newspaper and weekly magazines.

f. Provide the necessary information for those students who would like to take part in book clubs. Several companies have book clubs through which students can purchase books at discounted prices. These companies include (1) Arrow Scholastic Book Club, Scholastic Book Club, Inc., Jefferson City, Missouri 65102; (2) Troll Book Clubs, 320 Route 17, Mahway, New Jersey 07430; and (3) Trumpet Club, P.O. Box 604, Holmes, Pennsylvania 19043. Bonus points are awarded for each book ordered; these points can be accumulated and used to select books for the classroom library.

g. Include any books written by students. This reinforces the importance placed on their reading *and* their writing.

2. *Organizing your library.* As with any library, the classroom library must be organized so that students can locate books easily and efficiently. As books are collected, fill out and file three cards—Subject, Title, and Author—for each book. Older students can help with this procedure, using the school library's card catalog for help in setting up the cards. Cards can be alphabetized in boxes (i.e., shoe boxes) or in a Rolodex.

Give the books call numbers just as in the regular library.

Fiction books are coded with an *F* for fiction and the first letter of the author's last name. Biographies are coded with a *B* and the first letter of the subject's last name. Nonfiction books are organized according to the Dewey Decimal Classification System. Place a sticker with the book's call number on the bottom of the book's spine. You can also put different-colored pieces of tape on the spine to indicate genres; this procedure will make classifying and shelving the books easier.

OWL MOON

F

Yol

Yolen, Jane

Name	Date Out	Date Due

3. *Checking out books.* Ask your school librarian to help you obtain cardholders. Have students decorate them, and then attach one to the end page of each book. Place a card, containing the author and the title, in the cardholder. Remember to leave room on the card for the name of the student checking out the book, the date the book is checked out, and the date it is returned. The book card on page 260 provides a sample for you to use.

When a book is checked out, stamp both the card and the cardholder with the date the book is due. Have the class establish rules for dealing with late, lost, and damaged books. Teach students the procedure for checking out books, and show them how the books are organized. Schedule specific times when students are permitted to check out books, and post these times to avoid confusion. Each month, select student librarians who are responsible for helping students locate and check out books, as well as for shelving books that have been returned.

4. *Setting up the classroom library.* Place bookshelves in an easily accessible area of the classroom. Shelves should be labeled so that there is a place for fiction, biographies, and nonfiction. An area should also be established for materials such as newspapers, periodicals, and reference books.

A special reading area can be decorated and furnished with large pillows and carpeting so that students can get comfortable as they become engrossed in their reading. A "reading room" such as the "Green Dragon Castle" can be constructed using refrigerator cartons and lots of imagination. The reading room can be changed throughout the year to reflect the themes being studied or different genres.

13

Reaching Beyond the Classroom: Parent Involvement in Reading

In most cases, the parent is the first and most important teacher a child will ever have. The parents, not professional educators, teach many of the important basic skills. Try to imagine what life would be like today if you knew only what you had been taught in school? Most likely, you learned many of the important lessons of life from a parent or guardian, not from a teacher.

As the poem "Unity" so beautifully illustrates, success can be achieved when the teacher and parents work together.

Unity

I dreamed I stood in a studio
and watched two sculptors there.
The clay they used was a young child's mind,
And they fashioned it with care.
One was a teacher; the tools he used
Were books, and music, and art;
One, a parent with a guiding hand,
And a gentle, loving heart.
Day after day the teacher toiled,
With touch that was deft and sure
While the parents labored by his side
And polished and smoothed it o'er.
And when at last their task was done,
They were proud of what they had wrought.
For this thing they had molded in the child
Could neither be sold nor bought.
And each agreed he would have failed
If he had worked alone,
For behind the parent stood the school
And behind the teacher, the home.

Author Unknown

The significance of "Unity"—the teacher and parents sharing the responsibility of educating a child—is recognized by many researchers. For example, Iverson, Brownlee, and Walberg (1981) found that parent–teacher contact with the goal of providing at-home reading instruction resulted in significant gains in reading. Tizard, Schofield, and Hewison (1982) found that children whose parents listened to them read at home had markedly higher reading attainment at ages seven and eight than children who did not receive support.

In the Commission on Reading's report *Becoming a Nation of Readers* (1985), leading experts presented the following interpretations of the current knowledge and research on parents and reading:

- "The single most important activity for building the knowledge required for eventual success in reading is reading aloud to children."

- "Research shows that parents of successful readers have a more accurate view of their children's performance."

- "Most children will learn how to read. Whether they will read depends in part upon encouragement from their parents. Several researchers recently studied the amount of reading that middle-grade students do at home. Those who read a lot show larger gains on reading achievement tests. They tend to come from homes in which there are plenty of books, or opportunities to visit the library, and in which parents and brothers and sisters also read."

- "The more knowledge children are able to acquire at home, the greater their chance for success in reading."

- "Wide experience alone is not enough, however. The way in which parents talk to their children about an experience influences what knowledge the children will gain from the experience and their later ability to draw on the knowledge when reading."

- "A long-term study that followed children from age one to seven found that the content and style of the language parents used with their children predicted the children's school achievement in reading."

If parent involvement is so important, why aren't more parents involved? The answer to this question varies. First, many parents feel inadequate in terms of their qualifications to help with academics. Second, more women than ever before are working outside the home, therefore many parents simply do not have time to become involved with their children's education. Third, some parents feel that the school and the teacher are responsible for educating their child. Finally, there are those few parents who do not want to be involved in the education of their child. They simply are not interested!

LETTERS TO PARENTS

If parents are reluctant to become involved in their children's education, you need to help them overcome this reluctance. One approach is to develop a way in which they can feel successful in their endeavors with their children. To do this, you must provide specific tasks that all parents can accomplish. These tasks should be stated in a clear, concise manner and the parent should feel comfortable about doing them. In addition to providing activities, giving feedback to the parent is essential. The parent needs to know if what he or she is doing is indeed correct. When possible, communicate with the parent about specific progress the child is making as a result of the parent's extra help or interest. Also, when a parent does something for the child or the class, express your appreciation by sending a thank-you note or by calling and saying thank you.

The checklist on page 267 can help parents evaluate their reading involvement with their child. This checklist will also help parents discover activities to do with their children. You can adapt the parent letters on pages 268–274 to fit the specific needs of your class in terms of age, ability, curriculum, and so on. The letters provide guidelines to assist parents in creating quality reading time with their children.

Dear Parents,

The following checklist provides activities that encourage listening, speaking, reading, and writing. Using the following scale, rate yourself on each of the statements:

Sincerely,

1	2	3
Never	Sometimes	Frequently

_____ I listen to my child and answer his or her questions.

_____ I make time each day to talk with my child.

_____ My child and I go to the library and select books.

_____ I show my child that reading is important by reading books, magazines, newspapers, and so on.

_____ My child and I talk about books, magazines, or other things that we have read.

_____ I read aloud to my child.

_____ I limit TV viewing so that there is at least equal time for reading.

_____ I write messages to my child and encourage return messages in whatever form he or she chooses.

_____ I give and suggest reading and writing materials as gifts for my child.

Dear Parents,

Reading to your child regularly is very important in developing his or her ability to read and in fostering a love for reading. The following guidelines are important for making the reading time profitable and enjoyable for both of you. So sit back, relax, and enjoy a good book with your child!

Sincerely,

1. Select from a variety of books that reflect your child's interests.

2. Try to set aside a "special" time each day for a story, maybe at bedtime, naptime, or after dinner.

3. Find a quiet, comfortable place to read.

4. Ask a few prereading discussion questions, such as: "Look at the cover. What do you think this book might be about?"

5. Be sure your child can see the illustrations as you read.

6. Read with expression. Gestures, sound effects, and voice inflections add interest to many books.

7. Encourage your child to participate in the reading when appropriate.

8. The main objective of reading to your child is to provide an opportunity to relax and enjoy the magic of good literature. However, a few appropriate questions can enhance your child's comprehension and interest. The following questions can serve as a guide:

    Which character would you most like to be friends with?

    How would you change the ending of the story?

    How would the story be different if it took place at a different time or place?

    Compare this story with other stories we have read on the same subject or other books written by the same author.

9. Stop at strategic points and discuss what your child thinks will happen next.

10. When the book is finished, allow your child to respond in some way. This might be done by making an illustration of a favorite character or part of the book or by making a puppet to role-play the story.

Most teachers are required to do a weekly lesson plan. Using this plan, send a letter like the following one to the parents each Friday that outlines what you are planning to do during the following week and ways in which the parent can assist their child or you in the classroom.

Dear Parents,
This will be the first of a series of weekly newsletters informing you of what is happening in our class. Please use this information to talk with your child about the day's activities or to practice some of them at home.

Monday's curriculum will include reading Tana Hoban's *Is It Red? Is It Yellow? Is It Blue?* Then we will finish our tree pictures (coloring the tree trunks brown and the leaves green). We will put together puzzles that require matching colors (red, yellow, blue). In the afternoon, we'll review the numerals 1, 2, and 3 by playing a game where the children must follow one-, two-, or three-part commands in the right order: First, go to the back of the room; second, turn around; and third, jump up in the air!

Ideas for home:
1. Visit your local library and get other color- or number-related books such as *Colors* by John Reiss or Eric Carle's *Count-Up*. Read these books with your child and discuss the concepts presented.
2. As you and your child do routine chores around the house, count the knives, forks, and spoons that you put on the table. Or talk about colors of the dishes, glasses, towels, drapes, or clothes. You could also play a game "I Spy" by saying, "I spy something that is red." Let the child guess what you are thinking of. He or she can then give the "I spy" statement.
3. Provide your child with plenty of crayons, pencils, and paper. Encourage your child to draw a certain number of a familiar item and then make each one a particular color. (P.S. I'd love to see the finished product!)

On *Tuesday* we will write our own stories about colors. Each child will construct a sentence in which he or she names the color of something he or she is wearing: "My name is John, and I am wearing a yellow shirt." "My name is Sally, and my socks are pink." Once the story is written, we will read it aloud together and each child will make an illustration to go along with his or her sentence. Next, using color pattern cards, the children will sort beads and string them according to the colors on the cards. To help in developing the fine motor control that is so important for writing, the children will do an activity that involves putting on and taking off bottle tops and jar tops. In the afternoon, the children will sing about colors. Their favorite song is Hap Palmer's "Colors."

Ideas for home:

1. Put 1/2 cup of macaroni in a small covered container. Add 1/4 teaspoon of food coloring and a few drops of alcohol, shake well, and pour onto a sheet of newspaper to dry. Follow the same procedure to make at least three different colors of macaroni. When the macaroni is dry, ask your child to sort the macaroni by color. When finished with the sorting activity, string the macaroni using a large needle with thread. The macaroni can be strung following a color pattern (i.e., 1 blue, 1 red, 1 yellow). When completed, the ends of the thread can be tied together to make a necklace or bracelet.
2. Sit down with your child in a particular room of the house. Tell your child to tell you sentences in which he or she names an item and its color (i.e., The chair is blue). As the child tells you the sentence, write it down. When he or she is finished, read the sentences together. As an additional activity, your child could draw and color items to match each of the sentences. Later the sentences could be cut apart and pasted onto each picture. The pages could then be stapled together to make a book.

Sincerely,

(*Note:* Continue this outline for the entire week.)

Dear Parent,

The attached monthly calendar provides you with literature-based activities that you and your child can enjoy. Display this calendar in a conspicuous place and make it part of your daily routine to do as many of the activities with your child as possible. Enjoy!

Sincerely,

Send a monthly calendar (pages 273 and 274) to the parents that suggests specific daily literature-related activities for the child that reinforce the objectives of the school program. To gather information for calendars and to find out about events that are free or available at a nominal fee, check TV guides, read local newspapers, and get schedules of activities from museums and libraries.

**LITERATURE
AND THE
READING PROGRAM**

FEBRUARY

1	2	3	4	5	6	7
Take your child to the library and check out books for you and your child to read.	Read a story to your child, stopping now and then, allowing him to predict what will happen next.	Read a story to your child and ask her to illustrate a favorite character.	Storytelling hour at the public library; 4:00–5:00 P.M. Take your child.	Read headlines or a favorite cartoon from the newspaper. Point to the print as you read.	Help your child decorate his bedroom door like a favorite bookcover or character.	Buy an inexpensive cassette tape. Make a tape of a favorite story and play it in the car.

8	9	10	11	12	13	14
Staple together writing paper, with a construction paper cover. Title it "Books I Have Read." Encourage your child to keep a record of the books and authors read.	Take your child to the exhibition of Dr. Seuss books and related materials at the Children's Youth Museum: 6:00–8:00 P.M., Feb. 9–Feb 16.	Ask your child to tell you a story. Write exactly what she says. Reread the story together.	Prepare a special place for your child to keep his books (i.e. bookshelves, cardboard box, drawer).	PBS showing of *The Reluctant Dragon:* 7:00–8:00 P.M. Watch this show with your child.	Find *The Reluctant Dragon* by Kenneth Grahame at the library, and other related dragon books, such as *Alexander and the Dragon* by Katherine Holabird. Read.	Read your child your favorite story from childhood and tell why it is your favorite childhood book.

REACHING BEYOND
THE CLASSROOM:
PARENT INVOLVEMENT
IN READING

15	16	17	18	19	20	21
Invite another member of the family (i.e. father, brother, sister, to join you during your reading time).	Provide modeling clay for your child. Ask her to make a replica of her favorite character or scene.	Help your child write a letter to a friend telling him why he should read a particular book.	Storytelling hour at the public library: 4:00–5:00 P.M. Take your child.	Provide your child with paper, pencil, crayons, etc. Discuss what a bookmarker is and help your child make one.	Discuss TV commercials with your child, then help your child make up a commercial for his favorite book. Write it down or illustrate it.	Read a story to your child. Ask her to illustrate her favorite part of the story.
22	**23**	**24**	**25**	**26**	**27**	**28**
Watch the PBS showing *Sleeping Princess*, 7:00–8:00 P.M., with your child.	Get the book *Sleeping Princess* from the library, as well as other related books, such as *The Sleeping Beauty* by Brothers Grimm. Read.	Read a book with several characters, then ask your child to role-play one of them. You guess the character. Switch roles.	"Puppet Show" at the public library: 4:00–5:00 P.M.	Help your child make a simple paper-bag puppet using paper bag, yarn, construction paper, crayons, etc.	Using a large brown paper grocery bag, help your child make a costume representing a character from a book. Have your child wear this costume and pretend to be the character.	Read a book with your child. When you are finished, ask your child to think of a different ending.

It is important to involve not only mothers and fathers in the education of their child, but also grandparents, aunts, uncles, and other relatives. This can be done by declaring a particular month as "Visitor Reading Month." Send the letter on page 276 home inviting members of each family to be involved in the "Visitor Reading Month."

Once the forms are returned, make a schedule of visitors and send it home with the child. It is a good idea to follow up with a phone call, at least two days before the visitor's presentation, to confirm the time and date and to ask if any assistance is needed.

OTHER ACTIVITIES

In addition to the letters, the following activities that involve parents, and the community as well, can be initiated.

1. Have a "Picnic Reading Day." Invite family members to come on a particular day at a specific time, and request that the children and family members pack a picnic lunch. In addition, ask each child to select several books that he or she would like to have read. At the designated time, the family members join the child for a picnic lunch as they read the book(s) together. If some children do not have a family member at the picnic, invite them to join other children and their family members.

2. Conduct a Read-a-Thon—a whole day to read! Have students bring pillows, blankets, and books from home. If weather permits, they can read outdoors, as well as in the classroom. Ask for parent volunteers to help supervise.

3. Invite parents and other interested people to "An Author's Night" to celebrate the young authors in the class. This could be combined with a potluck or dessert feast. Ask each child to read something he or she has written to the very appreciative audience.

4. Schools with lower-income families can participate in Reading Is Fundamental programs in which each child is given a free book. For more information, contact Reading Is Fundamental, 600 Maryland Avenue S.W. 1, Suite 500, Washington, D.C. 20560, (202) 287-3220.

5. Pizza Hut, Inc., sponsors an excellent reading incentive program called Book It! For more information, contact The Book It Program, c/o Pizza Hut, Inc., P.O. Box 428, Wichita, Kansas 67201-0428, (800) 4-BOOK-IT.

Dear Parent,

This is "Visitor Reading Month" in our classroom, and we would like to invite someone from your family to participate. Mothers, fathers, grandparents, uncles, aunts, and cousins are invited. A checklist of activities you might like to do during your visit, along with a choice of days and times, is provided below. Please complete and return to me by _____ . We are looking forward to having a member of your family with us during "Visitor Reading Month."

                                    Sincerely,

— — — — — — — — — — — — — — — — —

I _____ would like to participate in "Visitor's
        name
Reading Month."

I will be happy to:

_____ select a book and read it aloud to the class.

_____ take a group of children to the school library.

_____ monitor the classroom library and assist students as needed.

_____ assist students with writing projects.

_____ tell a favorite story.

Other _____

Choice of day   Choice of time

_____   _____ 9:00 – 10:00 A.M.

_____   _____ 10:00 – 11:00 A.M.

_____   _____ 1:30 – 2:30 P.M.

                                  Other _____

Signature: _____

Relationship _____

6. At Back to School Night, take time to explain the reading and writing program to the parents. This opportunity can help alleviate problems and misunderstandings that might occur later. Educate the parents about the research that supports the methods being used. Finally, recruit parents who will volunteer, on a regular basis, to listen to the children read and to read to the children.

SUGGESTED BOOKS FOR CHILDREN

Carle, Eric. *Count-Up*. Philomel, 1984.
Hoban, Tana. *Is It Red? Is It Yellow? Is It Blue?* Greenwillow, 1978.
Reiss, John. *Colors*. Bradbury, 1969.

REFERENCES

Anderson, R. C., E. H. Hiebert, J. A. Scott, and I. Wilkinson. *Becoming a Nation of Readers: The Report of the Commission on Reading*. Washington, D.C.: National Institute of Education, 1985.

Iverson, B. K., G. D. Brownlee, and H. J. Walberg. "Parent-Teacher Contacts and Student Learning." *Journal of Educational Research 74,6* (July/August 1981): 394–396.

Tizard, J., W. N. Schofield, and J. Hewison. "Collaboration Between Teachers and Parents in Assisting Children's Reading." *British Journal of Educational Psychology 17* (February 1982): 509–514.

CONNECTIONS

Affective Response to Literature

Literature for Critical and Creative Thinking

**The Reading-Writing Connection:
Writing Process Approach
Language Experience Approach**

**Literature and the Curriculum —
A Thematic Approach**

LITERATURE AND THE READING PROGRAM

Strategies for Reading

Literature and the Basal Reading Program: Extending the Basal Literature-Based Materials

A Model for Literature-Based Reading Programs

Using the Library

Reaching Beyond the Classroom: Parent Involvement

THE LITERATURE CONNECTION

DEVELOPING INTEREST IN READING

The Read-Aloud Program

Shared Reading

Sustained Silent Reading

Storytelling

Extending and Sharing Literature

GENRES AND ELEMENTS

**Exploring Genres:
Picture Books, Realistic Fiction,
Historical Fiction,
Fantasy/Science Fiction,
Traditional Literature, Poetry,
Informational Books, Biographies**

**Analyzing Elements:
Characterization, Plot,
Setting, Theme, Point of View,
Evaluating Genres and Their
Elements**

Involving Students in Selecting Genres

P A R T F O U R

CONNECTIONS

Literature is a reflection of life, and as such, its benefits extend far beyond the scope of the reading program. Part IV of *The Literature Connection* illustrates ways to incorporate literature throughout the curriculum as the heart of an integrated approach to learning. This approach directly coincides with whole language, a philosophy in which children become totally immersed in all aspects of language. "Whole language surrounds children with literature. . . . It enriches children's lives with a tremendous variety of experiences and enables children to enjoy those experiences as if they were participants. It uses excellent form and written expression and is relevant to children's interest and needs . . ." (Brountas, 1987). Through a whole-language philosophy, all aspects of language are taught developmentally. Writing, reading, speaking, and listening are not taught as isolated contents, nor are their implicit skills taught in isolated lessons. Instead, these aspects of language are integrated through various approaches, many of which will be described in this section of *The Literature Connection* and many of which were described earlier, such as reading aloud, shared reading, Sustained Silent Reading, storytelling, and activities for sharing literature. It is important to remember that a well-balanced curriculum includes using many such approaches. Children benefit in different ways from different kinds of reading experiences.

From the time words were first printed, people realized that books had the ability to affect thoughts and feelings. Therefore, literature is the perfect vehicle through which children can increase their knowledge of themselves, gain confidence, clarify values, and better understand and relate to others. Through reading children can identify with book characters, empathize with their situations, and discover ways to deal with their own problems, as well as learn more about themselves and the world in which they live. Chapter 14, "Affective Response to Literature," introduces a variety of topics, including friendship, prejudice, handicaps, strengths and weaknesses, fears, and life changes, along with related works of literature and activities that allow children the opportunity to explore each topic. "As students discuss their feelings with one another as well as read about problems similar to the ones they are experiencing, they will begin to realize that their problems are not unique and that they certainly are not alone. As they discover how others handled similar situations, they may gain insight into their own problems—insight which will aid them in the choices they will ultimately have to make!" (Meinbach and Rothlein, 1989, vi).

A fundamental element that underlies the use of literature is critical and creative thinking. Children react to what is being read; they analyze, organize their thoughts, make their own connections, and respond in oral and written form. Chapter 15 describes strategies and models that have been successful in fostering critical and creative thinking and presents a framework that can be adapted to any work of literature to promote and extend students' thinking skills. The latter part of the chapter illustrates the ways in which each strategy can be used in conjunction with a specific work of literature.

Reading and writing are closely related skills; each is a catalyst for the other. Literature stimulates students to write in journals, create new endings to classics, change pivotal sections of books to create new scenarios, react to ideas, explore feelings stimulated by a reading, and experiment with style as they use literary works as models for their own writing. Two methods that link reading and writing are the Writing Process and Language Experience. Both approaches, described in Chapter 16, are important in the acquisition of language skills and enhance a literature-based program.

Chapter 17 details the development of thematic units in order to expose students to a variety of reading sources, to extend their interests, to arouse their curiosity, to provide opportunities to uncover discrepancies in information, and to stimulate a desire to learn more. No matter what the concept or idea being explored, there are usually excellent examples of literature on the same subject. Four sample thematic units are provided.

Regardless of the label we assign to the use of literature in the classroom, the main ingredient for success is the use of real reading and real writing for real-life purposes. As a result, we bring the beauty of the written word to the forefront and empower students in the selection of words that will give meaning to their ideas and allow them to express new ideas and create new images.

REFERENCES

Brountas, Marie. "Whole Language Really Works." *Teaching K–8*, November–December 1987, pp. 57–60.

Meinbach, Anita M., and Liz Rothlein. *Circles and Square Pegs: Activities and Literature to Help Children Accept Self, Others and Change.* Hawthorne, N.J.: Educational Impressions, 1989.

14

Affective Response to Literature

Benjamin S. Bloom (1956) and several associates developed a taxonomy of educational objectives that they classified into three domains: cognitive, affective, and psychomotor. The cognitive domain deals with general types of learning, including concepts, principles, verbal association, and problem solving. The affective domain relates to attitudes and values. The psychomotor domain refers to skill development in areas such as fine motor development, eye–hand coordination, and so on.

Although all three domains can be developed through the use of children's literature, this method has been found to be especially effective in developing the affective domain (Krathwohl et al., 1964). In many books the main character has the same social or emotional problem as the reader, and often the reader identifies so closely with the character that he or she is able to successfully solve his or her own problem or crisis. S. S. Dreyer's *The Bookfinder* (1985) provides an annotated bibliography of books, by topic, that are useful in helping children adjust socially and emotionally.

BIBLIOTHERAPY

The term *bibliotherapy* was coined in the early 1900s to identify printed materials that influence the way people think and feel and help them solve problems. Much research has been done in the area of bibliotherapy, and its use in the school curriculum has become more popular over the years.

In *The Bookfinder* (1985), S. S. Dreyer identifies three main steps in the process of bibliotherapy:

1. *Universalization.* Through reading, children learn that they are not the only ones with certain fears or problems. They are

able to see themselves in various characters. They may also see similarities between and among book characters and their family or friends.

2. *Catharsis*. By identifying with certain characters, children can empathize with situations and discover ways to deal with their own problems or fears.

3. *Insight*. Through reading, children may learn more about themselves and others and the world around them.

ACTIVITIES

The following activities will provide students with an opportunity to read and react to selected books that may help them deal with a variety of emotions or conflicts and better understand themselves and others.

Looking Different

Many students may feel that they are not as beautiful or handsome as they would like to be, and some may develop a complex about their appearance. Either read aloud or provide the following books for students to read.

The Ugly Duckling, by Hans Christian Andersen

Freckle Juice, by Judy Blume

The Snow Goose, by Paul Gallico

After reading the book(s), ask the following questions and complete the activity.

1. What problem did the main character have?

2. How did the main character deal with the problem?

3. Do you agree with the way the main character dealt with the problem?

4. What other ways might this character have dealt with the problem?

Collect pictures of people with different appearances by cutting them out of magazines or taking photos of your own. For example, collect pictures of people who are tall, short, thin, or heavy; people who wear glasses, have freckles, large noses, button noses; and so forth. Make a collage of these pictures and then write a poem or short story that reflects your feelings about the differences in appearance that you see in your collage. For example,

People

Tall people, short people,
    Thin people, fat;
    Lady so dainty
    Wearing a hat.
Straight people, dumpy people,
    Man dressed in brown,
    Baby in buggy,
    These make a town.

Author unknown

Success/Failure

Read *The One in the Middle Is the Green Kangaroo*, by Judy Blume. Then ask the students to pretend they are Freddy Dissel, the middle child in the family, who finds success as he plays the part of the Green Kangaroo in a school play and thus develops his individuality. Next, ask the students to write a journal entry that Freddy could have written to describe his successes and failures. Finally, ask them to each write about one success they have had and then share their successes with the class.

Friendship

Read *Charlotte's Web*, a beautifully written book about the friendship between Wilbur the pig and Charlotte the spider. Identify, list, and discuss the qualities that Charlotte possessed that made her such a good friend. Keeping these qualities in mind, ask the students to complete the following:

1. If you could see friendship, what color would it be? _____

_____

Why? _____

2. What type of animal best represents friendship? _____

_____

Why? _____

3. If friendship were a shape, what shape would it be? _____

_____

Why? _____

4. What would friendship sound like? _____

_____

Why? _____
Finally, ask the students to draw a picture depicting what friendship would look like.

Getting Along
After reading *Ramona the Pest*, by Beverly Cleary, ask the students to write a letter to Ramona suggesting how she might handle some of the situations differently than she did in the book so that people wouldn't consider her such a pest.

Insecurity/Self-Confidence
Some students may feel insecure and lack self-confidence because they think they are too big or too little. Read *The Runt of Rodgers School*, by Harold Verne Keith (ages 9–12), or *The Smallest Boy in the Class*, by Jerrold Beim (ages 5–8). Then, as a group, complete the following:
1. List famous people who may be considered too big—either too heavy or too tall. Summarize their accomplishments.
People   *Accomplishments*

_____   _____

_____   _____

_____   _____

2. List famous people who may be considered too small—either too thin or too short. Summarize their accomplishments.
People   *Accomplishments*

_____   _____

_____   _____

_____   _____

3. Finally, discuss whether the body size of the people listed interfered with or aided them in their accomplishments and explain why.

Individual Strengths and Weaknesses

In *The Secret Garden*, by Frances Hodgson Burnett, Mary, one of the main characters, has some good as well as some bad qualities. Ask the students to read the book and then list Mary's strengths and good qualities. Finally, tell them to write a testimonial speech about Mary citing these special qualities.

Stereotypes

After reading *Little House in the Big Woods*, by Laura Ingalls Wilder, discuss the specific roles or jobs that the men and boys assumed and those that the women and girls assumed. In other words, the men and boys were expected to behave in certain ways, as were the women and girls. After this discussion, ask students to complete the following activity, based on current expectations of boys and girls.
1. List five expectations for boys and five expectations for girls.
2. Analyze the expectations listed for your own gender and tell how well you follow those expectations. Explain.
3. Should you follow these expectations? Why or why not?
4. Do you want to follow these expectations. Why or why not?
5. In your opinion, is following these expectations important or not? Explain.

Death

An *obituary* is a published death notice, whereas a *eulogy* is a speech honoring a person and is often delivered at the funeral. Things that are worth remembering about the deceased make up the eulogy.

In *Bridge to Terabithia*, by Katherine Paterson, Leslie Burke has an accident and is killed. After reading the book, ask the students to complete the following:
1. Think of ten good things that are worth remembering about Leslie Burke and write them down.
2. Using the ten good things worth remembering about Leslie, create a eulogy that could be delivered at her funeral.

Fears

In *Call It Courage*, by Armstrong Sperry, Mafatu felt like a coward until he proved to himself that he could do things that required courage. After reading this book, ask the students to each describe a time when they felt they lacked courage to do something. Finally, ask each student to read the following letter and complete the worksheet on Problem-Solving Steps on page 290.

July 22, 1989

Dear Advice Columnist,

I am nine years old and I don't know what to do or who to go to for help. I feel like such a failure because I can't live up to the expectations of being an island chief's son. I am supposed to be brave, but I am not! I am afraid of the sea because it killed my mother when I was a baby, and yet I live on this seafaring island where the people worship courage. People call me a coward. I even heard my best friend, Kana, call me a coward, and now I feel as if I have no friends. Please tell me what I can do.

Signed,

The Coward

PROBLEM-SOLVING STEPS

Pretend that you are an advice columnist for your school newspaper. You have received a letter from The Coward and must respond to it. Before you give your response, complete the problem-solving steps listed. Then plan and write your response.

1. Underline key words and phrases in the letter that help you understand the problems.

2. Identify the problems from the letter.

   _____

   _____

3. Select what you believe to be the major problem and write a problem statement for it by completing the following: "In what ways might I help The Coward to . . .

   _____

   _____

4. Think of as many solutions as you can to solve the problem stated in Step 3. List these solutions below.

   _____

   _____

   _____

5. Look over the solutions in Step 4, and put a star next to those that would be possible for The Coward to accomplish.

6. Answer the letter from The Coward based on the best possible solutions identified in Step 5.

```
                    July 22, 1989
Dear Coward,

_____

_____

_____

_____

                    Signed,
```

Getting Old

People sometimes have difficulty dealing with the idea of aging parents or grandparents. After reading *How Does It Feel to Be Old*, by Norma Farber, ask the students to think about all the good and bad things suggested in this book about growing old. Make a list on the chalkboard. Next, have the students role-play a situation by having a conversation with the grandmother about the positive side of growing older.

Prejudice/Discrimination

In *Sounder*, by William Armstrong, the father was discriminated against and not given a fair trial because he was a sharecropper. Read the book and describe the prejudice displayed in the book. Discuss whether similar situations occur today.

Read *Navajo Victory: Being a Native American*, by Jane Claypool Miner. Then have the students write an editorial for the local newspaper or school newspaper to support the young teenage Indian boy who was being discriminated against.

Handicaps

Golden Daffodils, by Marilyn Gould, is about Janis, a fifth-grade student who is handicapped because she has cerebral palsy. She is being mainstreamed into a regular classroom. Have students imagine that Janis is going to be coming into your classroom. Ask them to make a list of the changes that could be made in the classroom and the surrounding environment to make life easier. Often changes are not made because there isn't enough money available. Ask students to prepare a two-minute speech to persuade the legislature to use funds to make the changes they feel are necessary.

Many successful people in history have had some type of handicap: Helen Keller, Louis Braille, Franklin D. Roosevelt. Have the students read a biography or autobiography about such a person and then answer the following questions:
1. What obstacles did the person have to overcome?
2. What were his or her contributions?
3. What were his or her important qualities?
4. Did success come easily to the person you read about? Explain.

Life Changes

Changes in life such as divorce, moving, or death are often very difficult to handle. Read one of the following books: *My Mother Is Not Married to My Father*, by Jean Davies Okimoto; *I Don't Live Here!* by Pam Conrad; or *Where the Lilies Bloom*, by Vera Cleaver and Bill Cleaver. Have the students each pretend to be a main character in the book he or she has read. As that character, ask them to write a letter to an advice columnist. Have them give the letter to a friend and ask that person to write a response and return it. When they get the response, compare it with what actually happened in the book.

SUGGESTED BOOKS FOR CHILDREN

Looking Different

Andersen, Hans Christian. *The Ugly Duckling*. Macmillan, 1955.
Blume, Judy Sussman. *Freckle Juice*. Four Winds, 1971.
First, Julia. *Look Who's Beautiful!* Watts, 1980.
Gallico, Paul. *The Snow Goose*. Knopf, 1940.
Landis, James David. *The Sisters Impossible*. Knopf, 1979.

Success/Failure

Avi. *S.O.R. Losers*. Bradbury, 1984.
Blume, Judy Sussman. *The One in the Middle Is the Green Kangaroo*. Bradbury, 1981.

Holl, Krista D. *First Things First*. Atheneum, 1980.
Lord, Bemen. *Rough Ice*. Walck, 1983.
Van Leeuwen, Jean. *Benjy the Bootball Hero*. Dial Books, 1985.

Friendship
Conford, Ellen. *Anything For a Friend*. Little, Brown, 1979.
Fisher, Lois I. *Radio Report*. Dodd, 1985.
Glenn, Mel. *Play-By-Play*. Clarion, 1950.
Moore, Emily. *Just My Luck*. Unicorn, 1982.
Robins, Nancy K. *Veronica the Show Off*. Four Winds, 1981.
White, E. B. *Charlotte's Web*. Harper & Row, 1952.

Getting Along
Cleary, Beverly. *Ramona the Pest*. Illustrated by Louis Darling. Morrow, 1968.
Estes, Eleanor. *The Hundred Dresses*. Illustrated by Louis Slobodkin. Harcourt Brace Jovanovich, 1944.
Miles, Betty. *All It Takes Is Practice*. Knopf, 1976.
Smith, Doris Buchanan. *Laura Upside-Down*. Viking, 1984.
———. *Salted Lemons*. Four Winds, 1980.

Insecurity/Self-Confidence
Beim, Jerrold. *The Smallest Boy in the Class*. Morrow, 1949.
Greene, Bette. *Get on out of Here, Philip Hall*. Dial Books, 1981.
Honeycutt, Natalie. *Invisible Lissa*. Bradbury, 1985.
Hurwitz, Joanna. *Yellow Blue Jay*. Atheneum, 1986.
Keith, Harold Verne. *The Runt of Rodgers School*. Lippincott, 1971.
Manes, Stephen. *Be a Perfect Person in Just Three Days*. Clarion, 1982.

Individual Strengths and Weaknesses
Bachmann, Evelyn Trent. *Tressa*. Viking, 1966.
Burnett, Frances Hodgson. *The Secret Garden*. Illustrated by Tasha Tudor. Lippincott, 1962.
Herman, Charlotte. *Millie Cooper*. Dutton, 1985.
Naylor, Phyllis Reynolds. *Eddie Incorporated*. Atheneum, 1980.
Pfeffer, Susan Beth. *What Do You Do When Your Mouth Won't Open?* Delacorte, 1981.

Stereotypes
Baker, Rachel Mininberg. *The First Woman Doctor: The Story of Elizabeth Blackwell, M.D.* Messner, 1944.
Douglas, Barbara. *Skateboard Scramble*. Westminster, 1979.
Dygard, Thomas J. *Winning Kicker*. Morrow, 1978.

Knudson, R. Rozanne. *Zanbanger*. Harper & Row, 1977.

Wilder, Laura Ingalls. *Little House in the Big Woods*. Illustrated by Garth Williams. Harper & Row, 1953.

Death

Hermes, Patricia. *You Shouldn't Have to Say Goodbye*. Harcourt Brace Jovanovich, 1982.

Little, Jean. *Mama's Going to Buy You a Mockingbird*. Viking, 1984.

Mann, Peggy. *These Are Two Kinds of Terrible*. Doubleday, 1977.

Paterson, Katherine. *Bridge to Terabithia*. Illustrated by Donna Diamond. Thomas Y. Crowell, 1977.

Voigt, Cynthia. *Dicey's Song*. Atheneum, 1983.

Fears

Bachmann, Evelyn Trent. *Tressa*. Viking, 1966.

Dalgliesh, Alice. *The Courage of Sarah Noble*. Illustrated by Leonard Weisgard. Scribner's, 1954.

Sperry, Armstrong. *Call It Courage*. Macmillan, 1968.

Stolz, Mary. *A Dog on Barkham Street*. Illustrated by Leonard Shortall. Harper & Row, 1963.

Weiman, Eiveen. *Which Way Courage?* Atheneum, 1981.

Getting Old

Beckman, Delores. *My Own Private Sky*. Dutton, 1980.

Blue, Rose. *Grandma Didn't Wave Back*. Illustrated by Ted Lewin. Watts, 1972.

Faber, Norma. *How Does It Feel to Be Old?* Illustrated by Trina Schart Hyman. Dutton, 1979.

Lowry, Lois. *Anastasia Again!* Illustrated by Diane de Groat. Houghton Mifflin, 1981.

Mathis, Sharon Bell. *The Hundred Penny Box*. Illustrated by Leo and Diane Dutton. Viking, 1975.

Skorpen, Liesel M. *Grace*. Harper & Row, 1985.

Prejudice/Discrimination

Armstrong, William. *Sounder*. Illustrated by James Barkley. Harper & Row, 1969.

Blue, Rose. *The Preacher's Kid*. Watts, 1975.

Madden, Betsy. *The All-American Coeds*. Criterion, 1971.

Miner, Jane Claypool. *Navajo Victory: Being a Native American*. Crestwood, 1982.

———. *The Tough Guy: Black in a White World*. Crestwood, 1982.

Screen, Robert Martin. *With My Face to the Rising Sun*. Harcourt Brace Jovanovich, 1977.

Sebestyen, Ouida. *Words by Heart*. Little, Brown, 1977.

Taves, Isabella. *Not Bad for a Girl*. Evans, 1972.

Tobias, Tobi. *Arthur Mitchell*. Thomas Y. Crowell, 1975.

Handicaps

Byars, Betsy. *Summer of the Swans*. Viking, 1974.

Davidson, Margaret. *Helen Keller*. Hastings, 1964.

Donovan, Pete. *Carol Johnson: The One-Armed Gymnast*. Children's Press, 1982.

Gould, Marilyn. *Golden Daffodils*. Addison-Wesley, 1982.

Litchfield, Ada. *A Button in Her Ear*. Whitman, 1976.

Mathis, Sharon. *Ray Charles*. Thomas Y. Crowell, 1973.

Peterson, Jeanne. *Claire and Emma*. Day, 1977.

White, Paul. *Janet at School*. Thomas Y. Crowell, 1978; Children's Press, 1982.

Life Changes

Cleary, Beverly. *Dear Mr. Henshaw*. Illustrated by Paul Zelinsky. Morrow, 1983.

Cleaver, Vera, and Bill Cleaver. *Where the Lilies Bloom*. Illustrated by Jim Spanfeller. Lippincott, 1969.

Conrad, Pam. *I Don't Live Here!* Dutton, 1984.

Gordan, Shirley. *The Boy Who Wanted a Family*. Illustrated by Charles Robinson. Harper & Row, 1980.

Mann, Peggy. *My Dad Lives in a Downtown Hotel*. Illustrated by Richard Cuffari. Doubleday, 1973.

Okimoto, Jean Davies. *My Mother Is Not Married to My Father*. Putnam, 1979.

Paterson, Katherine. *The Great Gilly Hopkins*. Thomas Y. Crowell, 1978.

REFERENCES

Bloom, Benjamin S., ed. *Taxonomy of Educational Objectives: Handbook 1: Cognitive Domain*. New York: McKay, 1956.

Dreyer, S. S. *The Bookfinder: A Guide to Children's Literature About the Needs and Problems of Youth Aged 2 and Up*. Circle Pines, Minn.: American Guidance, 1984.

Krathwohl, David R., Benjamin Bloom, and Bertram B. Masia. *Taxonomy of Educational Objectives. Handbook II: Affective Domain*. New York: McKay, 1964.

15

Literature for Critical and Creative Thinking

If one of the main goals of education is to prepare students for the real world, then education should focus on helping them acquire a base of information, skills to acquire additional information, and the ability to process this knowledge to identify problems, formulate alternatives, and arrive at meaningful, thoughtful, effective decisions and solutions. Therefore, skills in critical and creative thinking are vital.

Many definitions have been offered for each of these skills. In general, creative thinking can be defined as a "mental process by which an individual creates new ideas or products, or recombines existing ideas and products, in a fashion that is novel to him or her" (Gallagher, 1985, p. 303). Creativity must be nurtured in an accepting environment where new ideas are encouraged, valued, and discussed freely, without fear of a judgmental teacher or classmates. Creative thinking is enhanced as students react to questions and solve problems that promote divergent responses rather than convergent ones.

Critical thinking has been defined as "reasonable reflective thinking that is focused on deciding what to believe or do" (Ennis, 1985, p. 54). A critical thinker "strives to analyze arguments carefully, looks for valid evidence, and reaches sound conclusions. The goal of critical thinking is to develop people who are fair minded, and objective and committed to clarity and accuracy" (Marzano et al., 1988, p. 18). Learning situations should be based on a variety of issues and current events, and opportunities should be provided for the discussion of these issues. An open, accepting environment is equally important to fostering critical thinking if students are to gain confidence in their ability to draw conclusions and to express them to others.

"People tend to view critical thinking as primarily evaluative and creative thinking as primarily generative. But the two types of thinking are not opposites; they complement each other and even share many attributes" (Marzano et al., 1988, p. 17). Critical and creative thinking work together; both are necessary for successful problem solving and decision making. Once students are skilled in critical and creative thinking, they are more likely to see all the possibilities in a situation, viewing it from many different perspectives. And, once all possibilities are compiled, they will be better prepared to analyze and evaluate each alternative, as well as effectively communicate solutions, findings, and conclusions.

Many strategies or techniques or models have been developed to help facilitate growth in both critical and creative thinking. The strategies described in this chapter are only a sampling of those that can be used in conjunction with literature to help students enhance their critical and creative thinking skills. The strategies provide a framework on which meaningful, extending activities can be built and from which questions can be formulated that ask students to discover those connections relevant to their own lives, and good literature provides an excellent catalyst for thought, causing children to wonder, to dream, and to imagine. Examples of using these strategies with literature appear on pages 310–315.

THINKING MODELS OR STRATEGIES

Shared Inquiry (Junior Great Books)

The Great Books Foundation (1984) established Junior Great Books to provide a liberal arts program for grades 2–12, through the reading and discussion of outstanding literary works. The foundation publishes paperback sets of literary works and offers training courses to prepare and certify teachers and discussion leaders to conduct Great Books groups.

The program is based on a method called *shared inquiry*, through which groups discuss and explore ideas offered by the classics. In shared inquiry, participants discover for themselves certain meanings in the literature, and they must be able to support their views with facts and evidence from the writings. Shared inquiry helps develop critical thinking skills, encourages divergent answers, models an inquiry style of learning, provides a framework for classroom discussion, helps students interpret what they read, and promotes independent and reflective thought.

Steps.

1. Before beginning the first shared-inquiry discussion, students should be familiar with the rules for shared inquiry: (a) each participant must have read the selection, (b) only the selections that everyone has read can be discussed, (c) opinions must be backed with evidence from the selection, and (d) the teacher or leader can only *ask* questions, not answer them.

2. Prior to the discussion, develop questions that cause students to think for themselves. Questions must pose a real problem about the meaning or idea of the story and reflect your doubts as well. Questions must be specific and clear. The initial question should be interpretive (explaining character motives, making connections between passages, giving opinions about meaning, etc.). Subsequent related questions can be factual (one correct answer), interpretive, or evaluative (based on individual values and choice of action).

3. Students must read a specific selection before the group discussion. Encourage them to read the selection a second time.

4. Seat students in a circle for the discussion. This organization has been found to stimulate discussion.

5. Have students write down the question you ask. Give a set time (approximately one to two minutes) for each student to come up with his or her interpretive answer.

6. As students respond, ask frequent follow-up questions to challenge and encourage in-depth answers, as well as to give them the opportunity to explain their views more clearly.

7. Try to call on each participant at least three times during the discussion. A seating chart can help you keep track of respondents.

8. At the end of the discussion (usually about twenty minutes), attempt to bring the group to resolution. To do this, repeat the initial interpretive question and call on students to repeat their answers. Try to call on those students who may not have been as verbal during the discussion. At this point, all participants should have an answer and should be able to support their responses.

Implications for Literature. Shared inquiry encourages students to read whole books of literature and fosters their ability to think critically, listen more attentively, and recognize the value in others' positions. Shared inquiry can be based on any quality work of literature representing any genre. Interpretation can focus on words or passages or on the entire work. Before the discussion, students should read the selection a second time, or as an alternative, they should read the selection orally or listen to a taped version.

Taba Strategies (Hilda Taba Teaching Strategies)

Hilda Taba (1964, 1966) has developed a series of generic questioning techniques that can be used with any content area or can be based on a variety of materials to promote growth in thinking skills at different levels of depth and abstractness. The four strategies, though not necessarily sequential, can be used sequentially as students build on the knowledge and understanding they've gained through each strategy. The focus of each strategy is evident from its name: concept development, interpretation of data, application of generalizations, and interpretation of feelings, attitudes, and values. No matter which strategy or combination of strategies is used, develop good focusing questions to guide the students. Questions should also ask students to clarify their responses, respond with more divergency, support their answers, and so on.

Strategies and Their Steps.

1. Concept development. In this step, students form a concept and then clarify their understanding of it. Concept development is also a good evaluative tool to assess their knowledge of a specific subject. The following steps will guide students in concept development:
   a. Listing. Have students list all the words that relate to a specific word, whether abstract or concrete.
   b. Grouping. Have students group items from the list in a way that is meaningful to them.
   c. Labeling. Have students find a word or a group of words that gives meaning to each grouping identified.
   d. Subsuming. Have students determine which labels can be grouped together in meaningful ways.

e. Recycling. Have students go through Steps b, c, and d once again to establish new perspectives from the original information listed.

2. Interpretation of data. In this strategy, students interpret the material presented and form conclusions and generalizations dealing with relationships (i.e., cause and effect), based on the inferences generated and evaluated. The following steps will lead students in the interpretation of data:

a. Listing data. Have students list observations and information dealing with a specific subject.

b. Inferring cause and effect. Have students appraise the information and generate inferences to identify and explain relationships among data.

c. Inferring prior causes and subsequent effects. Have students attempt to determine other happenings that would explain the resultant data and support their inferences.

d. Making conclusions. Based on the information and discussions, have students formulate the best conclusion possible to explain the existing data and relationships.

e. Generalizing. Have students take their conclusion a step further and form a more global and encompassing generalization, transferring understandings from one situation to a different one in which they might hold true.

3. Application of generalizations. Ask students to make predictions based on their understandings and the conclusions reached on a subject. The following steps will lead students in the application of generalizations:

a. Making predictions. Have students list all possible results of a related situation and justify their responses.

b. Inferring conditions. Have students explain what must happen for the prediction to come true.

c. Inferring consequences and conditions. Repeat Steps a and b to give students additional opportunities to consider other conditions and outcomes.

d. Drawing conclusions. Have students make a judgment about which conditions would lead to the predictions made.

e. Examining a generalization. Have students analyze the generalization made to assess appropriateness, accuracy, and so on.

4. Interpretation of feelings, attitudes, and values. Guide students in an approach to resolve conflict-type situations and gain insight into their feelings as well as the feelings of others. The following steps can be used to help with this process:

    a. Listing. Have students list the facts of the situations.

    b. Inferring reasons and feelings. Have students assess the information and make inferences to explain the situation and the motives of those involved.

    c. Generating alternatives and examining their consequences. Have students examine possible ways to solve the problem and evaluate the consequences of each alternative.

    d. Evaluating. Have students determine which alternative is the best one, considering all aspects of the situation.

    e. Applying it to real life. Have students go through each step based on a real-life situation.

    f. Generalizing. Have students form a generalization to explain how people deal with similar situations.

Implications for Literature. Each of the four strategies can be used to enhance a discussion based on any (or on a combination of) literary elements and themes. The strategies not only foster growth in cognitive and affective thinking skills, but they also give students skill in using strategies that cross content areas and that will help them in their own lives as they manipulate ideas to form conclusions.

Taxonomy of Educational Objectives:
Cognitive Domain (Benjamin S. Bloom)

The Cognitive Taxonomy was developed by Benjamin Bloom and his colleagues (1956) to classify educational objectives according to the level of thinking required. These six levels— knowledge, comprehension, application, analysis, synthesis, and evaluation—are hierarchical; that is, each level depends on those below it.

Since its inception, the taxonomy has become an invaluable tool for developing questions and activities for students. Implicit in its use is the belief that as students tackle questions and activities representative of each succeeding level of the taxonomy, they become more skilled thinkers.

Levels (Least Complex to Most Complex).

1. Knowledge. Students recall facts and information. Activities and questions can be completed using only the information given. Knowledge questions or activities may include arranging the events of the story in sequence, recalling details about the plot, characters, setting (Who said . . . ?), identifying the main characters.

2. Comprehension. This is the lowest level of understanding, and it is made up of three skills:

    a. Translation—stating an idea in one's own words

    b. Interpretation—summarizing

    c. Extrapolation—extending ideas

Comprehension questions or activities may include explaining what happened, explaining the character's actions, describing a character's feelings or attitudes toward a situation, organizing and summarizing the story's events (What will happen next? How would you describe a favorite character or setting?), illustrating a special event, character, or setting.

3. Application. Students apply information or knowledge in a new way. Application questions or activities may include giving examples of someone who has a similar problem to the one in the book (How could it be solved? How would the character's life be different if he or she lived fifty years ago?), solving a problem presented in a different way, enacting a favorite scene from the story, classifying the main characters (according to predetermined criteria).

4. Analysis. Students break down the whole into parts and examine the elements and their relationships. Questions encouraging analysis may include Why is the story considered a good example of (name genre)? How was the plot affected by the characters? How did the setting affect the plot? Activities may include analyzing the main character's motives or comparing the main characters from two related stories.

5. Synthesis. Students put parts together in a different way to produce something unique. Synthesis questions or activities may include developing a new ending, creating a diary as if you were the main character, writing a biopoem to describe a selected character, creating a new character for the story and discussing how this character's presence will change the plot or affect other characters.

6. Evaluation. Students form judgments or opinions based on selected criteria. Evaluative activities may include judging the actions and behavior of a specific character, writing a review that discusses your evaluation of a story, defending the points of view of two different characters in the story. Which character would you most like to know? is an example of an evaluative question.

Implications for Literature. Too often, students are involved in numerous questions and activities that require only cursory knowledge of the selected literature and little reflective thought. Since the taxonomy represents all levels of thinking, it enables you to focus and plan questions and activities based on any literary work to stimulate all levels of thinking, especially those considered higher level (analysis, synthesis, evaluation). This, in turn, will increase students' ability to think critically, understand human behavior and social issues, and reflect on their own values.

Creative Problem Solving (Sidney Parnes, Director, Creative Problem Solving Institute, State University of New York at Buffalo)

Creative Problem Solving (CPS) is a technique that approaches problem solving through the use of imagination (Parnes, 1977). It provides a framework for problem solving that encourages the generation of as many solutions as possible. Creative Problem Solving results in innovative problem solving, and helps promote more creative thinking in general. Many industries and businesses have had their employees trained in CPS, and its importance in education is now being recognized.

Steps.
1. Fact finding. Students are provided with what is referred to as the "mess." Students collect as much information as possible about the problem (mess) and try to find out all the facts relating to it.
2. Problem finding. Students view the "mess" and the information gathered from different perspectives to focus on the main problem that needs to be solved. State the problem using the formula IWWMI (In What Ways Might I . . .).

3. Idea finding. Students brainstorm, listing as many ideas as they can to solve the problem. The rules for brainstorming include defer judgment, hitchhike on the ideas of others, and quantity produces quantity.

4. Solution finding. Students list the most appropriate criteria for evaluating the ideas that were generated. The following matrix can be used to help evaluate the possible solutions.

ALTERNATIVE SOLUTIONS	CRITERIA					TOTAL
	1	2	3	4	5	
1.						
2.						
3.						
4.						
5.						
6.						
7.						
8.						

List the alternative solutions, and evaluate each one according to the criteria selected. Rank each solution according to each criterion on a scale of 1 to N (N being the number of alternatives listed). Total the points for each alternative to find the solution that best meets the criteria.

5. Acceptance finding. Students create a plan of action to explain how they would carry out the solution chosen, keeping in mind the needs of those who will ultimately be evaluating the plan.

Implications for Literature. In almost every literary work, there is some problem that must be solved. Often, students have faced or are facing similar problems in their lives. As the literary work brings the problem to the surface, students can work together, or individually, to generate alternatives to help solve the problem. Literature also reflects universal problems such as crime, pollution, and aging. Students have the opportunity to apply the CPS skills to real-world problems. The framework provided by CPS will encourage students to use their imagination in problem solving to formulate solutions that might not have been apparent from the beginning.

Discussion of Moral Dilemmas (Lawrence Kohlberg)

Kohlberg's approach to moral education was formulated as a result of the belief that certain universal, ethical principles, must be considered when making decisions involving moral questions. Kohlberg (1971) identified fixed stages of moral development through which all people pass, although not everyone stops at the same stages along the way. Kohlberg also found that most people do not act solely on the basis of their own personal stage of reasoning. Instead, most decisions are based on group identification. Therefore, in the highest level of moral development, the individual makes decisions based on certain moral principles regardless of the thoughts or decisions of others. Kohlberg's research found that teachers can help students reach higher levels of moral reasoning by giving them the opportunity to develop moral reasoning through the discussion of situations in which universal values come into conflict. The key word in Kohlberg's technique is *reasoning*. "Basic to the understanding of Kohlberg's theory is the realization that it is a cognitive approach . . . suggesting that educators attempt to develop moral *reasoning* rather than moral *behavior*. Sophisticated moral reasoning usually leads to ethical behavior, and educators should be concentrating on reasoning" (Maker, 1982, p. 140). The discussion of moral dilemmas stresses thought processes and patterns of thinking.

Steps. Moral dilemmas can be presented in numerous ways. When selecting dilemmas for classroom discussion, consider the following criteria: a central character must decide between alternatives, there are only two or three alternatives from which to choose, society provides at least some support for any of the alternatives, and at least one moral issue is involved.

1. Present the dilemma. There are many ways to present a dilemma to students. For example, you may read the dilemma aloud, students may read it individually, or the dilemma can be role-played.

2. Clarification of facts and issues. Encourage students to list the facts of the situation, summarizing events, the people involved, and possible alternatives.

3. Students choose an alternative. Students decide which alternative the main character should follow and offer at least three reasons for their decision. They should do this step individually and in written form.

4. Small-group discussion. By a show of hands, find out which alternatives students selected. If the class is fairly split on the issues, divide them into groups depending on their position. If a majority of the class selects the same position, place some students in the group that took an alternative position, or place them in groups depending on their reason for their position. (Those students who have a similar reason can be placed together.) Once in groups, have students discuss the position they took and focus on the most important reasons for taking the position.

5. Class discussion. Seat students in a circle to best promote group interaction. Allow time for students to discuss their positions and their reasons for it. Initiate discussion by having each group summarize their position and reasons for it, or a general discussion can follow your questions: "What should the character do? Why?"

During this discussion, it is important to be nonjudgmental and to encourage all students to participate and interact with one another. Help students clarify their own reasons and perceptions of the issue with questions.

6. Students reevaluate their positions. Encourage students to think about the facts, issues, and reasons discussed, and then individually record what they think the main character should do and the most important reason for taking this position. If the students did change their original positions, encourage them to write about what caused them to look at the issue differently. Do not attempt to reach a class consensus.

When students have completed their papers, compare responses to their earlier responses to see if any ideas changed.

You may also record the stage of moral reasoning as reflected by students' responses.

Implications for Literature. Many of the books that students read will include moral dilemmas that the characters had to face. These dilemmas can be adapted for use with the six steps outlined earlier. Often students will be facing similar dilemmas, and the discussion will help them in their own reasoning of the dilemma. Periodically, involve students in problem solving to encourage alternatives that were not considered in the original dilemma as it was presented. This, in turn, will make them more aware of the choices open to all of us.

Implementing Cognitive-Affective Behaviors in the Classroom (Frank E. Williams)

Williams (1970) has developed a three-dimensional model that illustrates the way in which the curriculum (content areas), pupil behaviors (both cognitive and affective), and teacher strategies interact to maximize students' education. Williams identifies cognitive behaviors as those thinking processes that include fluency (the generation of a quantity of responses), flexibility (the generation of divergent ideas, a variety of approaches), originality (the creation of unusual, novel, unique ideas), and elaboration (the embellishment of an idea). The affective behaviors include the processes of risk taking (the courage to defend ideas or take a guess), complexity (the challenge to seek alternatives, to delve into complex problems), curiosity (the willingness to be inquisitive, to wonder, to be open to puzzling situations), and imagination (the power to reach beyond, to visualize). Williams's model includes eighteen generic strategies that can be used to develop activities in any content area. These strategies include paradoxes; attributes; analogies; discrepancies; provocative questions; examples of change; examples of habit; organized random search; skills of search; tolerance for ambiguity; intuitive expression; adjustment to development; study of creative people and processes; evaluation of situations; creative reading skill; creative listening skill; creative writing skill; and visualization skill. Each of these strategies is outlined in detail in Williams's *Classroom Ideas for Encouraging Thinking and Feeling* (1970).

Implications for Literature. Williams's model provides an excellent framework for the development of questions and strategies based on literature that will foster selected cognitive and affective thinking processes. The model also aids in developing an interdisciplinary and multidisciplinary lesson or unit. The strategies are generic and lend themselves to literary analysis and critical reading.

USING THINKING MODELS OR STRATEGIES WITH LITERATURE

The following activities, based on *Tuck Everlasting* by Natalie Babbitt (Farrar, Straus & Giroux, 1988), illustrate ways in which these models or strategies can be incorporated with a work of literature to extend thinking skills and to integrate literature into other areas of the curriculum. *Tuck Everlasting* is the story of the Tuck family, who, through a strange trick of fate, discover that they are immortal. Most of the activities focus on the concept of *immortality* and are developed to help students gain insight into the importance of life and living each day to the fullest as they strive to make a difference in this world.

Shared Inquiry

The following interpretive questions may be used to stimulate discussion:

1. Making connections between passages. Throughout the story, the author repeatedly refers to a toad. What is the significance of the toad to the story?
2. Opinion as to meaning. What does Tuck mean when he says, ". . . we got to talk, and the pond's the best place. The pond's got answers."
3. Character motives. Is the stranger's motivation in solving the mystery of the Tuck family always based on greed?
4. Why something is put in an unusual way. Why doesn't the author give the stranger with the yellow suit a name?

Taba Strategies

1. Concept development. Guide students through the steps to formulate a concept for immortality.
2. Interpretation of data. After reading *Tuck Everlasting*, guide students as they interpret the data to answer the question, How would immortality change a person's life?

3. Application of generalizations. Once students have formulated a generalization for *immortality*, ask them to make predictions based on their generalization.

4. Interpretation of feelings, attitudes, and values. In the story, the Tucks find themselves in a conflict-type situation. They want to keep the spring a secret, but the stranger in the yellow suit wants to market the water. Guide students in the steps for resolving conflicts to see how the situation might have been solved differently, as well as how to solve problems that seem irreconcilable.

Taxonomy of Educational Objectives: Cognitive Domain

1. Knowledge. Who said, "You can't have living without dying. So you can't call it living, what we got . . ."?

2. Comprehension. What does Tuck mean by that quote? Summarize Tuck's views about immortality. What would happen if Tuck couldn't convince Winnie to keep the spring a secret?

3. Application. What affect would immortality have on different aspects of society, such as technology, living conditions (housing, food, crime), scientific research?

4. Analysis. Compare the attitudes concerning immortality of each of the following characters: Tuck, Mae, Miles, Jesse, the stranger, Winnie. What do these attitudes tell you about the kind of person each is?

5. Synthesis. Become *immortality*. What do you look like, taste like, smell like? How do you affect people? What do people think of you? Draw a portrait of yourself as immortality.

6. Evaluation. If you were given the opportunity to become immortal, would you choose to do so? Explain your answer.

Creative Problem Solving

Brainstorm the problems that were caused by immortality and list them on a chart or on the board. Have students choose one of these problems for the basis of a creative problem-solving technique. For example, students may select "having to move" as the "mess."

1. Fact finding. What problems arise from moving? Why is moving a problem? How do you feel when you have to move? How does it affect the family? Where did you move? What other questions can we list?

2. Problem finding. Change the fact-finding responses into problem statements. For example: "In what ways might we find new friends? In what ways might we make a move from another country easier? In what ways might we get used to getting around a new city?" Have students select the "best" problem.

3. Idea finding. Generate as many ideas as possible to help solve the problem. For example, if the problem selected were "In what ways might we make new friends?" ideas might include join a club, join a sports group such as Little League, become involved in after-school activities, invite classmates to your home after school to play, and so on.

4. Solution finding. Place the ideas on the matrix, select criteria on which to base them, and prioritize solutions. Criteria might include the fastest way to make friends or the easiest solution to implement.

5. Acceptance finding. Develop a plan of action for implementing the best solution.

Discussion of Moral Dilemmas

Present Winnie's dilemma and follow the steps outlined for Discussion of Moral Dilemmas. You can present the discussion as you read the dilemma aloud, or students can role-play the situation—one student reading the narration and others taking the parts of Tuck, Mae, Miles, and Jesse. During the class discussion in Step 5, ask questions that encourage students to focus and clarify responses. For example, have students explain their statements; focus on a moral issue (i.e., Is it ever all right to lie?); look at the situation from another viewpoint (Would Winnie's family want her to keep the spring secret?); determine universal consequences such as, What might happen if Winnie, her children, her children's children drank from the spring?; ask for reasons behind a statement (How might that cause over-population?); ask students to explain the responses of another student.

WINNIE'S DILEMMA

Winnie Foster is ten years old. She has lived a very sheltered, and often very lonely, life in Treegap. Her dream is to one day make a difference, to do something special in this world.

By chance, Winnie meets the Tuck family and stumbles on their secret. For the past eighty-seven years, ever since they drank from a mystical spring in the woods, Angus, Mae, Miles, and Jesse Tuck have not changed or aged. And, for the past eighty-seven years, blessed with . . . or doomed to . . . eternal life, the Tuck family wanders about trying to live as inconspicuously and comfortably as they can.

When she first heard about the spring, Winnie thought that "she, too, might live forever in this remarkable world she was only just discovering!" Angus Tuck tries to explain that living forever is unnatural, ". . . dying's part of the wheel, right there next to being born. You can't pick out the pieces you like and leave the rest. Being part of the whole thing, that's the blessing. But it's passing us by, us Tucks. Living's heavy work, but off to one side, the way we are, it's useless, too. It don't make sense. If I knew how to climb back on the wheel, I'd do it in a minute. You can't have living without dying. So you can't call it living, what we got. We just are, we just be, like rocks beside the road."

At 17, Jesse Tuck is quite happy with his life. Winnie adores him. He tries to convince Winnie to drink from the magical spring, "I been thinking it over . . . the thing is, you knowing about the water already, and living right next to it so's you could go there any time, well, listen, how'd it be if you was to wait till you're seventeen, same age as me — heck, that's only six years off — and then you could go and drink some, and then you could go away with me! We could get married, even. That'd be pretty good, wouldn't it! We could have a grand old time, go all around the world, see everything. Listen, Ma and Pa and Miles, they don't know how to enjoy it, what we got. Why heck, Winnie, life's to enjoy yourself, isn't it? What else is it good for? That's what I say. And you and me, we could have a good time that never, never stopped. Wouldn't that be something? . . . You think on it, Winnie Foster . . . All right?"

Implementing Cognitive-Affective Behaviors in the Classroom

The following activities or questions follow Williams's format: encouraging a specific process through certain content areas using selected strategies. When planning the activities or questions, tie those concepts being explored in the different content areas to the literature.

To Encourage: Fluency and Elaboration
Through: Language
Using: Strategy #2—Attributes
List all the attributes (adjectives) you can think of to describe Winnie. Decide which of these attributes you would like best in a friend. Write a paragraph examining this attribute and why it's so important to you.

To Encourage: Flexibility, Original Thinking: Risk Taking
Through: Language and Science
Using: Strategy #3—Analogies
Tuck made many analogies to explain how immortality affected his family's life. Discuss some of these analogies. Brainstorm the concept of *space*. Make comparisons (analogies) between *immortality* and *space*.

To Encourage: Fluency, Original Thinking: Curiosity
Through: Language and Social Studies
Using: Strategy #6—Examples of Change
The Tucks haven't changed for eighty-seven years, but the world has. Think back over the past eighty-seven years. What major changes have occurred in our country's relationship with other world powers (or focus on major trends, family dynamics, etc.)? Select one of the changes discussed. What changes do you predict for the next eighty-seven years?

To Encourage: Original Thinking, Elaboration: Complexity, Imagination
Through: Language
Using: Strategy #15—Creative Reading Skill
After a lesson on *foreshadowing*, list examples of foreshadowing found in the prologue and first three chapters. Seek alternatives as to what event(s) might occur. After reading the entire book, compare predictions to the events as they occurred in the story.

To Encourage: Original Thinking: Imagination
Through: Language and Science
Using: Strategy #5—Provocative Questions and Strategy #17—Creative Writing Skill
After studying the life cycles of certain animals, and after completing *Tuck Everlasting*, discuss the question, "How did *Tuck Everlasting* affect your feelings about the cycles of life?" Write a poem to reflect your feelings about the cycles of life.

REFERENCES

Bloom, Benjamin S., ed. *Taxonomy of Educational Objectives: Handbook I: Cognitive Domain*. New York: McKay, 1956.

Ennis, R. H. "Goals for a Critical Thinking Curriculum." In *Developing Minds: A Resource Book for Teaching Thinking*, edited by A. Costa. Alexandria, Va.: Association for Supervision and Curriculum Development, 1985.

Gallagher, James J. *Teaching the Gifted Child*. Boston: Allyn & Bacon, 1985.

Handbook on Interpretive Reading and Discussion. Chicago: Great Books Foundation, 1984.

Kohlberg, Lawrence. "Stages of Moral Development as the Basis for Moral Education." In *Moral Education: Interdisciplinary Approaches*, edited by C. M. Beck, B. S. Crittenden, and E. V. Sullivan. New York: Newman Press, 1971.

Krathwohl, David R., Benjamin Bloom, and Bertram B. Masia. *Taxonomy of Educational Objectives. Handbook II: Affective Domain*. New York: McKay, 1964.

Maker, June C. *Teaching Models in Education of the Gifted*. Rockville, Md.: Aspen Publication, 1982.

Marzano, Robert J., R. S. Brandt, C. S. Hughes, B. F. Jones, B. Z. Presseisen, S. C. Rankin, and S. Suhor. *Dimensions of Thinking*. Alexandria, Va.: Association for Supervision and Curriculum Development, 1988.

Parnes, Sidney J. "Guiding Creative Action." *Gifted Child Quarterly 21* (1977): 460–472.

Taba, Hilda. *Teaching Strategies and Cognitive Functioning in Elementary School Children*. (U.S.O.E. Cooperative Research Project No. 2404). San Francisco: San Francisco State College, 1966.

———. *Thinking in Elementary School Children*. (U.S.O.E. Cooperative Research Project No. 1574). San Francisco: San Francisco State College, 1964.

Williams, Frank E. *Classroom Ideas for Encouraging Thinking and Feeling*. Buffalo, N.Y.: D.O.K., 1970.

16

The Reading-Writing Connection

The writing process connects reading and writing. Writing is important because it helps the student better understand what writers do and how they think as they compose text. Writing also helps learning and self-expression. Students realize that reading and writing use the same language skills. To enable students to become better writers, they must be immersed in good literature. Literature serves as a model and a stimulus for writing (Calkins, 1986); in fact, the author actually becomes the teacher. By reading or being read to, children learn how to write. When they write, they use their knowledge of story structure and other literary techniques that they have gathered through their involvement with good literature. (A bibliography of books that help stimulate students' imaginations during the prewriting time is provided at the end of this chapter.)

THE WRITING PROCESS APPROACH

According to Hansen (1987), the following elements are essential to the writing process.

1. Time. Students need to be given time, on a regular, daily basis, to write. Ideally, they should write at a regularly scheduled time. Traditionally, writing programs include exercises in spelling, grammar, handwriting, and punctuation, in addition to writing papers on assigned topics that are then graded. However, researchers (e.g., Atwell, 1987) have recently compiled more realistic information about what "real" writers actually do. The writing process allows students to follow a process that is similar to that followed by "real" writers.

2. Choice. Students need to be given the freedom to choose their topics and to feel in control of their writing. They soon learn that it is their responsibility to decide what to write about. As Donald

Graves (1985) so poignantly stated, "The most important thing children can learn is what they know and how they know it."

3. Response. As part of the writing process, teachers and peers *respond* to the writers, not only on the finished product but also on their drafts. Also, teachers move among the students, responding and teaching as they write.

4. Structure. The writing process works best in classrooms with structures. According to Jane Hansen (1987), teachers who like order can often get a writing program organized more easily than those who are not organized. Once the writing process is organized, students know what to do—from choosing a topic, to editing a draft, to sharing with classmates.

5. Community. Developing a writing community in which students have an opportunity to share and listen to others share is very important to this whole process. Students value their own contributions as well as the contributions of others.

Stages of the Writing Process

When implementing the writing process, you must introduce its stages: prewriting, drafting, revising, editing, and publishing (Graves, 1983).

In the prewriting stage, the student chooses a topic. They may keep a notebook or folder that contains the topics they would like to share through writing. Then, they can select from these topics and begin writing.

During the drafting stage, students are taught to focus on their ideas and not on spelling, punctuation, handwriting, and so on. Invented spelling (Chomsky, 1979; Read, 1971) is encouraged. Priority is given to exploring thoughts, ideas, and feelings, rather than to adhering to mechanical rules. Not until the editing stage does instruction of mechanical skills take place.

When revising, students elaborate on the written text. They continue to work on their content by sharing ideas with their peers and teacher, who, in turn, contribute ideas that help in revising the draft.

During the editing stage, instruction in mechanical skills takes place. Spelling, punctuation, and capitalization are standardized and corrected. Students begin to learn these skills while working on their papers.

The final stage of the writing process is publishing.

Activities

The following activities enhance learning and motivate the students to publish their writings.

1. With the students, make a book, using the following materials and directions:

a. Materials

- Lightweight cotton fabric
- Dry-mount tissue (available in photography shops)
- Cardboard (medium-weight; needs to be heavier for larger books)
- Scissors
- Iron
- Construction paper (one piece for the end paper)
- Lightweight white paper (for the pages of the book)
- Needle and thread or long-arm stapler
- Glue or paste

b. Directions

- Cut cloth to desired size of book.
- Cut dry-mount tissue the same size as the cloth.
- Cut cardboard about an inch smaller all the way around than the dry-mount tissue and cloth.
- Cut the piece of cardboard in half.
- Place the dry-mount tissue evenly on top of the cloth.
- Place the two pieces of cardboard on top of the dry-mount tissue. Leave about ½ inch between the pieces of cardboard, placing them so that there is an equal amount of dry-mount tissue and cloth on all sides.
- Fold the cloth and dry mount at the corners, and with a hot iron press them down to the cardboard. The heat of the iron allows the dry mount to adhere the cloth to the cardboard.
- After all four corners are folded and ironed down, do the same to the remaining sides.
- Fold the book cover together, and iron the front and back to adhere the cloth to the cardboard more securely.
- Using construction paper, cut one piece that is ½ inch smaller than the book cover.
- Next, using the lightweight paper, make pages for the book. To do this, cut a pattern for the pages that is

¼ inch smaller than the construction paper previously cut. Using this as a pattern, cut the number of sheets needed for pages.

- Place the pages on top of the construction-paper page and fold in the center. Staple or sew these pages together.
- Rub glue or paste over the construction-paper sheet and carefully adhere it to the inside of the book cover. Hold the book open for several minutes to dry.

c. Contents. In addition to the text, the book can contain the following:
- A title page that includes the copyright date, a fictitious publishing company, dedication, and so on.
- A picture of the author along with a biographical sketch. This could be adhered to the front or back cover of the book.
- Illustrations of the text using either drawings or pictures from magazines. Students may also "hire" friends or classmates to do the illustrations, thus emphasizing that often books are illustrated by people other than the author.
- Four or five stories, instead of just one. In conjunction with this, make a table of contents plus an index. This helps the children learn the function of a table of contents and index, plus the index helps them learn such skills as main ideas, alphabetizing, and so on.

2. Set up a portion of the classroom library called "Famous Authors' Books" for all the books published by members of the class.

3. Provide cassette tapes so that the children can make tapes to accompany their books.

4. Provide a tall stool or captain's chair and label it "Author's Stool" (Graves and Hansen, 1983). Each day allow one child to sit in this chair as she or he reads the story she or he has written. Classmates can then ask questions about the story, tell what they like about the story, and so on.

5. Encourage and assist students in submitting their final writing products to one of the following magazines that publish the work of young writers:

Chart Your Course. P.O. Box 6448, Mobile, Alabama 36660. Ages 6–18.

Child Life. The Children's Better Health Institute, 1100 Waterway Blvd., Indianapolis, Indiana 46206. Ages 8–10.

City Kids. 1545 Wilcox, Los Angeles, California 90028. Ages 11–14.

Cobblestone: The History Magazine for Young People. 20 Grove Street, Peterborough, New Hampshire 03458. Ages 8–14.

Cricket. Box 100, LaSalle, Illinois 61301. Ages 5–13.

Ebony Jr.! 820 S. Michigan Ave., Chicago, Illinois 60605. Ages 6–12.

Paw Prints. National Zoo, Washington, D.C. 20008. Ages 6–14.

Spring. Scholastic, Inc. 730 Broadway, New York, New York 10003. Ages 9–11.

Stone Soup. P.O. Box 83, Santa Cruz, California 95063. Ages 6–13.

Teaching Writing as a Process

Nina Zaragoza (1987) has developed the following guidelines for teaching writing as a process:

1. Be consistent and committed. Schedule writing *every* day at the same time (i.e., first thing in the morning or after lunch) and for a good amount of time (20–30 minutes). This allows writing to develop from a habit to an exciting anticipation. Students begin to "think like a writer."

2. Allow the child control of the topic. Do *not* assign topics. Topic assignment, even "on the first day to give them an idea," will not make it easier for them. Instead, it will reinforce passivity and the misconception that what you think is what is most important. Be calm. Topic ideas will come through modeling, mini-lessons, discussions, sharing with peers, and reading children's literature.

3. Remember, writing is a process and a finished product should not be expected after every writing period. Be patient and accepting. Let the child think, experiment, and feel at ease within the process. Begin with the goal of fluency and enthusiasm.

4. Sit and write with the students at least once a week. This behavior will reinforce the idea that writing is important—to everyone. Students respond enthusiastically when teachers occasionally share something they've written.

5. Promote a literate environment in your classroom. Having

the opportunity to use a variety of writing or reading materials—pens, pencils, markers, crayons, white-out, scissors, tape, an assortment of papers, books, magazines, newspapers—will help children become comfortable with these materials used for communication. A writing center should also include a dictionary, thesaurus, poor speller's dictionary, and so on.

6. Keep the children in control during all phases of the process with questions and behaviors that exhibit respect for their decision-making ability. Say: "What do you think your title is going to be?" Not: "Why don't you use this title?" Ownership belongs with the children. We convey this even nonverbally. Sit at eye level with them and ask them to read what they've written.

7. Smile (it might take some practice!) when they hand you wrinkled, hole-ridden first drafts. Remember what really counts here are the ideas and the fact that you have positively accepted their writing. Focus first on the content.

8. Teach necessary skills within the context of the children's work and during the appropriate stage of the process (i.e., talk about handwriting when it is important—during publishing—not during the first draft). This allows them to focus on one aspect at a time instead of being overwhelmed with everything at once.

9. Allow the children to share daily with their peers. This sharing helps with topic ideas, gives them an audience to use as a resource, enables them to be a resource, and helps you maintain control and activity. Children can share with the whole class, in an Author's Chair (Graves, 1983) or in small response groups (Atwell, 1987).

10. Take it easy! In the beginning it might seem as if nothing is happening, but it is. Little by little, through daily, consistent writing, conferences, and using those once-isolated skills, a meaningful whole will form in the minds of the children who are allowed to write. Children will begin to see themselves as readers and as writers.

THE LANGUAGE EXPERIENCE APPROACH

The language experience approach (LEA) is a method of teaching reading based on translating personal experiences into written text and then reading them. The LEA involves stimulating oral expression, writing it down, reading it back, and then using the written material as the basis for developing reading and other language arts skills. It is simply teaching reading via compositions that have been developed with a child or a group of children.

The language experience approach has many advantages. One of its most significant advantages is that it integrates all the language arts skills—listening, speaking, reading, and writing. Second, although the LEA is often associated with beginning reading, it can be used successfully with upper-grade children in the beginning stages of reading, children whose backgrounds are not standard English, high-school dropouts, adult basic literacy learners, or children who are learning English as a second language. The LEA actually begins wherever the child is in terms of language development. It bridges the gap between "home language" and "school language." Along the same track, the basal reader is often criticized because the language patterns used are not typical of the way children actually speak; this is because of the controlled vocabulary that is used. The LEA does not limit vocabulary to high-utility words and is, therefore, much more natural and typical of children's speech. Another advantage is that children are motivated to read the selections because the text is centered around them and around something that is familiar to them. Finally, the LEA is very inexpensive to use. A pencil, marker, or chalk, and paper or chalkboard are the necessary equipment.

Steps in the Language Experience Approach

Implementation of the LEA follows prescribed steps. First, the children's thinking needs to be stimulated in some way; for example, by reading a story; experiencing an event such as a field trip, a special holiday, a cooking activity, or a science experiment; displaying an interesting picture or photograph; and so on. Second, the students discuss the event and listen as others express their ideas and thoughts. Next, the ideas and thoughts are written down on a large piece of chart paper or on the chalkboard. The final result is a story that interests the children *and* that they *can* read and understand because the words, the information provided, and the text are all familiar. The children are the authors! This process enables children to better understand that the books and stories that they read are someone else's ideas, experiences, or fantasies.

Once the story has been written, it can be used to teach a variety of reading skills. For example, if you want to work on punctuation skills, decisions can be made about punctuation as the sentences are being written. You can demonstrate that if the sentence asks something, a question mark is used, whereas if the sentence tells the reader something, a period is needed, or if something is being said by someone, quotation marks are used. Activities such as these make learning more meaningful than simply putting in punctuation marks on a skill sheet or workbook page. In addition, these skills can be transferred to other materials the students are reading.

Activities

The following activities can be initiated using the language experience (LE) stories to encourage children to become actively involved in the reading process.

1. Have the children make an individual book of each of their stories, or the stories can be collected over time and made into one book. To make the books, have the children copy the stories from the wall chart or chalkboard onto smaller sheets of paper. Staple these pages together and make a construction paper cover. (Books can also be made following the directions on pages 320–321.) These books can be catalogued into the school library or classroom library, thus allowing each child to have his or her copy of the book of LE stories to read at school or at home. Or, you can punch holes in the chart paper and use large metal rings to hold the pages together. For more durability, the pages can be laminated. Children enjoy lying or sitting on the floor reading the collection of stories, or you can use this book in much the same way as a Big Book (see Chapter 2). Big Books can also be made by neatly printing or typing the text of the LE stories onto separate sheets of paper and then having the children illustrate each page. These books can then be used during shared reading time.

2. Make a cassette tape to accompany each LE story. A child, a group of children, a parent, or a volunteer can help. The tape, along with the book, can be put in the library or the listening center for other children to enjoy.

3. Encourage students to read their books to other students. This can be done in class, or by arranging with another teacher

for students to bring their LE booklets to the class and read to individual students or to a small group.

4. Develop a class newspaper using the LE stories, as well as other news items, advertisements, and so on. This could be done on a monthly basis to allow parents to enjoy the rich stories developed by the class.

In summary, the writing process approach and the language experience approach encourage the development of oral and written expression. They help convey the idea that writing is a way of recording language and experiences and that reading reconstructs the language and the experiences of the writer. Children begin, as Frank Smith states (1983), to read like a writer and write like a reader.

BOOKS FOR STIMULATING THE WRITING PROCESS

Adoff, Arnold. *The Cabbages Are Chasing Rabbits.* Harcourt Brace Jovanovich, 1985.

Allard, Harry. *Miss Nelson Is Missing.* Houghton Mifflin, 1985.

Barrett, Judy. *Cloudy with a Chance of Meatballs.* Atheneum, 1978.

Barrett, Ron. *Hi Yo, Fido.* Crown, 1984.

Chevalier, Christa. *Spence Isn't Spence Anymore.* Whitman, 1985.

Galdone, Paul. *The Teeny Tiny Woman: A Ghost Story.* Houghton Mifflin, 1984.

Graves, Robert. *The Big Green Book.* Macmillan, 1985.

Hasler, Eveline. *Winter Magic.* Morrow, 1985.

Joyce, William. *George Shrinks.* Harper & Row, 1985.

Lester, Allison. *Clive Eats Alligators.* Houghton Mifflin, 1986.

Lester, Helen. *It Wasn't My Fault.* Prentice-Hall, 1985.

Lorenz, Lee. *A Weekend in the Country.* Prentice-Hall, 1985.

Modell, Frank. *Look Out, It's April Fool's Day.* Greenwillow, 1985.

Nozaki, Akihiro. *Anna's Hat Trick.* Philomel, 1985.

Schwartz, David. *How Much Is a Million?* Lothrop, 1985.

Spier, Peter. *Dreams.* Doubleday, 1986.

Steig, William. *Solomon, the Rusty Nail.* Farrar, Straus & Giroux, 1985.

Stevenson, James. *Are We Almost There?* Greenwillow, 1985.

REFERENCES

Atwell, Nancy. *In the Middle.* New Jersey: Boynton, 1987.

Calkins, Lucy. *The Art of Teaching Writing.* Portsmouth, N.H.: Heinemann, 1986.

Chomsky, Carol. "Approaching Early Reading Through Invented Spelling." In *Theory and Practice of Early Reading,* vol. 2 (edited by L. B. Resnick and P. A. Weaver), pp. 43–65. Hillsdale, N.J.: Earlbaum, 1979.

Graves, Donald H. "All Children Can Write." *Learning Disability Focus 1*, no. 1 (1985): 36–43.

———. *Writing: Teachers and Children at Work*. Portsmouth, N.H.: Heinemann, 1983.

Graves, Donald H., and J. Hansen. "The Author's Chair." *Language Arts 60*, no. 2 (February 1983): 176–183.

Hansen, Jane. *When Writers Read*. Portsmouth, N.H.: Heinemann, 1987.

Read, Carol. "Pre-School Children's Knowledge of English Phonology." *Harvard Educational Review 41* (1971): 1–34.

Smith, Frank. "Reading Like a Writer." *Language Arts 60* (1983): 558–567.

Zaragoza, Nina. "The Writing Process." Unpublished manuscript, University of Miami, 1987.

17

Literature and the Curriculum: A Thematic Approach

Our literature incorporates all that we are and all that we hope to be. It includes the knowledge of ages past and present and dares us to imagine the future. Literature is the perfect vehicle for making connections as we strive to understand our world and our place in it. Literature can help bridge the gap between classroom lessons and reality, adding additional perspective to the curriculum and giving dimension to the concepts and themes being taught.

A thematic approach combines a variety of materials, activities, and content areas to teach a specific concept, idea, or theme, thus offering a multidisciplinary, as well as interdisciplinary, approach to learning. And literature, no matter what the genre, adapts easily to this process.

TOWARD A THEMATIC APPROACH

When using a thematic approach to learning, the following factors must be considered and developed:

1. Theme. The most abstract themes or concepts lend themselves more readily to a thematic approach since they allow for greater flexibility and encourage more divergent and critical thought processes (i.e., imagination, survival, pioneer life).

2. Focus. What understandings will be explored or emphasized? (For example, students will become aware of the changes and challenges facing the pioneers who settled in the American West.)

3. Objectives. Select specific objectives and goals from the guidelines established for your state, county, or district. These objectives should reflect the various content areas and develop growth in the affective (feeling) as well as the cognitive (thinking) domains.

4. Materials. Use a variety of materials to stimulate and motivate. Works of literature should reflect the various genres. Materials should be easily accessible to all students. Once a theme is determined, work with students to gather appropriate materials.

5. Activities. Above all, activities should be meaningful, and reflect student needs and interests. Activities based on works of literature should take students back into the books, as they analyze, synthesize, evaluate, problem solve, and make connections.

Topics for activities can be generated as students create webs based on a selected idea, concept, or theme. Webbing creates a framework for the integration of content areas and encourages students to use their own creativity, imagination, and interests to shape the curriculum. The topics and subtopics generated from this exercise can serve as a springboard to readings in a variety of genres and can aid in the planning of activities and research (both teacher- and student-directed) that enhance growth in the cognitive and affective domains. The following steps will help you and your students create a web, such as the one on page 332.

a. Determine the idea, concept, or theme to be explored.
b. Display a variety of materials related to the idea, concept, or theme, and allow time for students to peruse the materials.
c. Write the idea, concept, or theme in the middle of either a large piece of chart paper or the chalkboard.
d. Involve students in a brainstorming session, as they call out words related to the central term.
e. Write down the words generated, and connect them to the central term. As you go along, attempt to arrange words (topics and subtopics) under appropriate headings. Arrange and rearrange the words, and continue brainstorming until the web reflects all possible ideas.
f. Copy the web onto a piece of butcher paper or chart paper and display it so that students can refer to it from time to time.

6. Culmination. Involve students in an activity that encourages them to make connections leading to an understanding, a conclusion, or some newly formed viewpoint about the idea, concept, or theme being explored.

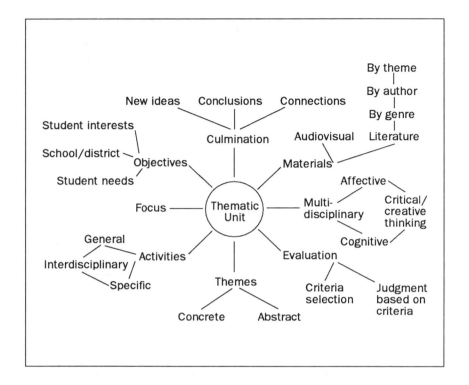

7. Evaluation. Select criteria to measure student growth (i.e., comprehension of information; ability to convey their own ideas concerning the idea, concept, or theme; creativity; ability to make connections concerning the idea, concept, or theme and some other aspect of life).

8. Related works of literature. Make a list of books that relate to the theme under investigation.

THEMATIC UNITS

This section contains sample thematic units developed to illustrate the ways in which literature can be used to supplement and enhance units of study. Two primary themes and two intermediate themes are included. At each level, one theme generally classified as social studies and one theme generally classified as science are described, however, the units are multidisciplinary in nature. The activities section has two parts: the general activities can be completed without the use of any particular book, while the specific activities are designed to be used with the designated books or with books of a specific genre. The activities section helps develop the unit objectives and guides students as they explore the focus of the theme. When developing your own thematic units, remember to take into account your own students' needs, interests, and motivation in selecting literature and planning the unit.

**LITERATURE AND
THE CURRICULUM:
A THEMATIC APPROACH**

Thematic Unit: Primary Level (Social Studies)

THEME: China.

FOCUS: Students will become familiar with Chinese culture by learning about the customs, foods, language, literature, art, and so forth.

OBJECTIVES: On completion of this thematic unit, students will
1. be familiar with a variety of Chinese foods
2. create Chinese characters to represent words such as *one, two, three, up, down.*
3. locate China on a world map
4. describe some similarities and differences between Chinese literature and American literature
5. be familiar with many of the Chinese customs
6. describe the differences and similarities between the architecture of Chinese homes and the architecture of American homes
7. speak a few words in Chinese by being able to sing "Happy Birthday" in Chinese
8. be familiar with Chinese cooking and eating utensils

MATERIALS:
1. Abacus.
2. Collection of books relating to China (see "Related Works of Literature" at the end of this section).
3. Cardboard and scissors for a tangram.
4. Menu from a Chinese restaurant.
5. Wok.
6. Selection of vegetables.
7. Student copies of the following:
   Tikki Tikki Tembo, written by Arlene Mosel and illustrated by Blair Lent. New York: Holt, Rinehart & Winston, 1968.

The Weaving of a Dream, by Marilee Heyer. New York: Viking Kestrel, 1986.

Passport to China, by Stephen Keeler. New York: Watts, 1987.

8. Variety of Chinese foods.
9. Chopsticks.
10. Art materials for a Chinese dragon: paper, tissue paper, glue, crayons, magic markers.
11. Samples of rice foods.
12. Pictures of brocades.
13. Large map of the world.

ACTIVITIES: It is not necessary, nor is it suggested, to use all the activities included. They are intended as a guide to illustrate the scope of activities that can be developed. Selection should be based on student needs, interests, objectives.

General Activities

1. Although the Chinese language is written in the same way throughout China, it is spoken in many different ways. Recently, the National Republic of China declared Mandarin Chinese the official language. Teach the students to sing "Happy Birthday" in Chinese to help them better understand what the Chinese language is like.

Happy Birthday
(Zuni Shenri)
English words: Hap py Birth day to you
Pinyin (system for writing Chinese words in English):
 Zu ni Shen ri kuai le
English sounds: zoo nee shen ree kwa lee

2. Most classrooms have an abacus. Show the abacus to the children and point out that this tool was created by the ancient Chinese to add, subtract, multiply, divide and to calculate square and cube roots. If you haven't taught them how to use the abacus, demonstrate it for them. Provide time for students to experiment with the abacus.

3. The Chinese do not have a written alphabet to form words like the English alphabet. Instead, they use a character (called *dz* in Chinese) to represent a word or an idea. For example, the characters on page 336 represent the English words indicated:

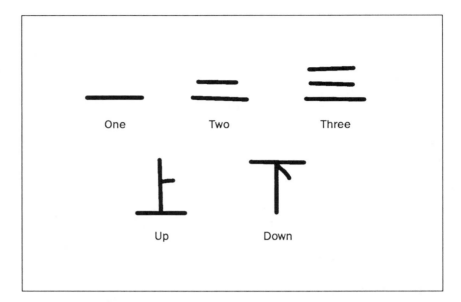

Obtain copies of the following books to help students investigate the art of Chinese writing in greater depth: *Chinese Writing: An Introduction*, by Diane Wolff, or *Chinese Calligraphy*, by Chiang Yee.

4. Every country seems to have its own versions of popular folktales and nursery rhymes. In China, for example, there is *Yeh-Shen, a Cinderella Story from China*, in which Yeh-Shen (Cinderella) wishes for pretty clothes to wear to a festival. Her stepmother has killed her magical fish, so Yeh-Shen wishes on the bones of the fish for pretty clothes. Suddenly, she is dressed in beautiful gold and feathers, and she goes to the festival. As she hurries from the festival, she leaves her golden slipper. A wealthy merchant finds the slipper and marries Yeh-Shen. Her wicked stepmother and stepsister are buried beneath an avalanche of heavy stones. Read other Chinese folktales such as *The Fox That Wanted Nine Golden Tales*, by Mary Knight, or Diane Wolkstein's *8,000 Stones: A Chinese Folktale* and *The Magic Wings*. In addition, use books such as Robert Wyndham's beautifully illustrated *Chinese Mother Goose Rhymes*, which has Chinese calligraphy decorating the borders of the pages, and Ray Wood's *The American Mother Goose* to compare and contrast the Chinese and American versions of these rhymes.

5. The Chinese developed a puzzle called a *tangram*, which

has only seven pieces. They use the tangram to make pictures of birds, fish, houses, and many other things. Provide pieces of cardboard and enlarged pieces of the puzzle (see the following tangram; tangrams are also available commercially). Allow time for each student to trace the puzzle's pattern pieces on the cardboard and cut them out. Then ask the students to create a design, using the tangram puzzle pieces. Share these designs.

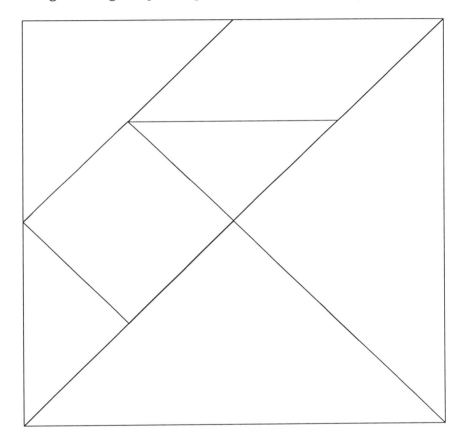

6. Many people enjoy Chinese food, and it is available in great variety. Using books such as *Chinese Food and Drink*, by Amy Shui and Stuart Thompson, and *Creative Wok Cooking*, by Ethel Graham and Richard Ahrens, provide information about Chinese food in general, food and festive occasions, cooking equipment, how to use chopsticks, and so on. If possible, bring in menus from Chinese restaurants. Discuss foods the students

may have tasted that are considered Chinese. Then prepare for a cooking activity using a wok. A wok is a popular cooking utensil in China because it cooks the food very quickly and does not use a lot of fuel. Using the following recipe, prepare the stir-fried vegetables so that everyone will get a small taste.

STIR-FRIED VEGETABLES

4 tablespoons vegetable oil

2 cloves garlic

6 cups vegetables (green beans, broccoli, mushrooms, pea
   pods, bean sprouts, Chinese celery, cabbage, etc.)

1 cup chicken broth

1 teaspoon salt

1 teaspoon sugar

2 teaspoons cornstarch in 2 tablespoons cold water

Heat oil in the wok. Brown and discard the garlic. Stir-fry the vegetables for three minutes. Add the chicken broth, salt, and sugar. Cover and steam over moderate heat for three minutes or until the vegetables are tender, but still bright colored and crisp. Stir the cornstarch mixture, and add it to the wok. Cook, stirring, until the sauce thickens. Serve at once.

Specific Activities: *Tikki Tikki Tembo*
Tikki Tikki Tembo, by Arlene Mosel, is a charming folktale that tells about Tikki Tikki Tembo and how his long name almost cost him his life. Using this book, select appropriate activities for your students from the following:

1. Tikki Tikki Tembo had a very long name because it was the custom in China many years ago to give the firstborn and honored sons long names. Have the students find out how the name they were given was decided. Using a large piece of chart paper, write each child's name and a brief explanation of how he or she got this name. When complete, this could become a newspaper, *How We Got Our Names*, which could be duplicated and sent home. As an addition to or variation of this activity, ask the students to find out what their name means. For example, *Tikki tikki tembo-no sa rembo-chari bari ruchi-pip peri pembo* means "the most wonderful thing in the whole wide world."

2. Tikki Tikki Tembo and Chang ate rice cakes. Discuss other foods that are typically Chinese. Make a list of these foods. Discuss who, in the class, has eaten these foods and who has not. Finally, obtain a variety of foods from a Chinese carry-out restaurant and have a tasting party. Include egg rolls, won-ton soup, chow mein, Chinese noodles, and, of course, fortune cookies. Have the children experiment with using chopsticks.

3. One of the illustrations in *Tikki Tikki Tembo*, illustrated by Blair Lent, is a picture of the Chinese Dragon. The Chinese Dragon symbolizes good fortune, strength, and wisdom and is present at most celebrations, especially at the New Year's parade. It is believed to keep the evil spirits away for the coming year. Provide students with a large sheet of paper, scraps of tissue paper, glue, crayons, magic markers, and so on. Ask them to create a Chinese Dragon of their own.

4. Show the students the illustrations depicting Tikki Tikki Tembo's house and the other houses in his small village. Discuss how these houses are similar to and different from the houses in which the students live.

5. Write the full name, *Tikki tikki tembo-no sa rembo-chari bari ruchi-pip peri pembo*, on the chalkboard. Develop a pencil (or chopstick) tapping rhythm to accompany this name. As the story is read aloud, have the students tap out this rhythm each time you read his name.

6. Parts of the story about Tikki Tikki Tembo were real or could actually have happened, but some of what happened was make-believe. After you finish reading the story, discuss the concepts of real and make-believe. Then, on the chalkboard, make a list of those things the students believe could have happened and those that were make-believe.

7. Tikki Tikki Tembo and his brother Chang were eating rice cakes as they stood by the well. Rice is a very popular food in China. Make a list of all the different products or dishes that the students have eaten that are made with or from rice (i.e., rice pudding, rice cereal). If possible, have students bring in samples of rice foods for a "rice day" tasting party.

Specific Activities: *The Weaving of a Dream*

The Weaving of a Dream, by Marilee Heyer, is a classic tale of love, loyalty, greed, and envy. It is based on an ancient Chinese legend. Using this book, select appropriate activities for your students from the following:

1. The widow thought the best life for her would be living in a beautiful palace like the one she saw in the painting. Using large sheets of paper, have the students create their own picture of how they would like their dream place to look.

2. Display pictures of brocades or bring in a real one, if possible. Ask students to use an 8½-by-11-inch sheet of paper to draw a pattern for a brocade they would like to have.

3. Discuss the feelings the students have toward the two sons, Leme and Letuie, who took the box of gold and went to the big city instead of returning home. Make a list of adjectives on the chalkboard describing these two boys: greedy, selfish. Next, ask the students to describe their feelings about Leje, the son who returned the brocade to this mother. Make another list on the chalkboard of words describing Leje: caring, loyal. Finally, discuss these descriptive words and have the children arrange the qualities from both lists in the order they feel is most important for a friend to possess, and also which is the most undesirable trait for a friend to possess.

4. *The Weaving of a Dream* is a folktale based on an ancient Chinese legend. Read other Chinese legends. For example, Jeanne Lee's *Legend of the Li River* explains the mysteries of nature such as the magical hills that line the Li River. Her *Legend of the Milky Way* provides an ancient Chinese explanation for the phenomenon of the galaxy. Have the class write a folktale based on one of the legends that they like best.

Specific Activities: *Passport to China*

Passport to China by Stephen Keeler is a nonfiction book that provides the reader with a complete, in-depth understanding of life in China and its role in today's world. Using this book, select appropriate activities for your students from the following:

1. Divide the topics presented in the table of contents—the people, pastimes and sports, transportation—among the students. Ask the students to research their assigned topic based on the community in which they live. Next, ask them to write the information in a brief, concise manner illustrating or inserting photographs whenever possible. When all the students have completed this assignment, develop a table of contents and put it together as a book, *A Passport to (the name of your community)*.

2. After studying the information in *Passport to China*, ask students to identify one thing they like about China and one thing they do not like. Discuss reasons for their likes and dislikes.

3. China is the world's third largest country, and as a result, there are big differences, depending on where you are, in weather, vegetation, population, and so on. After looking at the maps and pictures in this book, ask the students to select an area of China that they would most like to visit and tell why they selected it.

4. The following Chinese traditions, customs, or rules are very different from those that we find in the United States. Discuss each one to determine its advantages and disadvantages.

   a. People do *not* own their own homes.
   b. The government offers generous benefits to couples who have only one child and penalizes couples who have more than one.
   c. People are not allowed to change jobs or move to a different work unit other than the one in which they were born.
   d. It is common for three generations of a family (grandparents, parents, and children) to live in the same house, which is usually very small.
   e. There are almost no privately owned cars. Until recently, owning a car was not allowed.

CULMINATION: Hold an "Images of China" day in which students create skits, pantomimes, and demonstrations to describe their favorite Chinese customs or legends.

EVALUATION: The final culminating product can be evaluated according to the following criteria:

1. Does it reflect an understanding of China's culture and legends?

2. Does it allow the viewers to gain a better understanding of China's culture and legends?

3. Does the content of the project illustrate the differences and similarities between Chinese and American cultures and legends?

4. Does the project show creativity?

RELATED WORKS OF LITERATURE

Fiction

Bishop, Claire Huchet. *The Five Chinese Brothers*. Illustrated by Kurt Weise. Scholastic Book Services, 1938.

Jensen, Helen Zane. *When Panda Comes to Our House*. Dial Books, 1985.

Knight, Mary. *The Fox That Wanted Nine Tails*. Illustrated by Brigitte Bryan. Macmillan, 1969.

Lee, Jeanne. *Legend of the Li River*. Holt, Rinehart & Winston, 1983.

———. *Legend of the Milky Way*. Holt, Rinehart & Winston, 1982.

Wolkstein, Diane. *The Magic Wings: A Tale From China*. Illustrated by Robert Andrew Parker. Dutton, 1983.

———. *8,000 Stones: A Chinese Folktale*. Illustrated by Ed Young. Doubleday, 1972.

Wood, Ray. *The American Mother Goose*. Illustrated by Ed Hargis. Lippincott, 1940.

Wyndham, Robert, comp. *Chinese Mother Goose Rhymes*. Illustrated by Ed Young. World, 1968.

Informational Books

Graham, Ethel, and Richard Ahrens. *Creative Wok Cooking*. Ottenheimer, 1976.

Sadler, Catherine Edwards. *Two Chinese Families*. With photographs by Alan Sadler. Atheneum, 1981.

Shui, Amy, and Stuart Thompson. *Chinese Food and Drink*. Bookwright Press, 1987.

Wolff, Diane. *Chinese Writing: An Introduction*. Holt, Rinehart & Winston, 1975.

Yee, Chiang. *Chinese Calligraphy*, rev. ed. Harvard University Press, 1973.

Thematic Unit:
Primary Level
(Science)

THEME: Dinosaurs.

FOCUS: Students will learn about dinosaurs through stories and challenging activities.

OBJECTIVES: On completion of this thematic unit, students will
1. know the names of at least ten dinosaurs
2. distinguish between plant-eating dinosaurs and meat-eating dinosaurs
3. understand how scientists know as much about dinosaurs as they do
4. know when dinosaurs lived
5. identify dinosaurs that lived on land versus the prehistoric creatures that lived in the sea or flew in the air
6. compare various sizes, weights, and body shapes of the dinosaurs

MATERIALS:
1. *Science Adventures Dinosaurs*, by Kayne Quinn and Jan Hutchings. Los Angeles: Enrich-Education Division, Price/Stern/Sloan, 1987.
2. Plastic dinosaur figures.
3. Clay for making dinosaur models.
4. Dinosaur model sets (available in most toy stores).
5. Chicken or turkey bones.
6. Collection of books relating to dinosaurs (see "Related Works of Literature" at the end of this section).
7. Student copies of the following:
    If the Dinosaur Came Back, by Bernard Most. New York: Harcourt Brace Jovanovich, 1978.
    Danny and the Dinosaur, written by Syd Hoff and illustrated by Else Holmelund Minarik. New York: Harper & Row, 1958.

The Secret Dinosaur, by Marilyn Hirsh. New York: Holiday House, 1979.

Dinosaurs, written by Kathleen Daly and illustrated by Greg and Tim Hildebrandt. Racine, Wis.: Western, 1977.

ACTIVITIES: It is not necessary, nor is it suggested, to use all the activities included. They are intended as a guide to illustrate the scope of activities that can be developed. Selection should be based on student needs, interests, and objectives.

General Activities:

1. Provide students with large paper bags. Have them create a paper-bag puppet to represent their favorite dinosaur. Next, have students create skits with the puppets (i.e., a fight between a meat-eater and a plant-eater).

2. Tell students to use the names of dinosaurs to create new names for foods (i.e., Fabrosaurus French Fries, Megalosaurus Milk Shakes, Stegosaurus Spaghetti). Then have them write a menu for lunch using these "new foods." Allow time for students to share their menus.

3. Scientists have provided several reasons for the dinosaurs' disappearance (the earth became too cold, there wasn't enough food, etc.). Have students research the reasons provided and then divide them into groups, each group supporting one of the reasons. Provide time for them to discuss and defend their positions.

4. Ask the students to pretend that they want a dinosaur for a pet. Ask them to identify the dinosaur they would want and then tell how they would capture and tame it.

5. Using a variety of sources, list some dinosaurs and their lengths on the chalkboard. To help students understand how long the different dinosaurs were, measure their exact lengths with a ball of yarn (you have previously tied knots every five feet in the yarn). Count by fives as the yarn is unrolled. Use a meter stick to convert these lengths to meters.

6. Have students become paleontologists (a scientist who specializes in finding and studying ancient fossil remains) by bringing clean chicken or turkey bones to school. Place each bone in some wet, packed sand to make an imprint. Remove the bone, and pour plaster of paris into the imprint (or mold). Let it

harden and then remove it from the sand. Have students label and display their plaster of paris fossils.

7. Have students pretend that they want to move Tyrannosaurus Rex, the largest of the meat-eating dinosaurs that weighted approximately eight tons and was over twenty feet high, from a zoo in New York City to a zoo in Paris, France. Provide time for a brainstorming session on how this could be done.

8. Give each student a large piece of butcher paper, and have them draw their favorite dinosaur and color or paint it. Place a second sheet of paper under the first sheet and staple them together loosely, leaving a small opening for stuffing. Stuff the dinosaur with crumpled up newspaper and add legs, horns, tails, and so on. Label and display these stuffed dinosaurs.

9. Ask students to create riddles about dinosaurs (i.e., What is the best way to get a piece of paper out from under a dinosaur? Wait until it moves off it). Compile these riddles into a class booklet, *Dinosaur Riddles*.

10. Have students take on the role of a particular dinosaur. If possible, mime the dinosaur, in addition to giving one clue at a time:

I weigh _____.
I am _____ tall.
I eat _____.

Allow four clues. If students haven't guessed the dinosaur after four guesses, have the dinosaur-student provide the answer.

11. Plan a field trip to a museum of natural history to see dinosaur skeletons.

12. Provide students with plastic dinosaur figures, clay, dinosaur model sets, and so on. As a class, create a display or diorama that depicts a prehistoric time when dinosaurs roamed the world.

Specific Activities: *If the Dinosaurs Came Back*

If the Dinosaurs Came Back, by Bernard Most, is an imaginative and charming fantasy about a boy who dreams about having a dinosaur of his own and all the things they will be able to do, from pushing rain clouds back, to getting kites from trees. Using this book, select appropriate activities for your students from the following:

1. Select one of the dinosaurs that are illustrated and named on the last page of the book and draw its shape on a sheet of construction paper. Cut out the dinosaur and, using it as a pattern, make pages and construction paper covers for student dinosaur books. Allow students to use these materials to write their own stories about "if dinosaurs came back." Provide a time for the students to share their stories.

2. Tell students to use the last page of the book (where all the dinosaurs are pictured) as a guide and go back through the story to see how many dinosaurs they can recognize and name.

3. Ask students to select one of the dinosaurs in the story and write a letter to it saying why they would like it to come back or why they wouldn't.

4. Tell students to pretend that it is possible to bring back the dinosaurs; first, however, they must convince their community that it is a good idea. Divide the students into pairs, and ask them to create a full-page newspaper advertisement that will convince the community. Display these advertisements.

Specific Activities: *Danny and the Dinosaurs*
Danny and the Dinosaurs, by Syd Hoff, is a fantasy book that describes the joys of having a dinosaur as a pet. Using this book, select appropriate activities for your students from the following:

1. Ask students to pretend they have a dinosaur like Danny's and it gets lost. Have each student create a reward poster to get his or her dinosaur back.

2. Tell students to create their own list of activities for their pet dinosaur to do. Then ask them to illustrate their pet dinosaurs. Compile the illustrations and lists into a class booklet, *Our Dinosaur Pets*.

3. Have students conduct a survey among their classmates and neighbors. The question would be "If you had a dinosaur at home, what one job or task would you like it to do?" Have students compile the responses into a list by listing the person's name and what they'd like the dinosaur to do; that is:

Name of Interviewee	Job or Task
Mother	Wash windows

Duplicate this list and give each participant a copy.

Specific Activities: *The Secret Dinosaur*

The Secret Dinosaur, by Marilyn Hirsh, is a fantasy book that explains the difficulty Bill and Jane have in trying to hide a hungry dinosaur. Using this book, select appropriate activities for your students from the following:

1. Tell students to write a letter to their parents and neighbors convincing them that it would be beneficial for the students if they could keep the dinosaur, described in this book, as a pet.

2. Ask students to make a list of the possible places they might hide a dinosaur in their neighborhood. Allow time for them to share and discuss their lists of hiding places.

3. Create a contest in which students illustrate, on a 9-by-12-inch sheet of paper, a good hiding place for a dinosaur. Allow one week for them to submit their ideas. Then display all the ideas, and have students vote on the best illustrations in different categories such as most original, silliest, most unusual, most practical. Provide blue ribbons for the winners.

Specific Activities: *Dinosaurs*

Dinosaurs, by Kathleen Daly and illustrated by Greg and Tim Hildebrandt, is an informational book that provides the names and kinds of dinosaurs, their habitats, size, weight, and so on. Using this book, select appropriate activities for your students from the following:

1. Tell students to pretend that they could add another page with another dinosaur to this book. Create an imaginary dinosaur by drawing a picture of it and then writing a paragraph describing it. In the description, include the name of the dinosaur, its length, weight, and height, what it eats, where it lives, who its enemies are, and so on. Next, compile all of these illustrations and descriptions into a book, *Our Imaginary Dinosaur Friends*.

2. Tell students that after reading the book they should select one dinosaur and, using an encyclopedia, do additional research. Ask them to write a brief report of their findings and share it with their classmates.

3. Provide students with science books, encyclopedias, and other reference books, and ask them to investigate reptiles living today that bear some resemblance to dinosaurs (i.e., crocodiles, turtles, lizards). Tell them to make a list of these reptiles that

include the similarities and differences (i.e., what they look like, where they live, and what they eat); that is:

Name of Reptile	Similarities	Differences
Turtle	Four legs	Pulls head under shell

CULMINATION: There is at least one dinosaur name for each letter of the alphabet. Assign one letter to each student or group of students and tell them to find a dinosaur whose name begins with that letter. Next, have them draw the dinosaur and write a one-page summary describing it. The summary should include the following information: pronunciation of the dinosaur's name, its size, where it lived, what it eats, and so on. Finally, compile these reports into an *ABC of Dinosaurs*.

EVALUATION: The culminating product can be evaluated using the following criteria:
1. Do the illustrations and text reflect an understanding of the main types of dinosaurs and their characteristics?
2. Does the student-made ABC book allow the reader to gain a better understanding of the variety of dinosaurs and their characteristics?
3. Are the illustrations creative?

RELATED WORKS OF LITERATURE

Andrews, Roy Chapman. *All About Dinosaurs*. Illustrated by Thomas W. Voter. Random House, 1953.

Arnold, Caroline. *Dinosaur Mountain: Graveyard of the Past*. Photographs by Richard Hewett. Clarion, 1989.

Branley, Franklin. M. *Dinosaurs, Asteroids, and Superstars: Why the Dinosaurs Disappeared*. Illustrated by Jean Zallinger. Thomas Y. Crowell, 1982.

Brown, Marc, and Stephen Krensky. *Dinosaurs Beware! A Safety Guide*. Atlantic Monthly, 1982.

Cobb, Vickie. *The Monsters Who Died: A Mystery About Dinosaurs*. Illustrated by Greg Wenzel. Conrad-McCann, 1983.

Craig, Jean M. *Dinosaurs and More Dinosaurs*. Illustrated by George Solonevich. Four Winds Press, 1965.

Freedman, Russell. *Dinosaurs and Their Young*. Illustrated by Leslie Morrel. Holiday House, 1983.

Knight, David C. *"Dinosaurs" That Swam and Flew*. Illustrated by Lee J. Ames. Prentice-Hall, 1985.

Parish, Peggy. *Dinosaur Time*. Illustrated by Arnold Lobel. Harper & Row, 1974.

Rowe, Erna. *Giant Dinosaurs*. Illustrated by Merle Smith. Scholastic Book Services, 1973.

Sattler, Helen Roney. *The Illustrated Dinosaur Dictionary*. Illustrated by Pamela Carrol. Lothrop, Lee & Shepard, 1983.

———. *Dinosaurs of North America*. Illustrated by Anthony Rao. Lothrop, Lee, & Shepard, 1981.

Selsam, Millicent. *Tyrannosaurus Rex*. Illustrated with photos. Harper & Row, 1978.

Shuttlesworth, Dorothy. *To Find A Dinosaur*. Doubleday, 1973.

Stanton, Harry. *Now You Can Read About Dinosaurs*. Illustrated by Bob Hersey. Brimax Books, 1984.

Zallinger, Peter. *Dinosaurs and Other Archosaurus*. Random House, 1986.

Zim, Herbert. *Dinosaurs*. Illustrated by James G. Irving. Morrow, 1954.

LITERATURE AND
THE CURRICULUM:
A THEMATIC APPROACH

Thematic Unit:
Intermediate Level
(Social Studies)

THEME: Pioneer Life (Social Studies).

FOCUS: Students will become aware of the changes and challenges facing the pioneers who settled the American West and will understand the ways in which the pioneer spirit affects their own lives.

OBJECTIVES: On completion of this thematic unit, students will
1. use a map to trace the paths of pioneers as they moved west
2. use problem-solving strategies to generate solutions to some of the problems and dangers faced by the pioneers
3. describe the "pioneer spirit" and relate how it affects their lives today
4. relate the contributions of some of the great pioneer leaders
5. express insights into pioneer life gained through their reading of historical fiction, nonfiction, legends, and poetry
6. create works of art, music, and drama to retell the story of America's pioneers.

MATERIALS:
1. Slides of artwork depicting pioneers and pioneer life.
2. Copies of songbooks or records that convey the spirit of the West.
3. Small pieces of fabric for making a patchwork quilt.
4. Student copies of the following:
   Sarah, Plain and Tall, by Patricia MacLachlan. New York: Harper & Row, 1985.
   Little House on the Prairie, by Laura Ingalls Wilder. New York: Harper & Row, 1971.
   Prairie Songs, by Pam Conrad. New York: Harper & Row, 1985.
5. Large map of the United States.

6. A collection of informational books on pioneer life (see "Related Works of Literature" at the end of this section).
7. Photographs of pioneers and the journey West.

ACTIVITIES: It is not necessary, nor is it suggested, to use all the activities included. They are intended as a guide to illustrate the scope of activities that can be developed. Selection should be based on student needs, interests, and objectives.

General Activities:

1. With students, create a thematic web of pioneer life. Many of the activities in this portion of the unit were developed from the topics generated from the following web.

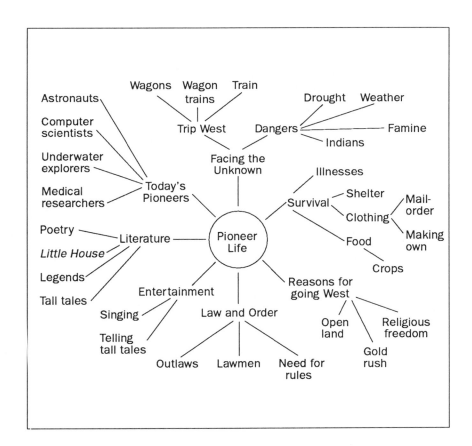

2. Hang butcher paper and allow students to continually add pictures and words that reflect their perceptions of pioneer life.

3. Display artwork that depicts life in the Old West and the days of the pioneers. Take photographs of artwork in books and display them in the form of slides or pictures. Have each student select a favorite picture and then try to recreate the image; have them write a brief biography of the artist and share their feelings about the work of art and what it represents.

4. Have each student select and learn a favorite song about pioneer life. Then have the students teach the song to a small group of students so that they can sing it at the festival campfire described in the culmination activity on page 359. (Many pioneer songs can be found in *America Sings*, by Carl Carmer.) Songs may include "Old Dan Tucker," "Davy Crockett," "Cumberland Gap," "John Henry," "Good-by Old Paint," "Get Along Cayuse," and "Home, Home on the Range."

5. Involve students in a problem-solving strategy based on difficulties encountered during a wagon-train trip. For example, students might wish to target the problem of leadership, and one of their solution ideas might center on the need for laws and rules on a wagon train. (See "Creative Problem Solving" in Chapter 15.)

6. Have students each choose ten personal items they would take with them if they had to leave their homes and journey by covered wagon across the continent. Once students have listed ten items, have them cut the list to five and defend their selections. This activity will help them prioritize values.

7. Provide each student with a 12-by-12-inch piece of fabric. On this piece of fabric, have each student illustrate a scene from pioneer life for a patchwork quilt of the Old West. Information on quilting can be obtained from books such as *The Quilt Story*, by Tony Johnson, or *The Quilt*, by Ann Jonas.

8. Hold a cooking class in which students make some of the foods discussed in the books about pioneer life. Students will have to research the foods to find recipes. A collection of these recipes can be combined to create a *Pioneer Cookbook*.

9. Involve students in a simulation of decision making on a wagon train using "Pioneers," published by Interact, P.O. Box 997-589, Lakeside, California 92040.

10. With students, brainstorm a list of today's pioneers. Have each student select one pioneer and create a chart to illustrate the dangers he or she faced. What connections can they make between the Old West pioneers and today's pioneers?

Specific Activities: Historical Fiction

Sarah, Plain and Tall, **by Patricia MacLachlan.** This is a touching story of a young woman who journeys West to begin a new life on the frontier. As students read *Sarah, Plain and Tall,* have them complete the following activities:

1. Write a travel diary as if you were Sarah, describing the journey West, her fears, and her reasons for leaving her home in Maine.

2. List details of frontier life as described in the book, and then look through nonfiction books and compare the details. Write a brief paper to explain why *Sarah, Plain and Tall* is considered "historical fiction."

3. Create a chart comparing the differences between life in Maine and life on the frontier as discussed in the book. Items compared can include animals, plants and vegetation, transportation, dangers, weather, and so on.

4. List clues and formulate a hypothesis as to where Sarah settled. Research this area to see if the facts back up your hypothesis.

5. Create a class book of illustrations for *Sarah, Plain and Tall* that reflects students' perceptions of the characters and setting.

Little House on the Prairie, **by Laura Ingalls Wilder.** This is one of a series of *Little House* books and relates the story of Laura Ingalls Wilder and her family as they travel by covered wagon through the West. As they read *Little House on the Prairie,* involve students in the following activities:

1. After reading *Little House on the Prairie,* write a paragraph to describe Laura Ingalls based on your perceptions. Read a biography of Laura Ingalls or an encyclopedia entry about her. Which material made you feel closest to Laura and which gave you a deeper understanding of her?

2. On the class map of the United States, trace the route Laura and her family followed.

3. Read another of the *Little House* titles. Create a sociogram (see "Characterization" in Chapter 7) based on this book and one based on *Little House on the Prairie* to describe Laura's relationship with the others in her family. Compare the two sociograms and discuss how Laura's relationships changed and reasons for these changes.

4. The pioneers were inventive and creative. They did not have the appliances and tools we have today, and they had to adapt available materials to accomplish a multitude of chores. Imagine that you are living in the 1800s. Using any of the materials described in *Little House on the Prairie*, create a leisure-time game for children to play. Make this game and teach others in the class to play it.

5. Participate in a shared inquiry lesson (see "Shared Inquiry" in Chapter 15): Are families better off today or during the time described in *Little House*?

6. Create a travel brochure to advertise the American West during the 1800s. Use descriptions included in *Little House* to help with the text.

7. Imagine what the Osage chief might have said to his tribe and to the other tribes to persuade them to ride off in peace rather than make war. Use your knowledge of the book's characters and their motivation to create and deliver a persuasive speech as if you were the chief.

8. Select one of the following:

a. In the book, Charles Ingalls says, "There's no great loss without some gain." Draw a cartoon to illustrate this quote.

b. When the Ingalls family was forced to leave their home, Charles Ingalls says, ". . . we're taking more out of Indian Territory than we took in." What does he mean? Give an example from your life that illustrates this philosophy.

Prairie Songs, by Pam Conrad. This is the story of a family living in the Nebraska prairie. Louisa, the main character, provides insights into prairie life and its paradoxical qualities. As students read *Prairie Songs*, have them complete the following activities:

1. Before reading the book, analyze the illustration on the title page. Describe the people; how are they dressed? Imagine the type of life they must have led and discuss it. Record these

ideas and compare them to what you uncover from reading the book to see how accurate your perceptions were.

2. Louisa describes a soddy in great detail. Based on her description, use sod and make a small soddy. Put the soddy outside and every day, for several weeks, record the temperature inside and outside the soddy. What did you discover? Why do you think the pioneers lived in this type of shelter?

3. Louisa speaks admiringly of Emmeline and often compares her mother to Emmeline. Fold a piece of paper lengthwise in half. List Emmeline's qualities on one side and Louisa's mother's qualities on the other. Place an asterisk next to the ten qualities you believe are most important for survival in pioneer days. Rank those qualities you choose by placing a 1 by the quality you think is most important, a 2 by the next most important, and so on. Discuss the rankings and, with your classmates, try to reach a consensus. Look at the list of qualities again. Which qualities are most admired today? What does this tell you about our values?

4. Create a monologue that one of the characters might have delivered to describe life on the prairie.

5. List the pros and cons of pioneer life. Prepare a skit that incorporates the paradoxical nature of the prairie. For example, the lonely prairie stretched endlessly in all directions, yet to Louisa, the prairie was far from lonely. To Louisa, the prairie was "like the comfort of a blank wall without too many things on it, or a stretch of clean, flawless sand down at the river."

6. Based on the problems described in the book, create a "Survival Guide" for a person traveling to the West in the 1850s.

Specific Activities: Informational Books

Many informational books relating to pioneer life and life in the American West have been written. The following generic activities can be adapted to extend learning from a variety of nonfiction materials:

1. Read about the hardships facing the pioneers. Write a paper to discuss "The Best of Times and the Worst of Times."

2. Read about a famous pioneer of the West. Compose a letter from this pioneer to friends in the East telling about his or her experiences.

3. Locate several photographs of pioneer times in a book. Ask your teacher to copy these photographs. Create questions that will ask other students to analyze the pictures. Then compare their analysis with information from the book, and share the comparison with the students who did the analysis.

4. Research one of the famous trails that took settlers west in the 1800s (i.e., the Oregon Trail, the Santa Fe Trail, the Donner Pass). Trace the trail on the classroom map. With a group of others, summarize any interesting stories connected with the trail and place the summary in the appropriate location on the map.

5. Select one of the following topics: clothing, crops, food, education, transportation, crafts, shelter, medical care, weather, Indian attacks, or other factors affecting pioneer life. Locate information on the topic and share the information in a creative way, either through poetry, art, music, or drama.

6. Create a time capsule that might have been left by the pioneers in the 1800s. It might contain pictures, letters, artwork, crafts, pieces of cloth, copies of songs, or poetry that reflect life at that time.

Specific Activities: Legends

As America grew and her people moved west, many heroes emerged. Tales of these heroes matched the vast open spaces of the West. The accomplishments of these heroes were hyperbole. As the pioneers overcame hardships, so did the heroes—and in a big way! Paul Bunyan, Captain Stormalong, Mike Fink, Daniel Boone, Davy Crockett, Johnny Appleseed, Windwagon Smith, John Henry, and Pecos Bill extolled the American virtues of courage, fortitude, and ingenuity. Some of these heroes were real people; others, embodying a cornucopia of qualities, became real through the yarns spun about them around the campfire. These legends, uniquely American, are often referred to as "tall tales." As students study frontier life, a knowledge of American tall tales helps them understand the humor and courage that have shaped our great nation.

1. What is a *tall tale*? Read several tall tales to students. (Tall tales are best told orally since they were passed along by word of mouth for generations.) Discuss the following questions and attempt to reach a consensus for a definition of a tall tale:

What did these stories have in common?

What factual information was included in each?

How is a tall tale like America?

How would you describe a tall tale?

2. Ask students to select a tall tale and read it with a partner. Have each pair create a chart that lists the facts and exaggerations included in the tale.

3. Watch filmstrips of several tall tales. Read poems about several tall-tale heroes such as those found in *America Forever New*, compiled by Sara and John Brewton. Have students select a favorite tall-tale character and create a caricature or poem.

4. Choral read the portion of Carl Sandburg's "The People, Yes" (included in *America Forever New*) that deals with heroes of the tall tale. Have students identify the characters being described in the verses. Ask students to add a verse to the poem that describes their favorite western hero and his or her feats.

5. Ask students to create a recipe for a "Whopper," write it on poster board, and illustrate it. For example:

Ingredients

1 giant hero

3 cups exaggeration

1 well-explained phenomenon

5 cups imagination

4 tablespoons historical facts

Directions: Mix ingredients thoroughly. Serve in large portions with a straight face. Store in a warm heart.

6. Have students create their own "Whoppers" based on a pioneer. Illustrate. Bind tales in tall books!

Specific Activities: Poetry

The following steps can help students gain a greater understanding and feeling for any of the poetry included in the thematic units:

1. Read the poem aloud to students.

2. Choral read the poem with the class.

3. Discuss each verse, focusing on the poet's purpose, the feelings and mood evoked, how the poet accomplished his or her purpose, and connections between the poem and the focus of the thematic unit.

4. Choral read the poem a second time.

5. At intervals, have students create their own verses, using the poem as a model of style.

Involve students in the following activities:

1. Read "The Pioneer" with students and discuss its theme and the mood it evokes. Group students and let each group select one of today's pioneers. Ask them to create a poem from this pioneer's perspective to describe his or her feelings about the accomplishments and contributions made. The original poem may be used as a model.

The Pioneer

Long years ago I blazed a trail
    Through lovely woods unknown till then
And marked with cairns of splintered shale
    A mountain way for other men;

For other men who came and came:
    They trod the path more plain to see,
They gave my trail another's name
    And no one speaks or knows of me.

The trail runs high, the trail runs low
    Where windflowers dance or columbine;
The scars are healed that long ago
    My ax cut deep on birch and pine.

Another's name my trail may bear,
    But still I keep, in waste and wood,
My joy because the trail is there,
    My peace because the trail is good.
             — Arthur Guiterman

2. Read the first two lines of "Immigrants" (from *America Forever New*). Ask students to relate who "these foreigners with strange and avid faces . . ." are. Read the final two lines of the poem and discuss who these immigrants are. Discuss the meaning of irony and discuss why this poem is a good example of irony. Have students relate, in written form, the way the poem made them feel and how it affected their feelings about immigrants.

Immigrants

"These foreigners with strange and avid faces
Crowding our shores, marring our pleasant places,
They must be curbed. . . ." So mused King Powhatan,
Hundred per cent, red-blood American.
                                        —Nancy Byrd Turner

CULMINATION: Have students use any communication form such as poetry, prose, art, or music to relate their interpretation of the "Pioneer Spirit." Encourage them to use quotations, facts, and information gained through literature. The final product should include the way in which a knowledge of pioneer life and the pioneer spirit affects their own outlook on life and how it relates to the present.

At the end of the unit, hold a "Pioneer Festival," in which participants are transported to the days of the pioneers' settling the American West. Recreate a scene from pioneer times and have students dress in pioneer garb. Many of the activities students have been involved with during this unit will result in products that can be shared during the festival. For example, decorate the room with student crafts, artwork, and writings. Simulate a campfire and have students sit around the "fire," singing songs, retelling stories and legends of pioneer days, and presenting original monologues, skits, stories, and poems. Serve the foods created in the cooking class. Invite parents, school administrators, other classes, and enjoy being a pioneer!

EVALUATION: The final culmination project, "Pioneer Spirit," can be evaluated based on the following criteria:
1. Was the student able to connect information gained from reading to their own personal philosophy?
2. Was the project creative?
3. Did the student understand the changes and challenges facing the pioneers of the American West (the unit's focus)?

RELATED WORKS OF LITERATURE

Historical Fiction

Aldrich, Rose. *A Lantern in Her Hand.* New American Library, 1983.
Brink, Carol R. *Caddie Woodlawn.* Macmillan, 1936.
Dalgliesh, Alice. *The Courage of Sarah Noble.* Scribner's, 1954.
Harvey, Brett. *My Prairie Year.* Holiday House, 1986.
Wilder, Laura Ingalls. The *Little House* Series. Harper & Row, 1953.

Informational Books

Carmer, Carol. *America Sings.* Knopf, 1942.
Felton, Harold. *Cowboy Jamboree—Western Songs and Lore.* Knopf, 1975.
Freedman, Russell. *Children of the Wild West.* Clarion Books, 1983.
Grant, Bruce. *Famous American Trails.* Rand McNally, 1971.
Johnson, Tony. *The Quilt Story.* Illustrated by Tomie de Paola. Putnam, 1985.
Jonas, Ann. *The Quilt.* Greenwillow, 1984.
Laycock, George and Ellen. *How the Settlers Lived.* McKay, 1980.
Place, Marian T. *American Cattle Trails, East and West.* Holt, Rinehart & Winston, 1967.
Rounds, Glen. *The Treeless Plains.* Holiday House, 1967.

Legends

Blair, Walter. *Tall Tale America: A Legendary History of Our Humourous Heroes.* Coward, McCann & Geoghegan, 1944.
Bowman, James C. *Pecos Bill.* Albert Whitman & Co., 1964.
Shephard, Esther. *Paul Bunyan.* Harcourt Brace Jovanovich, 1952.
Stoutenburg, Adrien. *American Tall Tales.* Viking Press, 1966.

Poetry

Brewton, Sara and John. *America Forever New. A Book of Poems.* Thomas Y. Crowell, 1968.
Guiterman, Arthur. *I Sing the Pioneer.* Dutton, 1926.
Lindsey, Vachel. *Johnny Appleseed and Other Poems.* Macmillan, 1928.
Sandburg, Carl. *Wind Song.* Harcourt Brace Jovanovich, 1960.
Wild, Peter, and Frank Graziano, eds. *New Poetry of the American West.* Logbridge Rhodes, 1982.

Thematic Unit:
Intermediate Level/
Middle School*
(Science)

THEME: Space Exploration (Science).

FOCUS: Students will analyze the contributions of space exploration and evaluate the need and importance of continued
funding for space exploration and space colonization.

OBJECTIVES: On completion of this thematic unit, students will
1. trace the development of space exploration and its contributions to our understanding of space and our own planet
2. identify contributions of space exploration to society and to
the individual's daily life
3. compare the astronauts' qualities with those of the early
pioneers who settled the West
4. analyze and evaluate the possibility of space colonization
5. support or refute the statement: "Yesterday's science fiction
is today's reality"
6. summarize various myths that relate to the constellations
and create original myths
7. use our Constitution as a model for creating a constitution for
a space colony
8. compare two works of science fiction and relate how they
affected their attitudes toward space exploration and colonization
9. design an experiment that can be carried out in a space lab

---

*Most of the objectives and activities are appropriate for both intermedi-
ate grades and middle school grades. However, the literature selected under
science fiction is more suitable for students in middle school, grades 6–9.

MATERIALS:

1. A collection of informational books dealing with space exploration, planets, constellations, space satellites, and space colonization (*Note:* A variety of articles, pamphlets, and brochures dealing with space exploration, planets, and satellites are available at no charge from NASA. NASA also has a film library that lends films without charge except return postage. Requests for a film catalog and the above mentioned written materials may be sent to: John F. Kennedy Space Center, Kennedy Space Center, Florida 32899, Attention: Educator's Resources Laboratory. Requests may be forwarded, depending on where you live, to one of nine resource centers around the country. Audiovisual materials—videotapes, slides, filmstrips—that trace NASA's research and technology can be obtained for a very nominal fee from CORE [Central Operations of Resources for Educators], Lorain County JVS, 15181 Route 58 South, Oberlin, Ohio 44074.)

2. Tapes or records of songs dealing with a space theme such as the themes from *2001 . . . A Space Odyssey*, *E.T.*, *Star Trek*, and *Star Wars*.

3. A collection of biographies of famous space pioneers (see "Specific Activities: Biographies" for a suggested list of names).

4. A collection of myths dealing with characters for whom the planets (Mercury, Venus, Mars, Jupiter, Saturn, Neptune, Uranus, and Pluto) and constellations (i.e., Andromeda, Cassiopeia, Centaurus, Hercules, Orion, Pegasus, and Perseus) were named.

5. Teacher's copy of *The War of the Worlds*, by H. G. Wells. New York: Bantam Books, 1988.

6. Student copies of *The Martian Chronicles*, by Ray Bradbury. New York: Bantam Books, 1988.

7. A collection of science fiction books (see "Related Science Fiction" at the end of this section).

ACTIVITIES: It is not necessary, nor is it suggested, to use all the activities included. They are intended as a guide to illustrate the scope of activities that can be developed. Selection should be based on student needs, interests, and objectives.

General Activities:

1. Create a thematic web of space exploration. Many of the activities in this portion of the unit were developed from the topics generated from the following web.

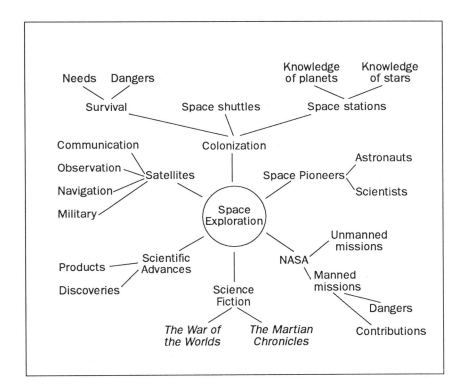

2. Create a bulletin board with the following quote: "Man must rise above the Earth . . . to the top of the atmosphere and beyond for only thus will he understand the world in which he lives" (Socrates). Encourage students to react to this quote and place reactions around the quotation.

3. Have students analyze the different portions of our country's Constitution. Have them create a constitution for a new colony in space. Be sure they include a Bill of Rights and a preamble.

4. Create a "Space . . . The Final Frontier" time line. As students read about the advances in space exploration, have them add events and dates to the time line.

5. Have students research the amount of spending that is allocated for space exploration. They can get this information by writing to their congressional representative or to NASA, Washington, D.C. 20546.

6. Have students design a papier-mâché model of our galaxy, keeping sizes relative.

7. Play music that is related to space, such as the themes from *2001 . . . A Space Odyssey*, *E.T.*, *Star Trek*, or *Star Wars*. Discuss how the music captures the mood of space. Have students create a picture or dance inspired by one of the pieces of music selected.

Specific Activities: Biography

Have each student research various space pioneers and select a biography of one of them. Space pioneers may include but are not limited to

Edward E. Aldrin, Jr.	Virgil Grissom
William A. Anders	Johannes Kepler
Neil A. Armstrong	James A. Lovell, Jr.
Guion S. Bluford, Jr.	(Sharon) Crista MacAuliffe
Frank Borman	Sir Isaac Newton
Scott M. Carpenter	Sally K. Ride
Nicolaus Copernicus	Alan B. Shepard
Robert L. Crippen	Valentina Tereshkova
Yuri Gagarin	Edward J. White
John H. Glenn, Jr.	Wernher von Braun
Robert H. Goddard	James W. Young

Based on the space pioneer selected and after reading a biography of the person, students may

1. become members of a "Panel of Space Pioneers." As a panel member, each student must dress as the pioneer may have dressed and relate to the rest of the class his or her background, contributions, successes, failures, motivation, and any other information that will allow others to better understand him or her.

2. write an article for *Space-Age News* about the space pioneer.

3. become part of the game show "What's My Line." Students prepare and ask questions of an individual (role-playing the space pioneer) to learn the identity of the pioneer, based on accomplishments.

4. list ten criteria for astronaut selection. Get together in a group of four or five and, from the criteria mentioned, choose the five criteria the group feels are most important. Now get together with the entire class and try to reach a consensus as to the five criteria most important in selecting an astronaut.

5. compare, in written or artistic form, the astronauts and other space pioneers with the early pioneers who settled the West.

6. become part of a four-member group and prepare a "Meeting of the Minds" in which each member role-plays the pioneer selected. Each group should discuss, before the rest of the class, a thought-provoking question. Questions can be of the group's own choosing or may include

Is it possible for humans to live in space for any length of time?

Is our government doing enough to foster space exploration?

Should we set up space colonies?

What problems might arise if we colonize space?

Who should "claim" the areas of space that are colonized?

Specific Activities: Mythology

Display a collection of myths in which the main characters are those for whom the planets (Mercury, Venus, Mars, Uranus, Saturn, Jupiter, Neptune, and Pluto) and the constellations (i.e., Andromeda, Cassiopeia, Centaurus, Hercules, Orion, Pegasus, and Perseus) were named. Also have available factual books dealing with the planets and constellations. Involve students in the following activities:

1. Create a new constellation, using the following steps:

a. Read a myth dealing with the origin of one of the constellations.

b. Summarize the myth. Be sure to include the following: name of the myth, summary of myth, name of constellation being explained.

c. Read factual information about the constellation. List three facts about the constellation.

d. Divide a piece of paper in half. On the left side, draw a picture of the constellation and include its name. On the right side of the paper, place the stars of the constellation, but connect them differently to form a new constellation and give it an original name.

e. Create a myth to explain the origin of this new constellation. Include actual mythological characters and at least three facts (see Step C above) about the constellation.

2. Select one of the planets. Research the planet and the name of the mythological character for whom the planet was named. Draw a picture of the planet, and briefly explain why the name was (or was not) a good choice.

3. Research other mythological characters. If Earth were to be renamed, choose a mythological character's name that you feel would be most appropriate and explain why.

Specific Activities: Poetry

Scientists, writers, and poets all look at the same heavenly bodies, yet they react to the beauty and mystery of space in different ways. Read the following haikus and involve students in the activities:

Moon moves down the sky
westward as true shadows flow
eastward and vanish.
—Buson

A full moon comes up
and stars, stars uncountable,
drown in a green sky.
—Skiki

O that moon last night!
no wonder everyone needs
an afternoon nap.
—Teitoku

O Moon, why must you
inspire my neighbor to chirp
all night on a flute!
—Koyo

1. Choral read each haiku. Discuss each haiku individually. What is the poet describing? Why is each haiku effective? What makes a poem a haiku? (three lines, with a total of 17 syllables: 5 in line one, 7 in line two, and 5 in line three) Why are these poems considered haikus even though they don't all have the correct syllables? (They were translated from Japanese.)

2. Have students select a planet, star, or the moon, and create their own haikus. Illustrations can be original or cut from magazines.

Specific Activities: Informational Books

1. Ask students to select a specific planet and read an informational book on the planet and
   a. prepare a skit to tell others about the planet. The skit should be factual as well as fictitious. For example, since Mercury is very hot on one side and very cold on the other, students might have a fashion show to describe the different types of clothing worn by Mercurians.
   b. write an essay to explain why the planet would, or would not, be a good choice for a space colony.
   c. design a futuristic space station based on the planet's actual needs and features.

2. Have students read an informational book dealing with space satellites—such as weather, observation, navigation, scientific, military—and
   a. develop a commercial for one of the space satellites being used today, describing its benefits (i.e., communication satellites send telephone calls and television pictures around the world).
   b. draw or make a model of one of the space satellites. Write a brief paragraph to accompany it that describes the uses and benefits of the satellite.

3. Have students read an informational book dealing with one of the following manned space programs: Mercury, Gemini, Apollo, Apollo-Soyuz Test Project, SkyLab, and the space shuttles (*Columbia*, *Challenger*, *Discovery*, and *Atlantis*). Have students select one mission from each of the programs. Have them write, on an index card, the name of the mission, the dates, the astronauts or cosmonauts, the main purpose of the mission, and its most significant contributions. Place the cards on the "Space . . . the Final Frontier" time line.

4. Have each student read nonfiction information dealing with one of the following NASA Planetary Exploration Missions: Mariner 2, 4, 5, 6, 7, 9, or 20; Pioneer 10 or 11; Viking 1 or 2; Pioneer Venus 1 or 2. Have the students write, on an index card, the name of the mission, the dates, the main purpose of the mission and its

most significant contributions. Place the card on the "Space . . . the Final Frontier" time line.

5. Have students read an informational book based on the space shuttles. Students may choose to

    a. list problems and needs related to living in space for a length of time (i.e., food, clothing, sleeping, coping with weightlessness). Select one of these problems and research how the crews have dealt with this problem. Draw a humorous cartoon to illustrate your findings.

    b. read about several experiments conducted in the space lab. Design an experiment to be conducted in space.

    c. write an application to be a member of a space shuttle crew as a payload specialist. A payload specialist is not an astronaut. He or she is a career scientist or engineer who is selected to perform a specific experiment or job.

6. Consider the future of space exploration. Read about the space station (a permanent multipurpose facility in orbit) that is being developed and will serve as a laboratory to conduct research, an observatory, a manufacturing plant, an assembly plant where structures can be put together, a storehouse to keep spare parts, and a garage where other spacecraft can be repaired. It will have both manned and unmanned facilities.

    a. Write and deliver a persuasive speech to get additional funding for the space station.

    b. Create an "artist's" rendering of a space station.

Specific Activities: Science Fiction

Before reading *The War of the Worlds* and *The Martian Chronicles*, involve students in the following activities:

1. A Taba lesson dealing with the formation of a concept of *science fiction* (see Chapter 15, "Taba Strategies," for steps to follow in *concept formation*.)

2. Ask students to listen to or read these science fiction novels with the following question in mind: Can yesterday's science fiction be today's reality? Encourage students to jot down ideas as they become involved with the readings.

After reading the two suggested books, involve students in the following activities:

1. Compare the two stories.

    In what ways were *The War of the Worlds* and *The Martian Chronicles* alike?

In what ways were these two stories different?

Which did you enjoy the most? Why?

In which story was the view of human qualities most accurate? Why?

Which story troubled you most? Why?

Which story seemed most believable? Why?

Which would you rate as the most outstanding example of science fiction? Why? Explain the criteria you are using to help you make this judgment.

2. Participate in a shared inquiry (see Chapter 15, "Shared Inquiry") to answer the question: Can yesterday's science fiction be today's reality?

***The War of the Worlds,* by H. G. Wells.** Written by one of the most famous writers of science fiction, *The War of the Worlds* is a classic that explores the possibility of intelligent life on Mars and describes the invasion of Earth by the Martians. (*Note:* We suggest that you read aloud *The War of the Worlds.* The chapters are brief enough that each can be read in a single read-aloud session.) Involve students in the following activities.

1. Have the class listen for "facts" that the author includes that make the plot seem plausible. Ask the class to list these facts. Have each student or group of students research one of the facts to check its accuracy and then report findings to the rest of the class.

2. After reading Chapter 3, ask students to write a paragraph describing what each believes the Martians will look like. Have students make a sketch of the Martians based on their description. Next, have them give their description to another student who can then draw the Martian from the description. Compare illustrations!

3. After reading Chapter 4, ask students to draw the beings from H. G. Wells's description and compare Wells's descriptions with their own. They may find, for example, that their Martians were more "humanlike," more "benevolent," and so on.

4. Have students create a new life form, a combination Martian–Earthling. Ask them to list the qualities of the Martians, as described in the book, and then make a list of human qualities. Then have them combine these qualities in a creative way, draw this new creature, and give him or her a name.

5. In *The War of the Worlds*, one of the most significant problems was the inability of the people of Earth to communicate with the aliens from Mars. Ask students to list as many nonverbal ways to communicate as they can. Then have each student or group of students choose one of the methods listed and use it to communicate a message.

6. Orson Welles adapted *The War of the Worlds*, changed the setting to the New York metropolitan area, and broadcast news of the Martian invasion over the radio. Listeners thought the broadcast was an actual news report and panicked, leaving their homes in droves. Have students create their own radio broadcast, modeling it after *The War of the Worlds* but changing the setting. Students can work in groups and use whatever special effects they can develop to make the report as realistic as possible. Optional: Play Orson Welles's broadcast *War of the Worlds*. Discuss what made it so effective.

7. After the death of the Martians, H. G. Wells wrote, "Surely, if we have learned nothing else, this war has taught us pity—pity for those witless souls that suffer our dominion." Have students write an editorial explaining and extending this thought. Have them also include what they learned from *The War of the Worlds*.

8. Engage students in a discussion of the following: Almost one hundred years after it was written, *The War of the Worlds* is still as startling and vivid as it was then. Why, when we have much more explicit science fiction books and films, does *The War of the Worlds* have the effect it does?

The Martian Chronicles, by Ray Bradbury. This classic chronicles the expeditions of Earth people who go to Mars to begin a new life and again find the "dream" that motivated earlier exploration and immigration. (*Note:* We suggest that each student has a copy of this book since many of the activities will require them to go back and analyze certain events that have been described. However, the book lends itself to being read aloud as well as silently.)

1. Ask students to describe the first four expeditions to Mars.

What were their missions?

Why did the first three fail?

How might failure have been avoided in each of the first three?

What did the crew of the fourth mission find when they arrived on Mars? Describe the Martian civilization and what happened to it.

Why did Spender begin to kill the other members of his crew? Were his fears well founded? Explain.

2. Benjamin Driscoll compared himself to Johnny Appleseed. Have students compare the first settlers on Mars to the pioneers who settled the American West and explain their responses.

3. *The Martian Chronicles* deals with many of the social problems we have on Earth: censorship, the large population of elderly, war, atomic weapons, prejudice. Make a list of these and the other problems described. Divide students into groups and have each group select one of the problems listed. Have them describe the problem as related in *The Martian Chronicles* and then describe the problem as it exists today. Have each group report orally on their comparison of findings in a creative manner.

4. *The Martian Chronicles* describes many lifelike robots that were built. Ask students to research the field of robotics to learn what progress had been made in the field by 1950 when *The Martian Chronicles* was first published and what strides have been made since then. Have students design and build a robot to carry out a specific task.

5. Many of the people of Earth left for Mars in the hope of building a better life. Involve students in a shared inquiry lesson (see Chapter 15) by asking them to formulate hypotheses to the following question: Will the people of Earth be able to create a new and improved civilization or are they bound to repeat the mistakes of the past?

6. Involve students in a discussion of the following dilemma, "A Scientist's Dilemma." (For the steps to follow in a discussion of moral dilemmas, see Chapter 15, "Discussion of Moral Dilemmas.")

A SCIENTIST'S DILEMMA

Dr. Julius Garelik, one of the world's foremost experts in bacteriology, has been with the space program for the past thirty years working on a top-secret project that will settle pioneers from Earth on Planet V. Planet V is the only planet that scientists have been able to discover that will sustain human life and that can be reached with technology as it now exists.

It is vital that Earth's inhabitants begin leaving at once for Planet V, since Earth has become a vast desert due to the intense heat caused by the greenhouse effect. Famine has hit the Earth and its people are dying by the tens of thousands.

Through experiments conducted of Planet V, scientists learn that intelligent life exists on the planet. By accident, Dr. Garelik learns that human settlement of Planet V will most certainly result in the extermination of all the planet's inhabitants, due to their lack of immune system. Dr. Garelik is the only person who possesses this vital information, and he also has the power to abort the entire mission. If he says nothing, the human race, as we know it, will continue to survive on Planet V. If he aborts the mission, the people of Planet V will survive. What should he do?

CULMINATION: Have students debate the issue: Should funding for space exploration and colonization be continued when money is so badly needed to solve social problems such as hunger, crime, and disease on Earth?

EVALUATION: The debate can be evaluated based on the following criteria:

1. Are the students able to connect information gained from reading to their argument?
2. Do they understand the contributions, moral obligations, and problems associated with space exploration and colonization?
3. Can they use the information persuasively?

RELATED SCIENCE FICTION:

Christopher, John. *When the Tripods Came*. Delacorte, 1988.
Engdahl, Sylvia L. *Journey Between Worlds*. Atheneum, 1970.
———. *Enchantress from the Stars*. Atheneum, 1970.
Fisk, Nicholas. *Grinny*. Elsevier-Nelson, 1974.
Harding, Lee. *The Fallen Spaceman*. Harper & Row, 1980.
Heinlein, Robert. *Podkaykne of Mars*. Putnam, 1963.
———. *Tunnel in the Sky*. Scribner's, 1955.
Hoover, H. M. *Orvis*. Viking, 1987.
Key, Alexander. *The Forgotten Door*. Westminster, 1965.
Lawrence, Louise. *Star Lord*. Harper & Row, 1978.
Walsh, Jill P. *The Green Book*. Farrar, Straus & Giroux, 1982.

A

Children's
Book Awards

Many awards, medals, and prizes
are given each year for outstanding children's literature in the
United States. The two best-known book awards are the Newbery Medal and the Caldecott Medal. The Newbery Medal is
awarded annually by the Children's Services Division of the
American Library Association to honor the most distinguished
contribution to literature for children published in the United
States during the previous year. The Caldecott Medal is awarded
annually to the illustrator of the most distinguished picture book
published in the United States during the previous year. Other
awards that are given to honor significant contributions in the
field of children's literature are as follows:

1. The Laura Ingalls Wilder Award is given every three years to
an author or illustrator whose books have made a substantial
and lasting contribution to children's literature.

2. The International Reading Association Children's Book Award,
which started in 1975, is awarded annually to an author who
shows universal promise in the field of children's literature.

3. The National Council of Teachers of English Award for Excel-
lence in Poetry for Children is given every three years to a living
American poet in recognition of his or her work of poetry.

4. The Hans Christian Andersen Award is given every two years to a living author who has made an important international contribution to children's literature. Since 1966 a medal has also been given to an outstanding illustrator.

5. The Children's Choice is a project of the International Reading Association and the Children's Book Council Joint Committee. The listing is a yearly selection by young readers of their favorite newly published books. The Choices are published in the October issue of *The Reading Teacher*.

THE NEWBERY MEDAL

1922 *The Story of Mankind* by Hendrik Willem van Loon, Liveright
Honor Books: *The Great Quest* by Charles Hawes, Little; *Cedric the Forester* by Bernard Marshall, Appleton; *The Old Tobacco Shop* by William Bowen, Macmillan; *The Golden Fleece and the Heroes Who Lived Before Achilles* by Padraic Colum, Macmillan; *Windy Hill* by Cornelia Meigs, Macmillan

1923 *The Voyages of Doctor Dolittle* by Hugh Lofting, Lippincott
Honor Books: No record

1924 *The Dark Frigate* by Charles Hawes, Atlantic/Little
Honor Books: No record

1925 *Tales from Silver Lands* by Charles Finger, Doubleday
Honor Books: *Nicholas* by Anne Carroll Moore, Putnam; *Dream Coach* by Anne Parrish, Macmillan

1926 *Shen of the Sea* by Arthur Bowie Chrisman, Dutton
Honor Book: *Voyagers* by Padraic Colum, Macmillan

1927 *Smoky, the Cowhorse* by Will James, Scribner's
Honor Books: No record

1928 *Gayneck, The Story of a Pigeon* by Dhan Gopal Mukerji, Dutton
Honor Books: *The Wonder Smith and His Son* by Ella Young, Longmans; *Downright Dencey* by Caroline Snedeker, Doubleday

1929 *The Trumpeter of Krakow* by Eric P. Kelly, Macmillan
Honor Books: *Pigtail of Ah Lee Ben Loo* by John Bennett, Longmans; *Millions of Cats* by Wanda Gág, Coward; *The Boy Who Was* by Grace Hallock, Dutton; *Clearing*

Weather by Cornelia Meigs, Little; *Runaway Papoose* by Grace Moon, Doubleday; *Tod of the Fens* by Elinor Whitney, Macmillan

1930 *Hitty, Her First Hundred Years* by Rachel Field, Macmillan
Honor Books: *Daughter of the Seine* by Jeanette Eaton, Harper; *Pran of Albania* by Elizabeth Miller, Doubleday; *Jumping-Off Place* by Marian Hurd McNeely, Longmans; *Tangle-Coated Horse and Other Tales* by Ella Young, Longmans; *Vaino* by Julia Davis Adams, Dutton; *Little Blacknose* by Hildegarde Swift, Harcourt

1931 *The Cat Who Went to Heaven* by Elizabeth Coatsworth, Macmillan
Honor Books: *Floating Island* by Anne Parrish, Harper; *The Dark Star of Itza* by Alida Malkus, Harcourt; *Queer Person* by Ralph Hubbard, Doubleday; *Mountains Are Free* by Julia Davis Adams, Dutton; *Spice and the Devil's Cave* by Agnes Hewes, Knopf; *Meggy Macintosh* by Elizabeth Janet Gray, Doubleday; *Garram the Hunter* by Herbert Best, Doubleday; *Ood-Le-Uk the Wanderer* by Alice Lide and Margaret Johansen, Little

1932 *Waterless Mountain* by Laura Adams Armer, Longmans
Honor Books: *The Fairy Circus* by Dorothy P. Lathrop, Macmillan; *Calico Bush* by Rachel Field, Macmillan; *Boy of the South Seas* by Eunice Tietjens, Coward; *Out of the Flame* by Eloise Lownsbery, Longmans; *Jane's Island* by Marjorie Allee, Houghton; *Truce of the Wolf and Other Tales of Old Italy* by Mary Gould Davis, Harcourt

1933 *Young Fu of the Upper Yangtze* by Elizabeth Foreman Lewis, Winston
Honor Books: *Swift Rivers* by Cornelia Meigs, Little; *The Railroad to Freedom* by Hildegarde Swift, Harcourt; *Children of the Soil* by Nora Burglon, Doubleday

1934 *Invincible Louisa* by Cornelia Meigs, Little
Honor Books: *The Forgotten Daughter* by Caroline Snedeker, Doubleday; *Swords of Steel* by Elsie Singmaster, Houghton; *ABC Bunny* by Wanda Gág, Coward; *Winged Girl of Knossos* by Erik Berry, Appleton; *New Land* by Sarah Schmidt, McBride; *Big Tree of Bunlahy* by Padraic Colum, Macmillan; *Glory of the Seas* by Agnes Hewes, Knopf; *Apprentice of Florence* by Anne Kyle, Houghton

1935 *Dobry* by Monica Shannon, Viking
      Honor Books: *Pageant of Chinese History* by Elizabeth
      Seeger, Longmans; *Davy Crockett* by Constance Rourke,
      Harcourt; *Day on Skates* by Hilda Van Stockum, Harper
1936 *Caddie Woodlawn* by Carol Brink, Macmillan
      Honor Books: *Honk, The Moose* by Phil Stong, Dod; *The
      Good Master* by Kate Seredy, Viking; *Young Walter Scott*
      by Elizabeth Janet Gray, Viking; *All Sail Set* by Arm-
      strong Sperry, Winston
1937 *Roller Skates* by Ruth Sawyer, Viking
      Honor Books: *Phebe Fairchild: Her Book* by Lois Lenski,
      Stokes; *Whistler's Van* by Idwal Jones, Viking; *Golden
      Basket* by Ludwig Bemelmans, Viking; *Winterbound* by
      Margery Bianco, Viking; *Audubon* by Constance Rourke,
      Harcourt; *The Codfish Musket* by Agnes Hewes, Dou-
      bleday
1938 *The White Stag* by Kate Seredy, Viking
      Honor Books: *Pecos Bill* by James Cloyd Bowman, Little;
      Bright Island by Mabel Robinson, Random; *On the Banks
      of Plum Creek* by Laura Ingalls Wilder, Harper
1939 *Thimble Summer* by Elizabeth Enright, Rinehart
      Honor Books: *Nino* by Valenti Angelo, Viking; *Mr. Pop-
      per's Penguins* by Richard and Florence Atwater, Little;
      "Hello the Boat!" by Phyllis Crawford, Holt; *Leader by
      Destiny: George Washington, Man and Patriot* by Jeanette
      Eaton, Harcourt; *Penn* by Elizabeth Janet Gray, Viking
1940 *Daniel Boone* by James Daugherty, Viking
      Honor Books: *The Singing Tree* by Kate Seredy, Viking;
      Runner of the Mountain Tops by Mabel Robinson,
      Random; *By the Shores of Silver Lake* by Laura Ingalls
      Wilder, Harper; *Boy with a Pack* by Stephen W. Meader,
      Harcourt
1941 *Call It Courage* by Armstrong Sperry, Macmillan
      Honor Books: *Blue Willow* by Doris Gates, Viking; *Young
      Mac of Fort Vancouver* by Mary Jane Carr, T. Crowell;
      The Long Winter by Laura Ingalls Wilder, Harper; *Nansen*
      by Anna Gertrude Hall, Viking
1942 *The Matchlock Gun* by Walter D. Edmonds, Dodd
      Honor Books: *Little Town on the Prairie* by Laura Ingalls
      Wilder, Harper; *George Washington's World* by

Genevieve Foster, Scribner's; *Indian Captive: The Story of Mary Jemison* by Lois Lenski, Lippincott; *Down Ryton Water* by Eva Roe Gaggin, Viking

1943 *Adam of the Road* by Elizabeth Janet Gray, Viking
Honor Books: *The Middle Moffat* by Eleanor Estes, Harcourt; *Have You Seen Tom Thumb?* by Mabel Leigh Hunt, Lippincott

1944 *Johnny Tremain* by Esther Forbes, Houghton
Honor Books: *These Happy Golden Years* by Laura Ingalls Wilder, Harper; *Fog Magic* by Julia Sauer, Viking; *Rufus M.* by Eleanor Estes, Harcourt; *Mountain Born* by Elizabeth Yates, Coward

1945 *Rabbit Hill* by Robert Lawson, Viking
Honor Books: *The Hundred Dresses* by Eleanor Estes, Harcourt; *The Silver Pencil* by Alice Dalgliesh, Scribner's; *Abraham Lincoln's World* by Genevieve Foster, Scribner's; *Lone Journey: The Life of Roger Williams* by Jeanette Eaton, Harcourt

1946 *Strawberry Girl* by Lois Lenski, Lippincott
Honor Books: *Justin Morgan Had a Horse* by Marguerite Henry, Rand; *The Moved-Outers* by Florence Crannell Means, Houghton; *Bhimsa, The Dancing Bear* by Christine Weston, Scribner's; *New Found World* by Katherine Shippen, Viking

1947 *Miss Hickory* by Carolyn Sherwin Bailey, Viking
Honor Books: *Wonderful Year* by Nancy Barnes, Messner; *Big Tree* by Mary and Conrad Buff, Viking; *The Heavenly Tenants* by William Maxwell, Harper; *The Avion My Uncle Flew* by Cyrus Fisher, Appleton; *The Hidden Treasure of Glaston* by Eleanore Jewett, Viking

1948 *The Twenty-one Balloons* by William Pène du Bois, Viking
Honor Books: *Pancakes-Paris* by Claire Huchet Bishop, Viking; *Li Lun, Lad of Courage* by Carolyn Treffinger, Abingdon; *The Quaint and Curious Quest of Johnny Longfoot* by Catherine Besterman, Bobbs; *The Cow-Tail Switch, and Other West African Stories* by Harold Courlander, Holt; *Misty of Chincoteague* by Marguerite Henry, Rand

1949 *King of the Wind* by Marguerite Henry, Rand
Honor Books: *Seabird* by Holling C. Holling, Houghton;

Daughter of the Mountains by Louise Rankin, Viking; *My Father's Dragon* by Ruth S. Gannett, Random; *Story of the Negro* by Arna Bontemps, Knopf

1950 *The Door in the Wall* by Marguerite de Angeli, Doubleday
Honor Books: *Tree of Freedom* by Rebecca Caudill, Viking; *The Blue Cat of Castle Town* by Catherine Coblentz, Longmans; *Kildee House* by Rutherford Montgomery, Doubleday; *George Washington* by Genevieve Foster, Scribner's; *Song of the Pines* by Walter and Marion Havighurst, Winston

1951 *Amos Fortune, Free Man* by Elizabeth Yates, Aladdin
Honor Books: *Better Known as Johnny Appleseed* by Mabel Leigh Hunt, Lippincott; *Gandhi, Fighter Without a Sword* by Jeanette Eaton, Morrow; *Abraham Lincoln, Friend of the People* by Clara Ingram Judson, Follett; *The Story of Appleby Capple* by Anne Parrish, Harper

1952 *Ginger Pye* by Eleanor Estes, Harcourt
Honor Books: *Americans Before Columbus* by Elizabeth Baity, Viking; *Minn of the Mississippi* by Holling C. Holling, Houghton; *The Defender* by Nicholas Kalashnikoff, Scribner's; *The Light at Tern Rock* by Julia Sauer, Viking; *The Apple and the Arrow* by Mary and Conrad Buff, Houghton

1953 *Secret of the Andes* by Ann Nolan Clark, Viking
Honor Books: *Charlotte's Web* by E. B. White, Harper; *Moccasin Trail* by Eloise McGraw, Coward; *Red Sails to Capri* by Ann Weil, Viking; *The Bears on Hemlock Mountain* by Alice Dalgliesh, Scribner's; *Birthdays of Freedom*, Vol. 1 by Genevieve Foster, Scribner's

1954 *. . . and now Miguel* by Joseph Krumgold, T. Crowell
Honor Books: *All Alone* by Claire Huchet Bishop, Viking; *Shadrach* by Meindert DeJong, Harper; *Hurry Home Candy* by Meindert DeJong, Harper; *Theodore Roosevelt, Fighting Patriot* by Clara Ingram Judson, Follett; *Magic Maze* by Mary and Conrad Buff, Houghton

1955 *The Wheel on the School* by Meindert DeJong, Harper
Honor Books: *The Courage of Sarah Noble* by Alice Dalgliesh, Scribner's; *Banner in the Sky* by James Ullman, Lippincott

1956 *Carry on, Mr. Dowditch* by Jean Lee Latham, Houghton
Honor Books: *The Secret River* by Marjorie Kinan Rawlings, Scribner's; *The Golden Name Day* by Jennie Lindquist, Harper; *Men, Microscopes, and Living Things* by Katherine Shippen, Viking

1957 *Miracles on Maple Hill* by Virginia Sorensen, Harcourt
Honor Books: *Old Yeller* by Fred Gipson, Harper; *The House of Sixty Fathers* by Meindert DeJong, Harper; *Mr. Justice Holmes* by Clara Ingram Judson, Follett; *The Corn Grows Ripe* by Dorothy Rhoads, Viking; *Black Fox of Lorne* by Marguerite de Angeli, Doubleday

1958 *Rifles for Watie* by Harold Keith, T. Crowell
Honor Books: *The Horsecatcher* by Mari Sandoz, Westminster; *Gone-Away Lake* by Elizabeth Enright, Harcourt; *The Great Wheel* by Robert Lawson, Viking; *Tom Paine, Freedom's Apostle* by Leo Gurko, T. Crowell

1959 *The Witch of Blackbird Pond* by Elizabeth George Speare, Houghton
Honor Books: *The Family Under the Bridge* by Natalie S. Carlson, Harper; *Along Came a Dog* by Meindert DeJong, Harper; *Chucaro: Wild Pony of the Pampa* by Francis Kalnay, Harcourt; *The Perilous Road* by William O. Steele, Harcourt

1960 *Onion John* by Joseph Krumgold, T. Crowell
Honor Books: *My Side of the Mountain* by Jean George, Dutton; *America Is Born* by Gerald W. Johnson, Morrow; *The Gammage Cup* by Carol Kendall, Harcourt

1961 *Island of the Blue Dolphins* by Scott O'Dell, Houghton
Honor Books: *America Moves Forward* by Gerald W. Johnson, Morrow; *Old Ramon* by Jack Schaefer, Houghton; *The Cricket in Times Square* by George Selden, Farrar

1962 *The Bronze Bow* by Elizabeth George Speare, Houghton
Honor Books: *Frontier Living* by Edwin Tunis, World; *The Golden Goblet* by Eloise McGraw, Coward; *Belling the Tiger* by Mary Stolz, Harper

1963 *A Wrinkle in Time* by Madeleine L'Engle, Farrar
Honor Books: *Thistle and Thyme* by Sorche Nic Leodhas, Holt; *Men of Athens* by Olivia Coolidge, Houghton

1964 *It's Like This, Cat* by Emily Cheney Neville, Harper

Honor Books: *Rascal* by Sterling North, Dutton; *The Loner* by Esther Wier, McKay

1965 *Shadow of a Bull* by Maia Wojciechowska, Atheneum
Honor Book: *Across Five Aprils* by Irene Hunt, Follett

1966 *I, Juan de Pareja* by Elizabeth Borten de Trevino, Farrar
Honor Books: *The Black Cauldron* by Lloyd Alexander, Holt; *The Animal Family* by Randall Jarrell, Pantheon; *The Noonday Friends* by Mary Stolz, Harper

1967 *Up a Road Slowly* by Irene Hunt, Follett
Honor Books: *The King's Fifth* by Scott O'Dell, Houghton; *Zlateh the Goat and Other Stories* by Isaac Bashevis Singer, Harper; *The Jazz Man* by Mary H. Weik, Atheneum

1968 *From the Mixed-Up Files of Mrs. Basil E. Frankweiler* by E. L. Konigsburg, Atheneum
Honor Books: *The Black Pearl* by Scott O'Dell, Houghton Mifflin; *The Egypt Game* by Zilpha Keatley Snyder, Atheneum; *The Fearsome Inn* by Isaac Bashevis Singer, Scribner; *Jennifer, Hecate, Macbeth, William McKinley, and Me, Elizabeth* by E. L. Konigsburg, Atheneum

1969 *The High King* by Lloyd Alexander, Holt, Rinehart & Winston
Honor Books: *To Be a Slave* by Julius Lester, Dial; *When Shlemiel Went to Warsaw and Other Stories* by Isaac Bashevis Singer, Farrar, Straus & Giroux

1970 *Sounder* by William Armstrong, Harper & Row
Honor Books: *Journey Outside* by Mary Q. Steele, Viking; *Our Eddie* by Sulamith Ish-Kishor, Pantheon; *The Many Ways of Seeing: An Introduction to the Pleasures of Art* by Janet Gaylord Moore, Harcourt Brace Jovanovich

1971 *The Summer of the Swans* by Betsy Byars, Viking
Honor Books: *Enchantress from the Stars* by Sylvia Louise Engdahl, Atheneum; *Kneeknock Rose* by Natalie Babbitt, Farrar, Straus & Giroux; *Sing Down the Moon* by Scott O'Dell, Houghton Mifflin

1972 *Mrs. Frisby and the Rats of Nimh* by Robert C. O'Brien, Atheneum
Honor Books: *Annie and the Old One* by Miska Miles, Atlantic-Little; *The Headless Cupid* by Zilpha Keatley Snyder, Atheneum; *Incident at Hawk's Hill* by Allan W.

Eckert, Little, Brown; *The Planet of Junior Brown* by Virginia Hamilton, Macmillan; *The Tombs of Atuan* by Ursula K. LeGuin, Atheneum

1973 *Julie of the Wolves* by Jean C. George, Harper & Row
Honor Books: *Frog and Toad Together* by Arnold Lobel, Harper & Row; *The Upstairs Room* by Johanna Reiss, Crowell; *The Witches of Worm* by Zilpha Keatley Snyder, Atheneum

1974 *The Slave Dancer* by Paula Fox, Bradbury
Honor Book: *The Dark Is Rising* by Susan Cooper, Atheneum

1975 *M. C. Higgins, the Great* by Virginia Hamilton, Macmillan
Honor Books: *Figgs and Phantoms* by Ellen Raskin, E. P. Dutton; *My Brother Sam Is Dead* by James Lincoln Collier and Christopher Collier, Four Winds; *The Perilous Gard* by Elizabeth Marie Pope, Houghton Mifflin; *Philip Hall Likes Me, I Reckon Maybe* by Bette Greene, Dial

1976 *The Grey King* by Susan Cooper, Atheneum
Honor Books: *Dragonwings* by Laurence Yep, Harper & Row; *The Hundred Penny Box* by Sharon Bell Mathis, Viking

1977 *Roll of Thunder, Hear My Cry* by Mildred Taylor, Dial
Honor Books: *Abel's Island* by William Steig, Farrar, Straus & Giroux; *A String in the Harp* by Nancy Bond, Atheneum

1978 *Bridge to Terabithia* by Katherine Paterson, Crowell
Honor Books: *Anpao: An American Indian Odyssey* by Jamake Highwater, Lippincott; *Ramona and Her Father* by Beverly Cleary, Morrow

1979 *The Westing Game* by Ellen Raskin, Dutton
Honor Book: *The Great Gilly Hopkins* by Katherine Paterson, Crowell

1980 *A Gathering of Days: A New England Girl's Journal, 1830–32* by Joan W. Blos, Scribner
Honor Book: *The Road from Home: The Story of an Armenian Girl* by David Kerdian, Greenwillow

1981 *Jacob Have I Loved* by Katherine Paterson, Crowell
Honor Books: *The Fledgling* by Jane Langton, Harper & Row; *A Ring of Endless Light* by Madeleine L'Engle, Farrar, Straus & Giroux

1982 *A Visit to William Blake's Inn: Poems for Innocent and Experienced Travelers* by Nancy Willard, Harcourt Brace Jovanovich
Honor Books: *Ramona Quimby, Age 8* by Beverly Cleary, Morrow; *Upon the Head of the Goat: A Childhood in Hungary, 1939–1944* by Aranka Siegal, Farrar, Straus & Giroux

1983 *Dicey's Song* by Cynthia Voigt, Atheneum
Honor Books: *The Blue Sword* by Robin McKinley, Greenwillow; *Doctor DeSoto* by William Steig, Farrar, Straus & Giroux; *Graven Images* by Paul Fleischman, Harper & Row; *Homesick: My Own Story* by Jean Fritz, Putnam; *Sweet Whispers, Brother Rush* by Virginia Hamilton, Philomel

1984 *Dear Mr. Henshaw* by Beverly Cleary, Morrow
Honor Books: *The Sign of the Beaver* by Elizabeth George Speare, Houghton Mifflin; *A Solitary Blue* by Cynthia Voig, Atheneum; *Sugaring Time* by Kathryn Lasky, Macmillan; *The Wish Giver* by Bill Brittain, Harper & Row

1985 *The Hero and the Crown* by Robin McKinley, Greenwillow
Honor Books: *Like Jake and Me* by Mavis Jukes, Alfred A. Knopf; *The Moves Make the Man* by Bruce Brooks, Harper & Row; *One-Eyed Cat* by Paula Fox, Bradbury

1986 *Sarah, Plain and Tall* by Patricia MacLachlan, Harper & Row
Honor Books: *Commodore Perry in the Land of the Shogun* by Rhoda Blumberg, Lothrop, Lee & Shepard; *Dogsong* by Gary Paulsen, Bradbury

1987 *The Whipping Boy* by Sid Fleischman, Greenwillow
Honor Books: *A Fine White Dust* by Cynthia Rylant, Bradbury; *On My Honor* by Marion Dane Bauer, Clarion; *Volcano: The Eruption and Healing of Mount St. Helen's* by Patricia Lauber, Bradbury

1988 *Lincoln: A Photobiography* by Russell Freedman, Clarion
Honor Books: *After the Rain* by Norma Fox Mazer, Morrow; *Hatchet* by Gary Paulsen, Bradbury

1989 *Joyful Noise: Poems for Two Voices* by Paul Fleischman, Harper & Row

Honor Books: *In the Beginning: Creation Stories from Around the World* by Virginia Hamilton, Harcourt Brace Jovanovich; *Scorpions* by Walter Dean Myers, Harper & Row

1990 *Number the Stars* by Lois Lowry, Houghton Mifflin
Honor Books: *Afternoon of the Elves* by Janet Taylor Lifle, Watts; *Shabanu: Daughter of the Wind* by Suzanne Fisher Staples, Knopf; *The Winter Room* by Gary Paulsen, Watts

THE CALDECOTT MEDAL

1938 *Animals of the Bible* by Helen Dean Fish, illustrated by Dorothy P. Lathrop, Lippincott
Honor Books: *Seven Simeons* by Boris Artzybasheff, Viking; *Four and Twenty Blackbirds* by Helen Dean Fish, illustrated by Robert Lawson, Stokes

1939 *Mei Li* by Thomas Handforth, Doubleday
Honor Books: *The Forest Pool* by Laura Adams Armer, Longmans; *Wee Gillis* by Munro Leaf, illustrated by Robert Lawson, Viking; *Snow White and the Seven Dwarfs* by Wanda Gág, Coward; *Barkis* by Clare Newberry, Harper; *Andy and the Lion* by James Daugherty, Viking

1940 *Abraham Lincoln* by Ingri and Edgar Parin D'Aulaire, Doubleday
Honor Books: *Cock-A-Doodle Doo . . .* by Berta and Elmer Hader, Macmillan; *Madeline* by Ludwig Bemelmans, Viking; *The Ageless Story* illustrated by Lauren Ford, Dodd

1941 *They Were Strong and Good* by Robert Lawson, Viking
Honor Book: *April's Kittens* by Clare Newberry, Harper

1942 *Make Way for Ducklings* by Robert McCloskey, Viking
Honor Books: *An American ABC* by Maud and Miska Petersham, Macmillan; *In My Mother's House* by Ann Nolan Clark, illustrated by Velino Herrera, Viking; *Paddle-to-the-Sea* by Holling C. Holling, Houghton; *Nothing at All* by Wanda Gág, Coward

1943 *The Little House* by Virginia Lee Burton, Houghton
Honor Books: *Dash and Dart* by Mary and Conrad Buff, Viking; *Marshmallow* by Clare Newberry, Harper

1944 *Many Moons* by James Thurber, illustrated by Louis Slobodkin, Harcourt
Honor Books: *Small Rain: Verses from the Bible* selected by Jessie Orton Jones, illustrated by Elizabeth Orton Jones, Viking; *Pierre Pigeon* by Lee Kingman, illustrated by Arnold E. Bare, Houghton; *The Mighty Hunter* by Berta and Elmer Hader, Macmillan; *A Child's Good Night Book* by Margaret Wise Brown, illustrated by Jean Charlot, W. R. Scott; *Good Luck Horse* by Chih-Yi Chan, illustrated by Plao Chan, Whittlesey

1945 *Prayer for a Child* by Rachel Field, illustrated by Elizabeth Orton Jones, Macmillan
Honor Books: *Mother Goose* illustrated by Tasha Tudor, Walck; *In the Forest* by Marie Hall Ets, Viking; *Yonie Wondernose* by Marguerite de Angeli, Doubleday; *The Christmas Anna Angel* by Ruth Sawyer, illustrated by Kate Seredy, Viking

1946 *The Rooster Crows* . . . (traditional Mother Goose) illustrated by Maud and Miska Petersham, Macmillan
Honor Books: *Little Lost Lamb* by Golden MacDonald, illustrated by Leonard Weisgard, Doubleday; *Sing Mother Goose* by Opal Wheeler, illustrated by Marjorie Torrey, Dutton; *My Mother Is the Most Beautiful Woman in the World* by Becky Reyher, illustrated by Ruth Gannett, Lothrop; *You Can Write Chinese* by Kurt Wiese, Viking

1947 *The Little Island* by Golden MacDonald, illustrated by Leonard Weisgard, Doubleday
Honor Books: *Rain Drop Splash* by Alvin Tresselt, illustrated by Leonard Weisgard, Lothrop; *Boats on the River* by Marjorie Flack, illustrated by Jay Hyde Barnum, Viking; *Timothy Turtle* by Al Graham, illustrated by Tony Palazzo, Viking; *Pedro, The Angel of Olvera Street* by Leo Politi, Scribner's; *Sing in Praise: A Collection of the Best Loved Hymns* by Opal Wheeler, illustrated by Marjorie Torrey, Dutton

1948 *White Snow, Bright Snow* by Alvin Tresselt, illustrated by Roger Duvoisin, Lothrop
Honor Books: *Stone Soup* by Marcia Brown, Scribner's; *McElligot's Pool* by Dr. Seuss, Random; *Bambino the*

Clown by George Schreiber, Viking; *Roger and the Fox* by Lavinia Davis, illustrated by Hildegard Woodward, Doubleday; *Song of Robin Hood* edited by Anne Malcolmson, illustrated by Virginia Lee Burton, Houghton

1949 *The Big Snow* by Berta and Elmer Hader, Macmillan
Honor Books: *Blueberries for Sal* by Robert McCloskey, Viking; *All Around the Town* by Phyllis McGinley, illustrated by Helen Stone, Lippincott; *Juanita* by Leo Politi, Scribner's; *Fish in the Air* by Kurt Wiese, Viking

1950 *Song of the Swallows* by Leo Politi, Scribner's
Honor Books: *America's Ethan Allen* by Stewart Holbrook, illustrated by Lynd Ward, Houghton; *The Wild Birthday Cake* by Lavinia Davis, illustrated by Hildegard Woodward, Doubleday; *The Happy Day* by Ruth Krauss, illustrated by Marc Simont, Harper; *Bartholomew and the Oobleck* by Dr. Seuss, Random; *Henry Fisherman* by Marcia Brown, Scribner's

1951 *The Egg Tree* by Katherine Milhous, Scribner's
Honor Books: *Dick Whittington and His Cat* by Marcia Brown, Scribner's; *The Two Reds* by William Lipkind, illustrated by Nicholas Mordvinoff, Harcourt; *If I Ran the Zoo* by Dr. Seuss, Random; *The Most Wonderful Doll in the World* by Phyllis McGinley, illustrated by Helen Stone, Lippincott; *T-Bone, the Baby Sitter* by Clare Newberry, Harper

1952 *Finders Keepers* by William Lipkind, illustrated by Nicholas Mordvinoff, Harcourt
Honor Books: *Mr. T. W. Anthony Woo* by Marie Hall Ets, Viking; *Skipper John's Cook* by Marcia Brown, Scribner's; *All Falling Down* by Gene Zion, illustrated by Margaret Bloy Graham, Harper; *Bear Party* by William Pène du Bois, Viking; *Feather Mountain* by Elizabeth Olds, Houghton

1953 *The Biggest Bear* by Lynd Ward, Houghton
Honor Books: *Puss in Boots* by Charles Perrault, illustrated and translated by Marcia Brown, Scribner's; *One Morning in Maine* by Robert McCloskey, Viking; *Ape in a Cape* by Fritz Eichenberg, Harcourt; *The Storm Book* by Charlotte Zolotow, illustrated by Margaret Bloy Graham, Harper; *Five Little Monkeys* by Juliet Kepes, Houghton

1954 *Madeline's Rescue* by Ludwig Bemelmans, Viking
Honor Books: *Journey Cake, Ho!* by Ruth Sawyer, illustrated by Robert McCloskey, Viking; *When Will the World Be Mine?* by Miriam Schlein, illustrated by Jean Charlot, W. R. Scott; *The Steadfast Tin Soldier* by Hans Christian Andersen, illustrated by Marcia Brown, Scribner's; *A Very Special House* by Ruth Krauss, illustrated by Maurice Sendak, Harper; *Green Eyes* by A. Birnbaum, Capitol

1955 *Cinderella, or the Little Glass Slipper* by Charles Perrault, translated and illustrated by Marcia Brown, Scribner's
Honor Books: *Books of Nursery and Mother Goose Rhymes*, illustrated by Marguerite de Angeli, Doubleday; *Wheel on the Chimney* by Margaret Wise Brown, illustrated by Tibor Gergely, Lippincott; *The Thanksgiving Story* by Alice Dalgliesh, illustrated by Helen Sewell, Scribner's

1956 *Frog Went A-Courtin'* edited by John Langstaff, illustrated by Feodor Rojankovsky, Harcourt
Honor Books: *Play with Me* by Marie Hall Ets, Viking; *Crow Boy* by Taro Yashima, Viking

1957 *A Tree Is Nice* by Janice May Udry, illustrated by Marc Simont, Harper
Honor Books: *Mr. Penny's Race Horse* by Marie Hall Ets, Viking; *1 Is One* by Tasha Tudor, Walck; *Anatole* by Eve Titus, illustrated by Paul Galdone, McGraw; *Gillespie and the Guards* by Benjamin Elkin, illustrated by James Daugherty, Viking; *Lion* by William Pène du Bois, Viking

1958 *Time of Wonder* by Robert McCloskey, Viking
Honor Books: *Fly High, Fly Low* by Don Freeman, Viking; *Anatole and the Cat* by Eve Titus, illustrated by Paul Galdone, McGraw

1959 *Chanticleer and the Fox* adapted from Chaucer and illustrated by Barbara Cooney, T. Crowell
Honor Books: *The House That Jack Built* by Antonio Frasconi, Harcourt; *What Do You Say, Dear?* by Sesyle Joslin, illustrated by Maurice Sendak, W. R. Scott; *Umbrella* by Taro Yashima, Viking

1960 *Nine Days to Christmas* by Marie Hall Ets and Aurora Labastida, illustrated by Marie Hall Ets, Viking

Honor Books: *Houses from the Sea* by Alice E. Goudey, illustrated by Adrienne Adams, Scribner's; *The Moon Jumpers* by Janice May Udry, illustrated by Maurice Sendak, Harper

1961 *Baboushka and the Three Kings* by Ruth Robbins, illustrated by Nicolas Sidjakov, Parnassus
Honor Book: *Inch by Inch* by Leo Lionni, Obolensky

1962 *Once a Mouse . . .* by Marcia Brown, Scribner's
Honor Books: *The Fox Went Out on a Chilly Night* by Peter Spier, Doubleday; *Little Bear's Visit* by Else Holmelund Minarik, illustrated by Maurice Sendak, Harper; *The Day We Saw the Sun Come Up* by Alice E. Goudey, illustrated by Adrienne Adams, Scribner's

1963 *The Snowy Day* by Ezra Jack Keats, Viking
Honor Books: *The Sun Is a Golden Earring* by Natalia M. Belting, illustrated by Bernarda Bryson, Holt; *Mr. Rabbit and the Lovely Present* by Charlotte Zolotow, illustrated by Maurice Sendak, Harper

1964 *Where the Wild Things Are* by Maurice Sendak, Harper & Row
Honor Books: *All in the Morning Early* by Sorche Nic Leodhas, illustrated by Evaline Ness, Holt, Rinehart & Winston; *Mother Goose and Nursery Rhymes* by Philip Reed, Atheneum; *Swimmy* by Leo Lionni, Pantheon

1965 *May I Bring a Friend?* by Beatrice Schenk de Regniers, Atheneum
Honor Books: *A Pocketful of Cricket* by Rebecca Caudill, illustrated by Evaline Ness, Holt, Rinehart & Winston; *Rain Makes Applesauce* by Julian Scheer, illustrated by Marvin Bileck, Holiday; *The Wave* by Margaret Hodges, illustrated by Blair Lent, Houghton Mifflin

1966 *Always Room for One More* by Sorche Nic Leodhas, illustrated by Nonny Hogrogian, Holt, Rinehart & Winston
Honor Books: *Hide and Seek Fog* by Alvin Tresselt, illustrated by Roger Duvoisin, Lothrop, Lee & Shepard; *Just Me* by Marie Hall Ets, Viking; *Tom Tit Tot* edited by Joseph Jacobs, illustrated by Evaline Ness, Scribner's

1967 *Sam, Bangs & Moonshine* by Evaline Ness, Holt, Rinehart & Winston

Honor Book: *One Wide River to Cross* by Barbara Emberley, illustrated by Ed Emberley, Prentice-Hall

1968 *Drummer Hoff* by Barbara Emberley, illustrated by Ed Emberley, Prentice-Hall
Honor Books: *Frederick* by Leo Lionni, Pantheon; *Seashore Story* by Taro Yashima, Viking; *The Emperor and the Kite* by Jane Yolen, illustrated by Ed Young, Harcourt Brace Jovanovich

1969 *The Fool of the World and the Flying Ship* by Arthur Ransome, illustrated by Uri Shulevitz, Farrar, Straus & Giroux

Honor Book: *Why the Sun and the Moon Live in the Sky: An African Folktale* by Elphinstone Dayrell, illustrated by Blair Lent, Houghton Mifflin

1970 *Sylvester and the Magic Pebble* by William Steig, Windmill/Simon & Schuster
Honor Books: *Alexander and the Wind-Up Mouse* by Leo Lionni, Pantheon; *Goggles!* Ezra Jack Keats, Macmillan; *The Judge: An Untrue Tale* by Harve Zemach, illustrated by Margot Zemach, Farrar, Straus & Giroux; *Pop Corn & Ma Goodness* by Edna Mitchell Preston, illustrated by Robert Andrew Parker, Viking; *Thy Friend, Obadiah* by Brinton Turkle, Viking

1971 *A Story, A Story* by Gail E. Haley, Atheneum
Honor Books: *The Angry Moon* by William Sleaton, illustrated by Blair Lent, Atlantic-Little; *Frog and Toad Are Friends* by Arnold Lobel, Harper & Row; *In the Night Kitchen* by Maurice Sendak, Harper & Row

1972 *One Fine Day* by Nonny A. Hogrogian, Macmillan
Honor Books: *Hildilid's Night* by Cheli Duran Ryan, illustrated by Arnold Lobel, Macmillan; *If All the Seas Were One Sea* by Janina Domanska, Macmillan; *Moja Means One: Swahili Counting Book* by Muriel Feelings, illustrated by tom Feelings, Dial

1973 *The Funny Little Woman* by Arlen Mosel, illustrated by Blair Lent, E. P. Dutton
Honor Books: *Hosie's Alphabet* by Hosea, Tobias, and Lisa Baskin, illustrated by Leonard Baskin, Viking; *Snow-White and the Seven Dwarfs*, translated by Randall Jarrell from The Brothers Grimm, illustrated by Nancy

Ekholm Burkert, Farrar, Straus & Giroux; *When Clay Sings* by Byrd Baylor, illustrated by Tom Bahti, Scribner's

1974 *Duffy and the Devil* by Harve and Margot Zemach, Farrar, Straus & Giroux
Honor Books: *Cathedral: The Story of Its Construction* by David Macaulay, Houghton; *The Three Jovial Huntsmen* by Susan Jeffers, Bradbury

1975 *Arrow to the Sun* by Gerald McDermott, Viking
Honor Book: *Jambo Means Hello: A Swahili Alphabet Book* by Muriel Feeings, illustrated by Tom Feelings, Dial

1976 *Why Mosquitoes Buzz in People's Ears* by Verna Aardema, illustrated by Leo and Diane Dillon, Dial
Honor Books: *The Desert Is Theirs* by Byrd Baylor, illustrated by Peter Parnall, Scribner's; *Strega Nona* by Tomie de Paola, Prentice-Hall

1977 *Ashanti to Zulu* by Margaret Musgrove, illustrated by Leo and Diane Dillon, Dial
Honor Books: *The Amazing Bone* by William Steig, Farrar, Straus & Giroux; *The Contest* by Nonny Hogrogian, Greenwillow; *Fish for Supper* by M. B. Goffstein, Dial; *The Golem: A Jewish Legend* by Beverly Brodsky McDermott, Lippincott; *Hawk, I'm Your Brother* by Byrd Baylor, illustrated by Peter Parnall, Scribner's

1978 *Noah's Ark: The Story of the Flood* by Peter Spier, Doubleday
Honor Books: *Castle* by David Macaulay, Houghton; *It Could Always Be Worse* by Margot Zemach, Farrar, Straus & Giroux

1979 *The Girl Who Loved Wild Horses* by Paul Goble, Bradbury
Honor Books: *Freight Train* by Donald Crews, Greenwillow; *The Way to Start a Day* by Byrd Baylor, illustrated by Peter Parnall, Scribner's

1980 *Ox-Cart Man* by Donald Hall, illustrated by Barbara Cooney, Viking
Honor Books: *Ben's Trumpet* by Rachel Isadora, Greenwillow; *The Garden of Abdul Gasazi* by Chris Van Allsburg, Houghton; *The Treasure* by Uri Shulevitz, Farrar, Straus & Giroux

1981 *Fables* by Arnold Lobel, Harper & Row
Honor Books: *The Bremen-Town Musicians* by Ilse
Plume, Doubleday; *The Grey Lady and the Strawberry
Snatcher* by Molly Bang, Four Winds; *Mice Twice* by
Joseph Low, Atheneum; *Truck* by Donald Crews,
Greenwillow

1982 *Jumanji* by Chris Van Allsburg, Houghton Mifflin
Honor Books: *On Market Street* by Arnold Lobel, illus-
trated by Anita Lobel, Greenwillow; *Outside over There*
by Maurice Sendak, Harper & Row; *A Visit to William
Blake's Inn: Poems for Innocent and Experienced Travel-
ers* by Nancy Willard, illustrated by Alice and Martin
Provensen, Harcourt; *Where the Buffaloes Begin* by Olaf
Baker, illustrated by Stephen Gammell, Warne

1983 *Shadow* by Blaise Cendrars, translated and illustrated
by Marcia Brown, Scribner's
Honor Books: *A Chair for My Mother* by Vera B. Williams,
Greenwillow; *When I Was Young in the Mountains* by
Cynthia Rylant, illustrated by Diane Goode, E. P. Dutton

1984 *The Glorious Flight Across the Channel with Louis Bleriot*
by Alice and Martin Provensen, Viking
Honor Books: *Little Red Riding Hood* by Trina Schart
Hyman, Holiday; *Ten, Nine, Eight* by Molly Bang,
Greenwillow

1985 *Saint George and the Dragon* by Margaret Hodges, illus-
trated by Trina Schart Hyman, Little, Brown
Honor Books: *Hansel and Gretel* by Rika Lesser, illus-
trated by Paul O. Zelinsky, Dodd, Mead; *Have You Seen
My Duckling?* by Nancy Tafuri, Greenwillow; *The Story of
Jumping Mouse* by John Steptoe, Lothrop, Lee & Shepard

1986 *The Polar Express* by Chris Van Allsburg, Houghton
Mifflin
Honor Books: *King Bidgood's in the Bathtub* by Andrew
Wood, Harcourt Brace Jovanovich; *The Relatives Came*
by Cynthia Rylant, Bradbury

1987 *Hey, Al* by Arthur Yorinks, illustrated by Richard
Egielski, Farrar, Straus & Giroux
Honor Books: *Alphabatics* by Suse MacDonald,
Bradbury; *Rumplestiltskin* by Paul O. Zelinsky, E. P.
Dutton; *The Village of Round and Square Houses* by Anne
Grifalconi, Little, Brown

1988 *Owl Moon* by Jane Yolen, illustrated by John Schoen-
herr, Philomel
Honor Book: *Mufaro's Beautiful Daughters: An African
Tale* by John Steptoe, Morrow
1989 *Song and Dance Man* By Karen Ackerman, illustrated by
Stephen Gammell, Knopf
Honor Books: *The Boy of the Three Year Nap* by Dianne
Snyder, illustrated by Allen Say, Houghton Mifflin; *Free
Fall* by David Wiesner, Lothrop, Lee, & Shepard;
Goldilocks and the Three Bears by James Marshall, Dial;
Mirandy and Brother Wind by Patricia C. McKissack,
illustrated by Jerry Pinkney, Knopf
1990 *Lon Po Po: A Red Riding Hood Story from China* by Ed
Young, Putnam
Honor Books: *Bill Peet: An Autobiography*, written and
illustrated by Bill Peet, Houghton Mifflin; *Color Zoo*,
written and illustrated by Lois Ehlert, Harper & Row;
Hershel and the Hanukkah Goblins by Eric A. Kimmel,
illustrated by Trina Schart Hyman, Holiday; *The Talking
Eggs* by Robert San Souci, illustrated by Jerry Pinkney,
Doubleday

THE LAURA INGALLS WILDER AWARD

1954 Laura Ingalls Wilder
1960 Clara Ingram Judson
1965 Ruth Sawyer
1970 E. B. White
1975 Beverly Cleary
1980 Theodor Geisel (Dr. Seuss)
1983 Maurice Sendak
1986 Jean Fritz
1989 Elizabeth George Speare

THE NATIONAL BOOK AWARD

1969 *Journey from Peppermint Street* by Meindert DeJong,
Harper
1970 *A Day of Pleasure: Stories of a Boy Growing Up in Warsaw*
by Isaac Bashevis Singer, Farrar
1971 *The Marvelous Misadventures of Sebastian* by Lloyd
Alexander, Dutton

1972 *The Slightly Irregular Fire Engine* by Donald Barthelme, Farrar

1973 *The Farthest Shore* by Ursula K. Le Guin, Atheneum

1974 *The Court of the Stone Children* by Eleanor Cameron, Dutton

1975 *M. C. Higgins, The Great* by Virginia Hamilton, Macmillan

1976 *Bert Breen's Barn* by Walter D. Edmonds, Little

1977 *The Master Puppeteer* by Katherine Paterson, Crowell

1978 *The View from the Oak* by Judith and Herbert Kohl, Sierra Club/Scribner's

1979 *The Great Gilly Hopkins* by Katherine Paterson, Crowell

THE AMERICAN BOOK AWARD

1980 Hardcover: *A Gathering of Days: A New England Girl's Journal, 1830–32* by Joan W. Blos, Scribner's
Paperback: *A Swiftly Tilting Planet* by Madeleine L'Engle, Dell

1981 *Fiction:*
Hardcover: *The Night Swimmers* by Betsy Byars, Delacorte
Paperback: *Ramona and Her Mother* by Beverly Cleary, Dell
Nonfiction: Oh, Boy! Babies! by Alison Cragin Herzig and Jane Lawrence Mali, Little

1982 *Fiction:*
Hardcover: *Westmark* by Lloyd Alexander, Dutton
Paperback: *Words by Heart* by Ouida Sebestyen, Bantam
Nonfiction: A Penguin Year by Susan Bonners, Delacorte
Picture Books:
Hardcover: *Outside Over There* by Maurice Sendak, Harper
Paperback: *Noah's Ark* by Peter Spier, Zephyr Books/Doubleday

1983 *Fiction:*
Hardcover: *Homesick: My Own Story* by Jean Fritz, Putnam
Paperback: *A Place Apart* by Paula Fox, Signet/NAL; *Marked by Fire* by Joyce Carol Thomas, Avon Flare
Nonfiction: Chimney Sweeps by James Cross Giblin, Crowell

Picture Books:
Hardcover: *Miss Rumphius* by Barbara Cooney, Viking;
Doctor De Soto by William Steig, Farrar
Paperback: *A House Is a House for Me* by Mary Ann
Hoberman, illustrated by Betty Fraser, Viking

INTERNATIONAL READING ASSOCIATION CHILDREN'S BOOK AWARD

1975 *Transport 7-41-R* by T. Degens, Viking
1976 *Dragonwings* by Laurence Yep, Harper
1977 *A String in the Harp* by Nancy Bond, McElderry/
Atheneum
1978 *A Summer to Die* by Lois Lowry, Houghton
1979 *Reserved for Mark Anthony Crowder* by Alison Smith,
Dutton
1980 *Words by Heart* by Ouida Sebestyen, Atlantic/Little
1981 *My Own Private Sky* by Delores Beckman, Dutton
1982 *Good Night, Mr. Tom* by Michelle Magorian, Kestrel/
Penguin (Great Britain); Harper (U.S.A.)
1983 *The Darkangel* by Meredith Ann Pierce, Atlantic/Little
1984 *Ratha's Creature* by Clare Bell, Atheneum
1985 *Badger on the Barger* by Janni Howker, McCray
1986 *Second Novel Prairie Songs* by Pam Conrad, Harper &
Row
1987 Children's Book: *The Line Up Book* by Marisabini Russo,
Greenwillow
Young Adult: *After the Dancing Days* by Margaret I.
Rostkowski, Harper & Row
1988 Children's Book: *The Third-Story Cat* by Leslie Baker,
Little, Brown
Young Adult: *The Ruby and the Smoke* by Philip Pullman,
Random House
1989 Children's Book: *Rechenka's Eggs* by Patricia Polaccko,
Putnam
Young Adult: *Probably Still Nick* by Virginia Euwer Wolff,
Holt

NATIONAL COUNCIL OF TEACHERS OF ENGLISH AWARD FOR EXCELLENCE IN POETRY FOR CHILDREN

1977 David McCord
1978 Aileen Fisher
1979 Karla Kuskin
1980 Myra Cohn Livingston
1981 Eve Merriam
1982 John Ciardi
1985 Lilian Moore

THE HANS CHRISTIAN ANDERSEN AWARD

1956 Eleanor Farjeon (Great Britain)
1958 Astrid Lindgren (Sweden)
1960 Erich Kästner (Germany)
1962 Meindert DeJong (U.S.A.)
1964 René Guillot (France)
1966 Author: Tove Jansson (Finland)
     Illustrator: Alois Carigiet (Switzerland)
1968 Authors: James Krüss (Germany), Jose Maria Sanchez-Silva (Spain)
     Illustrator: Jiri Trnka (Czechoslovakia)
1970 Author: Gianni Rodari (Italy)
     Illustrator: Maurice Sendak (U.S.A.)
1972 Author: Scott O'Dell (U.S.A.)
     Illustrator: Ib Spang Olsen (Denmark)
1974 Author: Maria Gripe (Sweden)
     Illustrator: Farshid Mesghali (Iran)
1976 Author: Cecil Bødker (Denmark)
     Illustrator: Tatjana Mawrina (U.S.S.R.)
1978 Author: Paula Fox (U.S.A.)
     Illustrator: Otto S. Svend (Denmark)
1980 Author: Bohumil Riha (Czechoslovakia)
     Illustrator: Suekichi Akaba (Japan)
1982 Author: Lygia Bojunga Nunes (Brazil)
     Illustrator: Zbigniew Rychlicki (Poland)
1984 Author: Christine Nostlinger (Austria)
     Illustrator: Mitsumasa Anno (Japan)
1986 Author: Patricia Wrightson (Australia)
     Illustrator: Robert Ingpen (Australia)

APPENDIX

B

Resources for Teaching Literature

American Library Association. "The USA Through Children's Books." *Booklist* (May 1, 1986 and May 1, 1988).

Bowker, R. R. *Children's Books in Print* Ann Arbor, Mich.: Bowker, annual.

Brozo, William, and Carl Tomlinson. "Literature: The Key to Lively Content Courses." *The Reading Teacher* (September 1985), pp. 493–497.

Butler, Andrea, and Jan Turnbill. *Towards a Reading-Writing Classroom.* Plymouth, N.H.: Heinemann, 1987.

Calkins, Lucy. *The Art of Teaching Writing.* Plymouth, N.H.: Heinemann, 1987.

Children's Book Council. *Children's Books: Awards and Prizes.* New York: Children's Book Council, 1986.

Cott, J., ed. *Masterworks of Children's Literature.* New York: Stonehill, 1986.

Cullinan, Bernice E., ed. *Children's Literature in the Reading Program.* Newark, Del.: International Reading Association, 1987.

Dreyer, S. S. *Fiction, Folklore, Fantasy, and Poetry for Children.* New York: Bowker, 1986.

————. *The Bookfinder: A Guide to Children's Literature about the Needs and Problems of Youth Aged 2 and Up.* Circle Pines, Minn.: American Guidance, 1984.

Gillespie, J. T., and C. B. Gilbert. *Best Books for Children: Preschool Through the Middle Grades.* New York: Bowker, 1985.

Goodman, Kenneth, Yetta M. Goodman, and Wendy Hood, eds. *The Whole Language Evaluation Book.* Portsmith, N.H.: Heinemann, 1989.

Graves, Donald H. *Writing: Teachers and Children at Work.* Portsmouth, N.H.: Heinemann, 1983.

Hains, Maryellen, ed. *A Two-Way Street: Reading to Write/Writing to Read.* Urbana, Ill.: National Council of Teachers of English, 1982.

Hancock, Joelie, and Susan Hill. *Literature and Basal Reading Programs at Work.* Portsmouth, N.H.: Heinemann, 1987.

Huck, Charlotte S., Susan Hepler, and Janet Hickman. *Children's Literature in the Elementary School,* 4th ed. New York: Holt, Rinehart & Winston, 1987.

Hunt, Mary Alice, ed. *A Multimedia Approach to Children's Literature*, 3rd ed. Chicago, Ill.: American Language Association, 1983.

International Reading Association. "Children's Choices." *The Reading Teacher.* Annually in October issue.

Jalongo, Mary Renck. *Young Children and Picture Books: Literature from Infancy to Six.* Washington, D.C.: National Association for the Education of Young Children, 1988.

Johnson, Terry D., and Daphne R. Louis. *Literacy Through Literature.* Melbourne, Australia: Methuen, 1985.

Lukens, Rebecca. A Critical *Handbook of Children's Literature.* Glenview, Ill.: Scott, Foresman, 1986.

McGowan, Tom, and Meredith McGowan. *Integrating the Primary Curriculum: Social Studies and Children's Literature.* Indianapolis, Ind.: Special Literature Press, 1988.

————. *Children, Literature and Social Studies: Activities for the Intermediate Grades.* Indianapolis, Ind.: Special Literature Press, 1986.

Maker, C. June. *Teaching Models in Education.* Rockville, Md.: Aspen Publication, 1982.

Meinbach, Anita M., and Liz Rothlein. *Circles and Square Pegs.* Hawthorne, N.J.: Educational Impressions, 1989.

Monson, Diane, ed. *Adventuring with Books: A Booklist for Pre-K to Grade 6*. Urbana, Ill.: National Council of Teachers of English, 1985.

Norton, Donna E. *Through the Eyes of a Child: An Introduction to Children's Literature*. Columbus, Ohio: Charles E. Merrill, 1983.

Noyce, Ruth M., and James Christie. *Integrating Reading and Writing Instruction in Grades K–8*. Boston: Allyn & Bacon, 1989.

Paulin, M. A. *Creative Uses of Children's Literature*. Hamden, Conn.: Shoestring Press, 1982.

Peterson, L. K., and M. L. Solt. *Newbery and Caldecott Medal and Honor Books: An Annotated Bibliography*. Boston: G. K. Hall, 1982.

Rothlein, Liz, and Terry Christman. *Read It Again!* Glenview, Ill.: Scott, Foresman, 1989.

Russell, W. F. *Classics to Read Aloud to Your Children*. New York: Crown, 1984.

Senick, G. J., ed. *Children's Literature Review*. Vols. 1–7. Detroit: Dale Research, 1984.

Somersand, Albert, and Janet Evans Worthington. *Response Guides for Teaching Children's Books*. Urbana, Ill.: National Council of Teachers of English, 1979.

Stott, J. C. *Children's Literature From A to Z: A Guide for Parents and Teachers*. New York: McGraw-Hill, 1984.

Sutherland, Zena, and May Hill Arbuthnot. *Children and Books*, 7th ed. Glenview, Ill.: Scott, Foresman, 1986.

Sutherland, Zena, and Myra Cohn Livingston. *The Scott, Foresman Anthology of Children's Literature*. Glenview, Ill.: Scott, Foresman, 1984.

Trelease, Jim. *The Read-Aloud Handbook*. New York: Penguin Books, 1982.

Tway, Eileen, ed. *Reading Ladders for Human Relations*, 6th ed. Urbana, Ill.: National Council of Teachers of English, 1981.

Winkle, L., ed. *The Elementary School Library Collection: A Guide to Books and Other Media*, 14th ed. Williamsport, Penn.: Brodart, 1984.

A P P E N D I X

C

Publishers and Addresses

Abingdon Press, 201 Eighth Ave. S., Nashville, TN 37202

Addison-Wesley Pub. Co., Inc., Reading, MA 01867

Allyn & Bacon, Inc., 7 Wells Ave., Newton, MA 02159

American Guidance Service, Inc., Publishers' Bldg., Circle Pines, MN 55014-1796

Association for Childhood Education International (ACEI), 1141 Georgia Ave., Wheaton, MD 20902

Atheneum Publishers, 115 Fifth Ave., New York, NY 10003

Atlantic Monthly Press, 8 Arlington St., Boston, MA 02116

Avon Books, 1790 Broadway, New York, NY 10019

Ballantine Books, Inc., 201 E. 50th St., New York, NY 10022

Bantam Books, 666 Fifth Ave., New York, NY 10103

R. R. Bowker Co., 205 E. 42nd St., New York, NY 10017

Bradbury Press, Inc. See Macmillan Pub. Co., Inc.

William C. Brown Group, 2460 Kerper Blvd., Dubuque, IA 52001

Cambridge University Press, 32 E. 57th St., New York, NY 10022

Carolrhoda Books, Inc., 241 First Ave. N., Minneapolis, MN 55401

CBS Educational Publishing, 383 Madison Ave., New York, NY 10007

The Chatham Press. See Devin-Adair Co., Inc.

Chelsea House Pub. Co., 432 Park Ave. S., New York, NY 10016

Child's World, Inc., P.O. Box 681, Elgin, IL 60120

Children's Book Council, Inc., 67 Irving Pl., New York, NY 10003

Children's Press, Inc., 1224 W. Van Buren St., Chicago, IL 60607

Collier-Macmillan, Inc., 866 Third Ave., New York, NY 10022

Coward, McCann & Geoghegan. See The Putnam Publishing Group

Creative Education, Inc., 123 S. Broad St., Mankato, MN 56001

Thomas Y. Crowell Co. See Harper & Row

Crown Publishers, Inc., One Park Ave., New York, NY 10016

Delacorte Press, 245 E. 47th St., New York, NY 10017

Dell Publishing Co., Inc., 245 E. 47th St., New York, NY 10017

Dial Books. See E. P. Dutton, Inc.

Dillon Press, Inc., 242 Portland Ave. S., Minneapolis, MN 55415

Dodd, Mead & Co., 79 Madison Ave., New York, NY 10016

Doubleday & Co., Inc., 245 Park Ave., New York, NY 10167

E. P. Dutton, Inc., 2 Park Ave., New York, NY 10016

Faber & Faber. See Harper & Row

Farrar, Straus & Giroux, Inc., 19 Union Square West, New York, NY 10003

The Feminist Press, Box 334, Old Westbury, NY 11568

Follett Pub. Co., 1010 W. Washington Blvd., Chicago, IL 60607

Four Winds Press. See Macmillan Pub. Co., Inc.

Franklin, (Chas.) Press, 18409-90 Ave. West, Edmonds, WA 98020

Garrard Pub. Co., 1607 N. Market St., Champaign, IL 61820

Golden Books, 850 Third Ave., New York, NY 10022

Greenwillow Books. See William Morrow & Co., Inc.

Grosset & Dunlap, Inc., 51 Madison Ave., New York, NY 10010

Harcourt Brace Jovanovich, Inc., 1250 Sixth Ave., San Diego, CA 92101

Harper & Row Publishers, 10 E. 53rd St., New York, NY 10022

Harvard University Press, 79 Garden St., Cambridge, MA 02138

Harvey House, Inc., 20 Waterside Plaza, New York, NY 10010

Hastings House Pub., Inc., 10 E. 40th St., New York, NY 10016

Heinemann Educational Books, 70 Court St., Portsmouth, NH 03801

Herald Press, 616 Walnut Ave., Scottdale, PA 15683

Holt, Rinehart & Winston, Inc., 521 Fifth Ave., New York, NY 10175

Houghton Mifflin Co., 3 Park St., Boston, MA 02108

Human Sciences Press, 72 Fifth Ave., New York, NY 10011

Kestrel Books. See Viking Penguin

Alfred A. Knopf, Inc., 201 E. 50th St., New York, NY 10022

Learning Corp. of America, 1350 Ave. of the Americas, New York, NY 10019

Library of Congress, Supt. of Documents, U.S. Government Printing Office, Washington, DC 20402

J. B. Lippincott Co., East Washington Sq., Philadelphia, PA 19105

Little, Brown & Co., 34 Beacon St., Boston, MA 02106

Live Oaks Media, Box 116, Selmer, NY 10589

Lodestar. See E. P. Dutton, Inc.

Longman, Inc., 1560 Broadway, New York, NY 10036

Lothrop, Lee & Shepard Co. See William Morrow & Co., Inc.

Macmillan Pub. Co., Inc., 866 Third Ave., New York, NY 10022

McDougal, Littell & Co., P.O. Box 1667, Evanston, IL 60204

McFarland & Co., Inc., Box 611, Jefferson, NC 28640

McGraw-Hill, Inc., 1221 Avenue of the Americas, New York, NY 10020

David McKay Co., Inc., 2 Park Ave., New York, NY 10016

Charles E. Merrill Pub. Co., 936 Eastwind Dr., Westerville, OH 43081

Merrimack Publishers Circle, 47 Pelham Road, Salem, NH 03079

Julian Messner. See Simon & Schuster, Inc.

Methuen, Inc., 733 Third Ave., New York, NY 10017

Morning Glory Press, 6595 San Haroldo Way, Buena Park, CA 90620

William Morrow & Co., Inc., 105 Madison Ave., New York, NY 10016

New American Library, Inc. (NAL), 1633 Broadway, New York, NY 10019

W. W. Norton & Co., Inc., 500 Fifth Ave., New York, NY 10010

Pantheon Books. See Alfred A. Knopf, Inc.

Parents Magazine Press, 685 Third Ave., New York, NY 10017

Parnassus Press. See Houghton Mifflin Co.

Penguin Books. See Viking Penguin

Pergamon Press, Inc., Maxwell House, Fairview Park, Elmsford, NY 10523

S. G. Phillips, Inc., P.O. Box 83, Chatham, NY 12037

Philomel Books, 51 Madison Ave., New York, NY 10010

Pied Piper Productions, P.O. Box 320, Verdugo City, CA 91046

Pocket Books, Inc., 1230 Avenue of the Americas, New York, NY 10020

Prentice-Hall, Inc., Englewood Cliffs, NJ 07632

Prometheus Books, 700 E. Amherst St., Buffalo, NY 14215

The Putnam Publishing Group, Children's Books Div., 200 Madison Ave., New York, NY 10010

Raintree Publishers, Inc., 330 E. Kilbourn Ave., Milwaukee, WI 53202

Rand, McNally & Co., 8255 Central Park Ave., Skokie, IL 60076

Random House, Inc., 201 E. 50th St., New York, NY 10022

St. Martin's Press, Inc., 175 Fifth Ave., New York, NY 10010

Schocken Books, Inc., 200 Madison Ave., New York, NY 10016

Scholastic, Inc., 730 Broadway, New York, NY 10003

Scott, Foresman & Co., 1900 East Lake Ave., Glenview, IL 60025

Charles Scribner's Sons, 115 Fifth Ave., New York, NY 10003

Simon & Schuster, Inc., 1230 Avenue of the Americas, New York, NY 10020

Stuart (Lyle), Inc., 120 Enterprise Ave., Secaucus, NJ 07094

Teachers College Press, Columbia University, 1234 Amsterdam Ave., New York, NY 10027

Time-Life Books, Inc., Alexandria, VA 22314

Triad Publishing Co., Inc., P.O. Box 13096, Gainesville, FL 32604

Tundra Books of Northern New York, P.O. Box 1030, 51 Clinton St., Plattsburgh, NY 12901

University of Chicago Press, 5801 S. Ellis Ave., Chicago, IL 60637

Van Nostrand Reinhold Co., 135 W. 50th St., New York, NY 10020

Viking Penguin, Inc., 40 W. 23rd St., New York, NY 10010

Walker & Co., 720 Fifth Ave., New York, NY 10019

Frederick Warne & Co., Inc., 40 W. 23rd St., New York, NY 10010

Warwick/Watts. See Franklin Watts, Inc.

Franklin Watts, Inc., 387 Park Ave. S., New York, NY 10016

Western Pub. Co., Inc., 1220 Mound Ave., Racine, WI 53404

The Westminster Press, 925 Chestnut St., Philadelphia, PA 19107

Weston Wood Studios, Inc., Weston, CT 06880

Westport Communications, 155 Post Road East, Westport, CT 06883

Albert Whitman & Co., 5747 W. Howard St., Niles, IL 60648

Windmill Books, Inc. See Simon & Schuster

INDEX